Space Travel and Culture:
From Apollo to Space Tourism

A selection of previous *Sociological Review* Monographs

Actor Network Theory and After*
eds John Law and John Hassard
Whose Europe? The Turn Towards Democracy*
eds Dennis Smith and Sue Wright
Renewing Class Analysis*
eds Rosemary Cromptom, Fiona Devine, Mike Savage and John Scott
Reading Bourdieu on Society and Culture*
ed. Bridget Fowler
The Consumption of Mass*
eds Nick Lee and Rolland Munro
The Age of Anxiety: Conspiracy Theory and the Human Sciences*
eds Jane Parish and Martin Parker
Utopia and Organization*
ed. Martin Parker
Emotions and Sociology*
ed. Jack Barbalet
Masculinity and Men's Lifestyle Magazines*
ed. Bethan Benwell
Nature Performed: Environment, Culture and Performance*
eds Bronislaw Szerszynski, Wallace Heim and Claire Waterton
After Habermas: New Perspectives on the Public Sphere*
eds Nick Crossley and John Michael Roberts
Feminism After Bourdieu*
eds Lisa Adkins and Beverley Skeggs
Contemporary Organization Theory*
eds Campbell Jones and Rolland Munro
A New Sociology of Work*
eds Lynne Pettinger, Jane Parry, Rebecca Taylor and Miriam Glucksmann
Against Automobility*
eds Steffen Böhm, Campbell Jones, Cris Land and Matthew Paterson
Sports Mega-Events: Social Scientific Analyses of a Global Phenomenon*
eds John Horne and Wolfram Manzenreiter
Embodying Sociology: Retrospect, Progress and Prospects*
ed. Chris Shilling
Market Devices*
eds Michel Callon, Yuval Millo and Fabian Muniesa
Remembering Elites
eds Mike Savage and Karel Williams
Un/knowing Bodies
eds Joanna Latimer and Michael Schillmeier

*Available from John Wiley & Sons, Distribution Centre, 1 Oldlands Way, Bognor Regis, West Sussex, PO22 9SA, UK

Most earlier monographs are still available from: Caroline Baggaley, The Sociological Review, Keele University, Keele, Staffs ST5 5BG, UK; e-mail srb01@keele.ac.uk

The Sociological Review Monographs

Since 1958, *The Sociological Review* has established a tradition of publishing one or two Monographs a year on issues of general sociological interest. The Monograph is an edited book length collection of research papers which is published and distributed in association with Blackwell Publishing Ltd. Our latest Monographs have been *Market Devices* (edited by Michel Callon, Yuval Millo and Fabian Muniesa), *Remembering Elites* (edited by Mike Savage and Karel Williams), *After Habermas: New Perspectives on the Public Sphere* (edited by Nick Crossley and John Michael Roberts), *Feminism After Bourdieu* (edited by Lisa Adkins and Beverley Skeggs), *Contemporary Organization Theory* (edited by Campbell Jones and Rolland Munro), *A New Sociology of Work* (edited by Lynne Pettinger, Jane Parry, Rebecca Taylor and Miriam Glucksmann), *Against Automobility* (edited by Steffen Böhm, Campbell Jones, Chris Land and Matthew Paterson), *Sports Mega-Events: Social Scientific Analyses of a Global Phenomenon* (edited by John Horne and Wolfram Manzenreiter) and *Embodying Sociology: Retrospect, Progress and Prospects* (edited by Chris Shilling). Other Monographs have been published on consumption; museums; culture and computing; death; gender and bureaucracy; sport and many other areas. We are keen to receive innovative collections of work in sociology and related disciplines with a particular emphasis on exploring empirical materials and theoretical frameworks which are currently under-developed. If you wish to discuss ideas for a Monograph then please contact the Monographs Editor, Chris Shilling, School of Social Policy, Sociology and Social Research, Cornwallis North East, University of Kent, Canterbury, Kent CT2 7NF C.Shilling@kent.ac.uk

Space Travel and Culture: From Apollo to Space Tourism

Edited by Martin Parker and David Bell

Wiley-Blackwell/The Sociological Review

BLACKWELL PUBLISHING
350 Main Street, Malden, MA 02148–5020, USA
9600 Garsington Road, Oxford OX4 2DQ, UK
550 Swanston Street, Carlton, Victoria 3053, Australia

First published 2009 by Blackwell Publishing Ltd

Library of Congress Cataloging-in-Publication Data

Space travel and culture : from Apollo to space tourism / edited by Martin Parker and David Bell.
   p.   cm.
   Includes bibliogrpahical references and index.
   ISBN 978-1-4051-9332-0
1. Astronautics–History.   2. Outer space–Exploration–History.   3. Astronautics–Social aspects.   4. Astronautics and civilization.   5. Astronautics–Political aspects.   6. Space tourism.   7. Popular culture.   I. Parker, Martin, 1962–   II. Bell, David, 1965 Feb. 12–
   TL794.5.S62 2009
   629.45–dc22

                                                                        2009013364

A catalogue record for this title is available from the British Library

Set in 10/12 Times NR MT

by SNP Best-Set Typesetter Ltd., Hong Kong

Printed and bound in the United Kingdom

by Page Brothers, Norwich

The publisher's policy is to use permanent paper from mills that operate a sustainable forestry policy, and which has been manufactured from pulp processed using acid-free and elementary chlorine-free practices. Furthermore, the publisher ensures that the text paper and cover board used have met acceptable environmental accreditation standards.

For further information on Blackwell Publishing, visit our website:
http://www.blackwellpublishing.com

Contents

Introduction: making space

Martin Parker and David Bell

It may often seem that sociologists, indeed all those studying social and cultural matters, have left no space unfilled. The relentless growth of the social sciences has meant that fields and sub-fields have proliferated, and it is almost inconceivable, now, that there could be any areas that have not been colonized by ambitious researchers and theorists. Despite the insistence of the term as an opening for work, 'gaps in the literature' are actually rather rare and often need to be manufactured through finer and finer distinctions as well as acts of disciplinary fragmentation and amnesia. It appears that there are actually few spaces left where more research is needed.

This is why it seems to us rather odd that so little has been written by social scientists about the space programmes, which reached their culmination in July 1969 but have continued in various ways since. At the time of writing, almost forty years later, it seems that most social scientists have been remarkably uninterested in this area, to the extent that it is worth asking why (when academics are constantly on the outlook for new areas to pioneer) this might be.[1] Of course it could be answered that there is simply not enough of interest here, or that it is too specific, too narrow. After all, it would make little sense to chide researchers for a lack of interest in the sociology of the ocean floor, or the psychology of cheese. But Apollo, along with all that preceded and post-dated it, is so central to any iconography of the twentieth century; what's more, the popular literature and culture around this topic is simply immense. More people on the globe probably know Neil Armstrong's name than that of the current US President, and space dust has been sprinkled over just about every conceivable product, service and media channel for the last half century. NASA is a global brand, and its achievements still resonate in the global imagination. Admittedly, this is (for most people) history rather than a contemporary concern, but it certainly can't be dismissed as a minor topic or arcane specialism.

Perhaps even more oddly, with a very slight shift in focus, more substantial academic literatures can be spotted nearby: on science fiction, for example, or technology, or complex project organization, or the cold war, the Soviet Union, the USA, the 1960s and so on. All these must figure in any account of space travel, but none of them is sufficient to explain it away. None of them can capture the multiplicity of events like the Moon landings, the monumentality and irrelevance of it all, and the myriad connections with both visions of social progress and the cold interests of capital. Perhaps, in this sense, the pre-history and legacy of Apollo is a superb example of an interdisciplinary topic, one that can only be captured by a lot of different starting points and trajectories. Hence, though it might be mentioned in a variety of literatures, it would never be central to any of them, and continues to be a liminal object in disciplinary terms. Perhaps this is why space appears as a gap? It seems as if Apollo has been skirted around, or sidled up to, but surprisingly rarely looked at head-on. The programme organized so many different interests, and resonated in so many different ways, that it shimmers in the distance, in a haze of its own making. Like the Saturn V rockets, it's a subject so vast that it can only be viewed either from a very long way, or in stages, as it moves across our collective field of vision.

We suspect, however, that the main reason for the neglect is simply that social scientists (of whatever political persuasion) find it easier to be knowing critics than sycophantic fans; and in the case of the 'Space Race', there is an awful lot to be critical about. If you begin with V2s and ICBMs, and add the interests of cold war generals and big aerospace, you can tell a story about war, money and interests. This account can be augmented with the paranoid politics of the cold war, which provided a powerful series of reasons for the military-industrial complex and the state to combine in painting flags on the sides of rockets. Neither can it be forgotten that these were projects mostly sponsored and controlled by white men, so both phallic and imperialist readings are easy enough to construct. Further, in post-everything times when science is an object of scepticism, it would be surprising if the technological grand narratives of such enterprises were not treated with a certain sniffiness, subject only to knowing deconstruction. Even the sort of science we 21st century citizens seem to be interested in is largely virtual and microscopic, not gigantic and noisy. And finally, the trump card – that all that money could have spent on eradicating poverty, building schools and keeping taxes down by leaving the nesting birds and alligators of Cape Canaveral alone. All that should be enough to ensure that this is a topic that people see little merit in exhuming.

Of course, all of these assessments are correct; and they have been made convincingly by many commentators from the 1960s onwards (see, for example, Etzioni, 1964; DeGroot, 2007; Dickens and Ormrod, 2007). But for us, this doesn't exhaust the sorts of things that might be said about Apollo and related matters. We think that there is something else of interest here, too, other stories to tell and to listen to. Something in the nature of myth, and a certain sort of promise that was never fulfilled. As Englishmen with childhood fascinations with space and science fiction, we could explain (away) this combination of nostalgia and fantasy biographically, as a form of adolescent sublimation (Bell, 2005: 80 *passim*; Parker, 2007). We should not assume that the desires and attachments of others are the same as ours, and we know that 'we' is a word that should always be treated with suspicion. But all that being said, and a slight guilt about boys' toys acknowledged, it still seems to us that this is an object with a certain sort of excess, in terms of disciplinarity for one thing, but also in terms of questions of effect and affect.

One way of beginning to explain what is going on here is simply to note that political and aesthetic judgements do not necessarily coincide. A person can be awestruck by something which is clearly dangerous and threatening. This is, of course, the central insight of hundreds of years of writing on the sublime, recently translated into questions of technology (including Apollo) by David Nye (1994). More recently still, the sublime has become rather politicized, with a variety of authors claiming that it represents a sort of gap in understanding that can open to radical change (Shaw, 2006). In other words, whether witnessing the towering mountain peak, or the Saturn V on a pillar of fire, the contingency of the everyday is exposed and (for a while) the world doesn't look quite the same. This is the sort of opening that many commentators have also found in science fiction, as a sort of longing for the world to be otherwise than it is (Jameson, 2005). So any form of alterity, whether expressed in terms of great distances in time and space, or objects of great power and size, might do enough to displace the observer from common sense, and allow them to see the world differently.

There are also, of course, more 'sociological' or 'cultural' ways of making an argument about the contemporary importance of space programmes. As Constance Penley (1997) has argued, what she calls 'NASA/Trek' articulates a sort of common-sense utopianism, a cultural text that blends technology and fiction to produce an image of a future that may well be better than the present. The commingling of the space programme and a science fiction programme produces a powerful, hopeful cultural resonance, of leaving Earthly troubles behind and starting anew. This sort of optimism is rare in policy and politics nowadays, and the innocence of people who might believe that rockets will make us happier seems laughable after Vietnam, Iraq, and global warming. But at Penley's more everyday cultural level, NASA/Trek is alive and well in many, many different ways (see Smith, 2005, for example). The popular culture of space is as diverse and vibrant as ever, from collecting space memorabilia to consuming various forms of science fiction and speculative science, or forms of conspiracy theory related to UFOs and unexplained mysteries (Parker, 2008). Clearly, there is a lot of cultural work still being done to process the utopian dreaming (and dystopian foreboding) of going into space.

It also shouldn't be forgotten that 2009 may well mark the first flight of the first commercial space tourism provider, Virgin Galactic. A great many other companies are attempting to follow, most of them claiming that their efforts represent the democratization of space for the masses. Space is being opened up once more, by a new kind of frontiersman, the entrepreneurial astronaut. Finally, even if we acknowledge that the popular interest in space programmes may well be less than it was in the 20th century in the USSR and the 'West', interest is growing in the 21st-century powers of India and China as they launch

3

their own programmes, and new space racers gather at the starting line, eyeing each other nervously. So rather than merely reflecting a dubious past, space is a topic with contemporary resonances in popular culture, frontier capitalism, and the restructuring of superpower status in the coming century.

In summary, there might be philosophical and sociological reasons not to dismiss Sunday July 21ˢᵗ 1969 too quickly, whatever the many criticisms that could be made about all that effort being expended sending two men 950 thousand miles to collect 40lbs of rock. As an event, we think it still matters, and wonder if its significance may not yet have been fully understood. The technological utopianism of the later 20th century found its most magnificent and pointless expression in the Apollo programme, but it has always been hard for social scientists to think and write about this topic for the disciplinary and political reasons we outlined above. Apollo is something we all know about, but rarely see any more. This book attempts to make space to see it again.

The chapters in this book represent a variety of disciplines – sociology, cultural studies, management, geography, archaeology – and focus on some very different topics. They are broadly organized as a movement from 'culturalist' to 'materialist' accounts, but this trajectory might imply a rather misleading narrative here. Politically, our authors cover the way in which images of space travel have functioned within the radical imagination, as well as the ways in which the interests of capital have been inscribed into the space programmes from the golden age onwards. They also understand their topic at very different levels of scale, from the crew member's check-list as an example of technology, or the launch pad as an archaeological site, to the political economy that produces the geography of satellites. No one account is sufficient, because the space programmes of the last fifty years rely on the settlement of detailed technological and organizational questions at the same time as they are implicated in questions about nations, states and worlds. So too are they implicated in questions of gender, ideas of heroism, and (perhaps most importantly) images of the future. They need to be looked at in many different ways, all at once. Apollo stands now as a future that never happened, or a history that seems not to connect with our present. But in remembering it, we might also begin to remember a sort of orientation to the future that is hard to sustain, as the ice caps melt and the credit crunch bites. The spaces opened in this volume ask some specific questions about the past and present, but imply some very big questions about the future. We think that is why it is worth making space for space.

Note

1 Which is not to say that nothing has been written, just that the paucity of academic writing seems dwarfed by the immensity of the object itself. The bibliographies in the essays that follow contain references to most of the writing on the topic that we have come across.

References

Bell, D., (2005), *Science, Technology and Culture*, Maidenhead: Open University Press.

DeGroot, G., (2007), *Dark Side of the Moon: The Magnificent Madness of the American Lunar Quest*, London: Jonathan Cape.

Dickens, P. and Ormrod, J., (2007), *Cosmic Society: Towards a Sociology of the Universe*, London: Routledge.

Etzioni, A., (1964), *The Moondoggle*, New York: Doubleday.

Jameson, F., (2005), *Archaeologies of the Future*, London: Verso.

Nye, D., (1994), *American Technological Sublime*, Cambridge, MA: MIT Press.

Parker, M., (2007), 'After the Space Age: Science, Fiction and Possibility', in M. Grebowicz (ed.), *SciFi in the Mind's Eye: Reading Science Through Science Fiction,* Chicago: Open Court: 275–288.

Parker, M., (2008), 'Memories of the Space Age: From Apollo to Cyberspace', *Information, Communication and Society* 11/6: 846–860.

Penley, C., (1997), *NASA/Trek*, London: Verso.

Shaw, P., (2006), *The Sublime*, London: Routledge.

Smith, A., (2005), *Moondust: In Search of the Men Who Fell to Earth*, London: Bloomsbury.

Checklist: The secret life of Apollo's 'fourth crewmember'

Matthew H. Hersch

Introduction

In Ron Howard's 1995 film account of the flight of Apollo 13, a lunar-bound space crew led by Jim Lovell (played by Tom Hanks) struggles to return their stricken Apollo spacecraft to the safety of Earth, only to be stymied by technical problems. In one scene, Hanks nervously performs arithmetic on an index card; in another, he waits anxiously for a procedure from ground control to restart his frigid, power-starved spacecraft. The film *Apollo 13* may have dramatized the travails of the crew, but the problems the astronauts faced – and the solutions – were very real: though tasked to pilot their craft in new and unexpected ways, the crew of Apollo 13 did not fly wholly on instinct or memory, but pursuant to complex series of instructions created in space and on the ground. In moments of peril, the astronauts' fortunes rose and fell in words and numbers – power, oxygen reserves, distance from home – and their safe return depended on the ability of flight and ground crews to revise and follow some of the most complex and unusual instruction manuals ever written.

The history of the American human spaceflight program, especially during the well-chronicled period from 1961 to 1975, offers an opportunity to study not only 'big' technology, but the constellation of 'small' technologies that made spaceflight possible, many of which had existed for centuries before astronauts began their journey to the Moon. Chief among these is the printed word: even with the arrival of the first lightweight digital electronic computers, the interior of a spacecraft of the 1960s was hardly a 'paperless office' – in fact, it could be a positively 19th-century environment, in which information moved in words and numbers printed in small pamphlets or handwritten on paper cards and notebooks. Astronauts and engineers of the National Aeronautics and Space Administration brought manuals and checklists with them from aviation where they were already well established; in space they proliferated. Composed in a language approximating English but mostly incomprehensible to the uninitiated, in-flight documentation has been the key to the complex technologies aboard all of America's spacecraft, the ignorance of which would doom crews to certain death (Thomas D. Jones, 2006: 35).

To historians, checklists at first appear to offer little of interest, but upon closer examination, the documents reveal themselves to be among Apollo's most audacious and evocative technological products. To historians of information technology, checklists, flight plans, and similar documents are the 'missing link' between the clearing house and the computerized office, durable pieces of 'analog' technology that flourished in an age of digital information (eg, Campbell-Kelly 1994). With their robust electromechanical systems and highly-trained operators, Apollo spacecraft still relied on standardized procedures and copious printed documentation of control and monitoring routines – sequences impossible for any human to remember and beyond the capacity of computers of the era.

If checklists validated the role of the printed word in space navigation, they also marked a shift in the occupational role of the aviator. Pilots who, in an earlier age, might have defined their skills in terms of valour, instinct, or memory, cooperated with – even encouraged – efforts to externalize their complex thought processes and reduce them to a stack of handheld reference cards. Like the legions of professional managers joining America's corporations of the 20th century, astronauts made themselves essential by mastering information technology and supervising its production. Rather than cowboy aviators gunning their rocket ships into deep space, astronauts acted as test engineers, laboratory scientists, and editors of technical information passed between their spacecraft and the armies of engineers, scientists, and physicians on the ground.

Enriched and perfected, the checklists themselves acquired agency, structuring and ordering the almost unimaginably opaque world of interplanetary navigation. More than simple lists of instructions, the checklists prompted users for sensory inputs and contemplated multiple decision pathways, synthesizing a human brain on paper. In Project Apollo, flight plans, checklists, navigation aids, and data cards, laboriously drafted, reproduced, and distributed to ground and flight crews, became what one astronaut called the spacecraft's 'fourth crewmember', and, in flight, its real commander (Michael Collins, 1974: 311). Indeed, checklists became, to one Apollo computer designer, a kind of 'program' that ran on people instead of machines (Mindell, 2008: 233).

Rise of the checklist

The rise of the modern checklist – a purpose-designed instruction set intended specifically for machine operators – appears to be a product of the industrial age, whose complex, mass-produced machines (often operated by mass-educated workers) lent themselves to standardized instructions (see generally, eg, Smith, 1977). As JoAnne Yates and others have written, late 19th-century capitalism was an environment of both mass production and mass information, necessitating new technologies for transmitting, processing, and storing numerical and other business data (Yates, 1989). Growing alongside business information systems were a new class of professional managers charged with organizing this creation, transmission, and use of information (eg, Chandler, 1977). The maintenance and transmission of schedules, timetables, and procedures could literally be a matter of life and death, spelling the difference between an efficient rail system and deadly collisions.

Examples of early checklists in aviation date back nearly to the dawn of heavier-than-air flight, but the ubiquity of the checklist is traced to the crash of a four-engine Boeing Model 299 airplane on takeoff in 1935 at Wright Field in Dayton, Ohio (Degani and Weiner, 1991: 2; Gawande, 2007). The crash claimed the lives of two experienced Army Air Corps test pilots, whose failure to deactivate a novel locking system on the plane's control surfaces rendered the plane uncontrollable in flight. Though attributed to pilot error, the proximate cause of the crash had been the complexity of the new aircraft; Boeing's solution to the 299's sophistication was a preflight checklist of takeoff procedures, a type of document that soon found widespread use among aircrews (Hallion, 1981: 140–41). The 299 would eventually serve in the US Army Air Forces as the illustrious B-17 'Flying Fortress,' while the checklist became the 'foundation' of 'cockpit safety,' despite little formal study of its effectiveness in flight testing (Degani and Weiner, 1991: 1).

Though seemingly de-skilling to the first pilots who used them, checklists in aviation eventually produced relatively little dissent among professional pilots, perhaps because the lives most often saved through their use were the pilots' own. America's increasingly well-educated aviators, versed in sophisticated mathematics and science, eventually became devotees of the technology, which approximated the mechanical precision of automated systems while enabling pilots to remain in charge of their vehicles. Test pilots would develop a particularly close relationship with checklists. If flying new aircraft seemed to other aviators like seat-of-the-pants adventure, to test pilots it was sophisticated laboratory work emphasizing precise procedures, reproducibility, and careful documentation. As aviators charged with making airplanes safe for their less-experienced peers, test pilots not only read flight manuals but wrote them, identifying problems and prescribing operational procedures (Michael Collins, 1974: 19–23). Unlike other workers who reacted to standardized procedures with disdain, test pilots (and, later, astronauts) carved out a professional niche in which the checklist became a mark of their sophisticated interaction with their machines. Test pilots asserted their professional competence by insisting that of all technical workers, they were the ones best qualified to prepare checklists and most fit to employ them in flight.

Checklists in American human spaceflight

Test pilots would find their relationship to documentation technologies – and their professional identities tested – most explicitly in space. Space vehicles contemplated by engineers of the late-1950s varied from piloted, hypersonic aircraft to capsules lobbed into orbit by ballistic missiles that would require about as much human piloting as the typical high-rise elevator. Some experienced test pilots publicly spurned America's nascent space programme, discouraged by the diminished role of the pilot in new vehicles that appeared roughly akin to cannonballs, and which were designed to land in the ocean, dangling helplessly beneath a parachute. If early astronauts could not fly the new spacecraft like the jet planes they knew best, though, they consoled themselves with the thought that they might at least have the opportunity to perform valuable engineering work, verifying the hardware and procedures that might someday make more extensive space voyages possible (Schefter, 1999: 88).

In the seven mid-career Air Force, Marine, and Navy test pilots NASA chose to be America's first astronauts, it found a community of technologists comfortable in the cockpits of dangerous machines. The men, though, were also familiar with the complex procedures of flight testing and the demands of data collection and analysis pursuant to an organized plan of research. Led, eventually, by Air Force test pilot Donald 'Deke' Slayton, they championed a vision of the astronaut as aviator-engineer-manager whose work, while often requiring little traditional piloting, entailed substantial responsibilities centered around the management of complex technological systems (Society of Experimental Test Pilots, 1978: 62; Schefter, 1999: 86–87; Mindell, 2008: 80). These would include critical life support and communications devices, navigational tools, scientific experiments, and thrusters to orient the vehicle and slow it down for its fiery, high speed plunge back into the atmosphere.

What Does an Astronaut Do?, a 1961 youth nonfiction book by Robert Wells, described the spacemen's role most succinctly:

> The astronaut sees to it that his spacecraft does the job assigned to it. Its control system for oxygen and air pressure, its control system which keeps the craft 'right side up' in flight – and most of its other systems – can work automatically. They usually do. Yet the astronaut is in command of these systems and their controls.
>
> He is manager of all these systems.

(Wells, 1961: 8–9). Instead of bemoaning the checklists as a deskilling intrusion on their traditional autonomy, America's pilot-astronauts embraced them as emblematic of the rigorous education, creative synthesis, and effective leadership they could bring to the space programme. While daring, reckless flying often characterized early airplane pilots, American spaceflight skipped the barnstorming stage and developed around highly standardized procedures from its very beginnings. Rather than climbing aboard the first space vehicles as artisans, astronauts approached them as professional managers.

A space vehicle workplace dominated by a skilled professional manager was not the only way to structure a space crew: in the Soviet Union, where test pilots had less influence in their country's space programme, legendary engineer-manager Sergei Korolev championed space vehicles flown by remote control and automated systems and a cosmonaut corps of young aviators trained principally to withstand physical stresses and follow orders from the ground, orders they had done relatively little to develop (Gerovitch, 2007: 141). In so effectively promoting their own skills as test pilots, though, NASA's astronauts (supported by NASA managers drawn from the flight test community) helped ensure that future space vehicles would be built to harness the astronauts' diverse abilities and would demand significant managerial attention from their crews.

The earliest pilots who embraced checklists had the luxury of working with aircraft already in existence; NASA's engineers – including its astronauts – would instead need to create in-flight documentation for vehicles that did not yet exist, flying to places that could not yet be reached. 'In manned space flight . . . there is no such thing as a "taxi test" or a "once-around-the-field" checkout,' wrote one NASA expert in 1964 (Kuehnel, 1964: 457). The extreme cost of space vehicle development required that NASA undertake research and development work with an operational space vehicle, requiring extensive preparation and constant communication between flight crews and ground personnel using detailed technical analyses and simulation technologies. While astronauts flew on predetermined trajectories, ground crews would monitor vehicle performance through voice communications and automated telemetry from vehicle systems and help resolve systems issues. Because launches entailed tight scheduling (and space vehicles move so quickly), space missions placed a premium on accurate real-time decision-making, requiring that flight planners anticipate major system malfunctions and plan appropriate responses in advance. Flight planning for any particular mission, one 1972 NASA summary report described, could embrace both a 'nominal' flight plan and a series of alternatives employed in the event of mechanical malfunction or other contingencies (O'Neill *et al.*, 1972: 35–36). As a result of these pressures, in-flight documentation grew to include a diverse array of materials, from the kind of navigational charts already well known to seafarers, to mathematical reference tables long-utilized in engineering work, to step-by-step descriptions of simple activities necessitated by NASA's lack of experience with orbital flight.

NASA's Manned Spacecraft Center (MSC) in Houston, Texas, eventually served to coordinate the production of in-flight documentation, which was only one highly-visible component of the large volume of technical literature produced by engineers and scientists to manage spaceflight training and operations. 'Mission rules,' for example, codified decision pathways, while other documents coordinated ground communication and work flows and described vehicle systems to ensure rapid troubleshooting of unexpected problems (Lewis and Lockhard, 1964: 451–53). Prepared in conjunction with medical and scientific experts, the mission's 'flight plan' was the most critical document, as it described how crewmembers would interface with their craft and served planning, training, and operational functions (O'Neill *et al.*, 1972: 3). The flight plan coordinated the diverse activities of the space mission into a single document comprising a 'time-referenced step-by-step list of the astronaut's activities,' compact procedure checklists, summaries of science experiments, and, often, supplemental maps and charts to be used by crews in-flight (Kuehnel, 1964: 458). Many of these documents might never be used in flight: 'contingency flight plans' provided procedures to be employed if mission objectives changed, while 'alternate' flight plans provided procedures to be used in case of alterations to the launch schedule (O'Neill *et al.*, 1972: 1). Together, though, these documents served as both a critical operational tool and a training device for future crews, created and tested using sophisticated, computer-controlled ground simulators that mimicked the operation of space vehicles (Faber and Johnson, 1964: 485; Lewis and Lockhard, 1964: 453; O'Neill *et al.*, 1972: 5).

While occasionally signed by their contributors and certified by NASA managers, flight plans and checklists bore an anonymous quality suited to the minimalist aesthetic of their era: crisp black-and-white text and artful line drawings and schematics intended to communicate information in the most clear manner possible (Lewis and Lockhard, 1964: 452). Indeed, the authors of two articles in a 1964 technical anthology described the creation of NASA's checklists without mentioning the name of a single individual responsible for it (Kuehnel, 1964; Lewis and Lockhard, 1964). While teams of 2–9 people laboured most closely over such documents, their creation required the cooperation of hundreds of individuals, most of whom never received any formal recognition for their efforts (O'Neill *et al.*, 1972: 26).

By 1963, MSC had become the base of both the Astronaut Office and of NASA's Flight Crew Support Division, which provided personal equipment training tools, and documentation for flight operations (Brooks *et al.*, 1979: 402–03). The first astronauts played an active role in the development of onboard documentation; Robert Gilruth, head of NASA's Space Task Group on human spaceflight, expected his astronauts to participate broadly in space vehicle design work and the astronauts enthusiastically exploited the opportunity. Eventually, this interaction was formalized in a procedure by which Slayton, acting as Chief Astronaut, assigned new astronauts to participate in various engineering projects associated with the space programme, including the finalization of vehicle design and the preparation of documentation. Several worked closely with contractors to produce NASA's Project Gemini (1965–66) and Apollo (1967–1975) vehicles, reviewing designs, suggesting improvements, and establishing procedures for their operation. Critically, development of spacecraft and the astronauts' training in their operation occurred roughly simultaneously.

America's earliest piloted space vehicles taxed their pilot's skill only minimally; the capsules of Project Mercury had little ability to manœuvre in orbit and were 'flown' remotely from the ground with chimpanzee passengers before human astronauts occupied them (Mindell, 2008: 77, 81). Even with its relative simplicity, though, a Mercury capsule under human control was a complex machine requiring a variety of booklets and data cards. In John Glenn's Friendship 7 Mercury spacecraft (now on display at the Smithsonian's National Air and Space Museum), a checklist mounted above the vehicle's periscope aided with in-flight tasks, supplemented by small, irregularly-shaped, typewritten data cards affixed to bare surfaces in the cockpit. In-flight equipment failures were commonplace in Project Mercury and could require substantial alterations to pre-planned procedures. Two relatively minor system failures during Gordon Cooper's 1963 Mercury flight required that ground personnel develop and communicate 22 procedural changes to Cooper over four hours, two of which were revisions of earlier changes necessitated by the second failure (Lewis and Lockhard, 1964: 452).

The enlarged two-man spacecraft of Project Gemini would offer crews more challenging responsibilities, including the need to control and navigate the vehicle during complex orbital manœuvres. Astronauts mastered these procedures with the help of the first onboard computers as well as more robust checklist technologies than those employed in Project Mercury (O'Neill *et al.*, 1972: 7). Gemini engineers actually integrated checklists into the vehicle's cockpit instrumentation: recessed into the instrument panel in the space between Gemini's two crew couches was a vertical reel-to-reel scrolling tape containing procedure lists visible to either crewmember. (Gemini's astronauts, literally, flew their checklist.) When venturing out of their spacecraft in the first space walks (extravehicular activity, or EVA), or intercepting other spacecraft in orbit, astronauts relied upon checklists and documentation they had prepared with ground engineers. Indeed, confronted with a radar failure prior to an attempted rendezvous on a 1966 Gemini mission, Pilot 'Buzz' Aldrin calculated the intercept by hand, using reference charts that he had mostly drafted himself (French and Burgess, 2007: 123).

If Gemini had increased the burden on astronauts, Apollo's Moon-bound space vehicles would tax them even further, tasking crews with the simultaneous management of two distinct spacecraft comprised of four separate modules, propelled into deep space by the largest rocket ever built. Apollo spacecraft permitted true interplanetary navigation aided by digital electronic computers and other complex instruments whose operation would be impossible without onboard documentation. While Apollo spacecraft maintained radio contact with ground control stations during their flights, contact remained intermittent and, when the vehicle disappeared behind the Moon, was impossible. Apollo would contain the technology to guide itself but, rather than relying totally on automation, spacecraft designers sought to give crewmembers as much control as was practical, harnessing their expertise to increase system reliability and justify a human presence aboard the vehicles (Mindell, 2008: 105). To do this, the astronauts would need instructions.

For Apollo, short schedules, overlapping timelines, and complex mission objectives would make documentation technologies a central aspect of mission planning. While NASA contractors at the Instrumentation Laboratory of the Massachusetts Institute of Technology devised the operating routines for the onboard guidance computers, for example, NASA's Mission Analysis and Planning Division devised lunar landing strategies. Using 'systems management' techniques pioneered in ballistic missile programmes in the 1950s, Apollo's managers utilized standard procedures for the implementation of design changes to ensure that all Apollo's hardware and documentation remained compatible through its development (O'Neill *et al.*, 1972: 2; Johnson, 2002). In the 30 days prior to the launch of Apollo 11, NASA considered over 1000 changes to the flight plan, but pre-flight documentation corrections could not be made haphazardly. Apollo was a system of connected technologies relatively intolerant of capricious change. Rather, a Crew Procedures Control Board (CPCB) coordinated these changes, insuring that seemingly small revisions did not create ripples that might alter mission objectives or crew procedures (O'Neill *et al.*, 1972: 40–41).

The volume of onboard materials required for lunar flight at first suggested the need for radical new technologies for storing and displaying them: the first Apollo mockup included a film reader that would project the entire universe of documentation required for each mission onto a screen inside the cabin. Instead, Apollo launched with a smaller library of printed works bound mostly in looseleaf binders, supplemented by more copious documentation on the ground. NASA, at Slayton's urging, also dropped plans to include a teletype printer aboard Apollo, saving weight and making the astronauts critical conduits for navigational information from the ground, which would be dispatched by voice radio by fellow astronauts in the Mission Control Center (MCC) and transcribed onboard by hand (David G. Hoag, 1976: 283; Mindell, 2008: 108–09).

Checklists to the moon

In Stanley Kubrick's 1968 adaptation of the Arthur C. Clarke novel *2001: A Space Odyssey*, the camera lingers on a space toilet whose instructions are not only impossibly complex, but appear to require that the operator actually read them while using the device. Such intensive integration of textual materials into vehicle operations was routine in America's actual space programme. Virtually every photograph or motion picture of Apollo's Command Module (CM) and Lunar Module (LM) depicts some kind of checklist, flight plan, data card, or timeline, affixed to a backing board lined with Velcro so that it could be mounted in any one of a number of locations around the cockpit.

Critical piloting tools, made safer after 1967 through the introduction of fireproof paper, checklists proliferated to every corner of Apollo's habitable environment.[1] Launch stowage lists for Apollo 11 detailed 34 separate pieces of documentation – letter-sized data cards, 8-inch-by-5.5-inch three-ring binders of white and red cardstock, and various other materials – provided for the crew's use during the mission (National Aeronautics and Space Administration, 1969b). Apollo 11's *Launch Operations Checklist* had 113 pages; its CM *Operations Checklist* more than 200. In excruciating detail, these books instructed crews on matters both obvious and obscure, including which switches to flip and when, where and how to stow or unstow equipment, and how to operate the onboard computers that would guide them to the Moon. Notation instructed astronauts when to monitor systems and provided blanks to record key data for later use. (Figure 1. *Apollo 11 Launch Operations Checklist:* 2–13, National Air and Space Museum NASM 9A05846, Smithsonian Institution.) No detail seemingly escaped the checklists' omniscience, instructing crews (in a clipped series of abbreviations and verbs) how to shut down the LM's descent engine

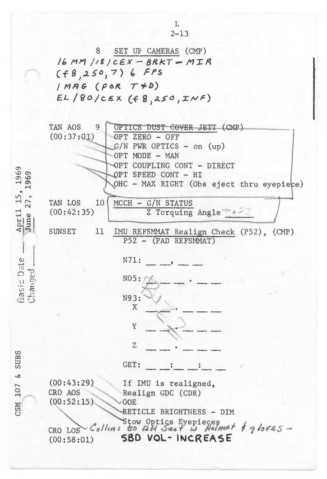

Figure 1: *Apollo 11 Launch Operations Checklists:* 2–13, National Air and Space Museum (NASM 9A05846), Smithsonian Institution.

or exit from an inverted CM so as not to bump their heads ('EXIT FEET FIRST') (Guidance and Control Procedures Section, 1971: 9–4; Mindell, 2008: 197). Even the hatch of Apollo 11's CM, now preserved at the Smithsonian's National Air and Space Museum, bore two checklists, describing the two dozen steps required to depressurize and repressurize the cabin. When freed from the confines of their craft, Apollo astronauts still relied upon checklists. Spacesuits carried various instructions; the left extravehicular gloves of Apollo 11 astronauts Neil Armstrong and Aldrin, for example, bore sewn-on cloth checklists of lunar surface activities. In time, though, the increasing complexity of Apollo's mission goals required separate 'cuff checklists,' small spiral-bound booklets affixed to the astronaut's wrist and containing more exacting instructions and diagrams, separated by tab dividers. (Figure 2: *Apollo 12 Lunar Module Pilot*

Figure 2: *Apollo 12 Lunar Module Pilot Alan Bean on lunar surface, with cuff checklist visible on left wrist.* NASA/JSC Photo AS12-49-7281.

Alan Bean on lunar surface, with cuff checklist visible on left wrist. NASA/JSC Photo AS12–49–7281.)

To aid in the production of these documents, the Astronaut Office, beginning with Apollo, assigned to each piloted flight a dedicated astronaut support crew (in addition to the traditional backup crew), to assemble and update the mission's flight plan, checklists, and mission rules, assembled in the 'Flight Data File' (O'Neill *et al.*, 1972: 4; Brooks *et al.*, 1979: 261 at †). Typically, the astronauts assigned to support duties were junior astronauts who, by virtue of their late arrival in NASA, could not receive immediate crew assignments and found themselves, instead, employed as engineers designing hardware that they hoped they might one day fly. Rather than bemoaning such work, astronauts embraced the opportunity to influence spaceflight operations and prepare for future flights. Junior astronauts Bill Anders and Alan Bean, selected in 1963 and anticipating their first flights as Lunar Module Pilot (LMP), conspired, while supervising construction of the spacecraft at the Grumman factory in Bethpage, New York, to prepare checklists that would enable them to disembark on the Moon's surface before their crewmates (French and Burgess, 2007: 297). Though eventually countermanded by a veteran astronaut, the change might have permitted one of the two men to become the first human to step foot on the Moon had they been assigned to the first lunar landing flight. Nonetheless, junior astronauts found drafting checklists to be among the more satisfying aspects of their work; in 1969, junior astronaut Gordon Fullerton found himself, with Ed Gibson, helping to write cuff checklists for Bean and fellow Apollo 12 astronaut

Pete Conrad, thrilled that only months into his tenure, NASA had entrusted him with such responsibility (Gibson, 2000: 21; Fullerton, 2002: 11).[2]

While support crews were charged also with less glamorous duties (like setting switches in cockpit simulators in advance of prime and back-up crews) familiarity with vehicle procedures gave them an advantage in future flights (Brooks *et al.*, 1979: 261 at †). As the astronauts' training entailed both reading checklists and writing them, flight crews often travelled into space having already logged long hours writing the manuals for the space vehicles they flew (Fullerton, 2002: 14). Training summaries for flight and backup crewmembers for Apollo 11, though, still allocated 100 hours to familiarization with these materials; Commander (CDR) Armstrong, Command Module Pilot (CMP) Michael Collins, and LMP Aldrin exceeded that quota by more than 40 hours each, and their backup LMP, Fred Haise, spent 131 hours (Training Office, 1974: Table 2.14). NASA's growing experience with lunar flight did not diminish the enthusiasm of crews for the robust information technology. Rather than relying upon these materials less as the program progressed, the last Apollo crew (of 1972's Apollo 17 mission), LMP Jack Schmitt later recalled, 'was more wedded to following checklists than other crews,' in part because they had trained with them so closely (Schmitt, 2000: 30).

As the authors and editors of checklists, astronauts were not mere automatons, performing scripts written by others. Rather, astronauts viewed checklists as their managerial responsibility, reading, discussing, and modifying them throughout the flight, and confidently expressing their disapproval when inevitable mistakes occurred. Collins, in particular, was intolerant of bad documentation produced by the engineers of the 'checklist world,' and noted, after Apollo 11, that one faulty checklist instruction required astronauts to throw a switch in a part of the craft before they had occupied it (Manned Operations Branch, 1969b: Sec. 4: 1).

Whenever possible, astronauts worked with ground controllers to resolve problems. Corrections to procedures might require a series of communications between the astronauts in space and the MCC in Houston; there, the Flight Activities Officer (FAO) coordinated crew procedures, including necessary revisions (O'Neill *et al.*, 1972: 6). Changes, though, might originate all over the country, including places like MIT, where engineers and scientists developed new sets of instructions to meet sudden problems. In one harrowing incident, a troublesome electrical short on Apollo 14 required a new procedure to be conveyed across the country and eventually to lunar orbit, where astronauts transcribed and implemented it (Mindell, 2008: 245).

Occasionally during flights, astronauts modified incorrect procedures on the fly, but contrary to their 'cowboy' image, they did so reluctantly. 'I don't enjoy making changes to procedures,' Collins declared in his post-flight briefing. 'It seems like the crew only does that when they feel there's some good need for it' (Manned Operations Branch, 1969a: Sec. 24: 45–46). Rather than defending the right of flight crews to alter checklists they found unwiely, Collins asserted that astronauts preferred to follow precise instructions and would hold ground engineers responsible for mistakes. Surrounded by complex systems, Apollo astronauts literally flew their vehicles to the Moon with book in hand, creating a personal relationship between people and the written word unseen since the Victorian era.

Mistakes to complex procedures discovered in flight, though, often required immediate written correction. Armed with a variety of writing implements (including the legendary pressurized-ink Fisher Space Pen, produced through a $1 million private research and development programme) (Dick, 2004), astronauts would alter procedures, enter data, check-off completed activities, or make notes for the future. Apollo 11 checklists used by Collins bear multiple annotations in neat black felt-tip pen concerning navigation, procedures, and systems monitoring. Other notations in blue ink and pencil attest to more harried jottings suggestive of a seafaring captain's log. Empty spaces on the checklists bear the occasional note for posterity, or for engineers combing the documents after the flight for information about the performance of flight hardware. The cover of the *Apollo 11*'s *Launch Operations Checklist*, for example, bears a penciled note in hurried script that a leg pocket of Armstrong's spacesuit 'interferes with abort handle,' a potentially mission-ending problem that Collins later described in his post-flight debriefing (National Aeronautics and Space Administration, 1969d). 'He was worried about that,' Collins noted, 'and I was worried about that' (Manned Operations Branch, 1969b: 3–12). Armed with their checklists, America's astronauts literally read themselves to the Moon.

Reflections of the workplace

As distillations of astronaut work, checklists were oddly representative of the human spaceflight programme, both in their obsession with well-planned technical details and carefully circumscribed space for individual expression. Checklists were a central aspect of the work culture of spaceflight; prepared by astronauts for astronauts, with little expectation that others would see them. While changes could be difficult to implement, though, even flawless checklists were not intended to be permanent articles of dogma. Just as 19th-century intellectuals consumed the latest tracts on natural science, annotating pages, tearing spines, and making books their own, astronauts laboured over binders intended to be fluid logs of their own achievements and stumbles, filled with paper and pencil checkmarks, annotations, and sometimes even bawdy humour (Secord, 2000: 236–39).

While critically involved in their construction, astronauts were not the only individuals with access to in-flight documentation, and ground personnel frequently annotated the materials with messages, cartoons, jokes, and their signatures. Expressions of support were frequent in in-flight materials, with ground crews poking fun at the astronauts but also praising Apollo 11's CM *Columbia* and LM *Eagle*, noting that 'COLUMBIA & EAGLE ARE THE GREATEST MAN HAS CREATED' and wishing the 'MOONMEN' luck on their voyage (National Aeronautics and Space Administration, 1969c). Cartoons depicting Snoopy, the daydreaming beagle of Charles Schulz's *Peanuts* cartoon strip, make particularly frequent appearances. First doodled on daily schedules by NASA pre-flight operations chief Ernie Reyes, Snoopy served as an unofficial mascot of the Apollo programme (Raul E. Reyes, 1992: 9–10). A 'Silver Snoopy' award honoured excellent performance by NASA employees and the black-and-white communications-carrying headgear Apollo astronauts wore was quickly dubbed the 'Snoopy Cap'; Apollo 10's LM even bore the cartoon beagle's name. In the unsigned cartoons drawn on various checklists, Snoopy appears as a narrator perched forlornly atop his doghouse describing mission events or, as a surrogate for the crew, clad in a spacesuit. Beneath their helmets, the characters wear Snoopy's distinctive leather flying helmet and goggles, known to readers from his imaginary duels with the famed World War I flying ace the Red Baron (Eric M. Jones and Glover, 2007). Apollo 11's 'Command Module Operations Checklist' bears two Snoopy cartoons, in which the dog wonders whether 'THEY HAVE DOGGIE BAGS ON THE MOON' and, later 'HOW CAN I EAT WHEN WE'RE APPROACHING A LUNAR LANDING?' One cartoon depicts Snoopy's doghouse as a surrogate for the Apollo spacecraft stack, with stick figure astronauts quietly smuggling personal items into the vehicles, a longstanding and occasionally controversial feature of the human spaceflight program (National Aeronautics and Space Administration, 1969c).

Checklists could also be, like many of America's early astronauts, imperfect, jocular, and blatantly sexual. On the lunar surface, Apollo 12 astronauts Bean and Conrad found that the cuff checklists had been littered with cartoons by Reyes depicting the astronauts as incompetent 'Snoopy'-style characters floundering on the lunar surface. In a 1998 interview Reyes described composing the cartoons at the request of an unnamed member of the Apollo 12 crew (possibly CMP Dick Gordon, who remained in lunar orbit as Bean and Conrad walked on the surface). Conrad apparently enjoyed them (Raul E. 'Ernie' Reyes, 1998: 77). Accompanying the cartoons, though, were black-and-white reproductions of *Playboy* magazine photographs of nude women, an addition for which Reyes denied responsibility.[3] The images bear smutty captions playing upon the scientific activities astronauts were assigned to complete while on the lunar surface, admonishing Bean to 'SURVEY HER ACTIVITY' and 'DESCRIBE THE PROTRUBERANCES,' and inquiring whether Conrad had 'SEEN ANY INTERESTING HILLS & VALLEYS?' (Eric M. Jones and Glover, 2007). Conrad and Bean later told a *Playboy* reporter that they hadn't noticed the Playmates in their checklists until well into their lunar EVA, and thoroughly enjoyed them (Rowe, 2007). Somewhat more tame was a mock glossary of abbreviations included on CDR Gene Cernan's Apollo 17 EVA-2 cuff checklist. Playing upon the arcane vernacular of checklists and NASA's penchant for cryptic acronyms, the glossary offered a range of observational terms unlikely to be of any use to Cernan on the Moon, including 'btw' ('big tall women'), 'cra' ('loco moon person'), and 'xln' ('Mr. Lincoln's ex-wife') (National Aeronautics and Space Administration, 1972). Such jokes were magnified by the profound distance between the author and recipient: on the surface of the Moon, no one could hear the astronauts groan.

Cartoons, jokes, and more staid notations about navigation, photography, and other operations appear throughout Apollo 11's checklists, but one Velcro-studded card in Apollo 11's 'Command Module Operations Checklist' invited more thoughtful commentary. Entitled in Gothic black script 'Ye Ole Lunar Scratch Pad,' the page, by mission's end, was filled with pencil scribbles and remarks apparently drafted by Collins, probably during the extended period in which he orbited the Moon as the vehicle's sole occupant (National Aeronautics and Space Administration 1969c). (Figure 3. *Apollo 11 Operations Checklist*, 'Ye Ole Lunar Scratch Pad.' National Air and Space Museum (NASM 9A05847), Smithsonian Institution.) While strings of numbers and lists of objects ('ROCK

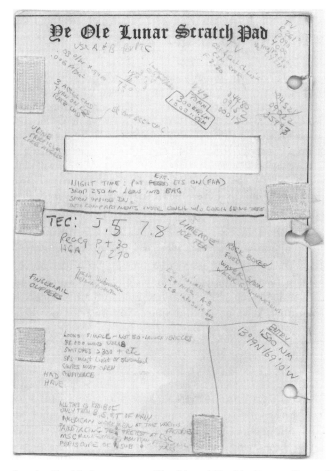

Figure 3: *Apollo 11 Operations Checklist, 'Ye Ole Lunar Scratch Pad.'* National Air and Space Museum (NASM 9A05847), Smithsonian Institution.

BOXES FOOD WATER SPOON'; 'Trash Underwear Helmet Protector') grace the sheet, so do random observations and musings. 'URINE PARTICLES LIKE ANGELS' reads one notation, as does the following, chilling description of the work of spaceflight:

LOOKS SIMPLE – NOT SO – LAUNCH VEHICLES
38,000 WORD VOCAB
SWITCHES >300 + etc
SPS[4] must light or stranded
CHUTES MUST OPEN
CONFIDENCE
HAD
HAVE

(National Aeronautics and Space Administration, 1969c). The checklist-style comments appeared to form a rough draft of the remarks Collins broadcast while returning to the Earth on July 23rd, in which he focused, not on the magnitude of his achievement, but upon the difficulty he had encountered managing *Columbia*'s huge cockpit:

> This trip of ours to the Moon may have looked, to you, simple or easy. I'd like to assure you that has not been the case. The . . . rocket which put us into orbit is an incredibly complicated piece of machinery. . . . This computer up above my head has a 38,000 word vocabulary. . . . This switch which I have in my hand now, has over 300 counterparts in the command module alone. . . . In addition to that, there are myriads of circuit breakers, levers, rods, and other associated controls. . . . The parachutes up above my head must work perfectly tomorrow or we will plummet into the ocean. We have always had confidence that all this equipment will work, and work properly, and we continue to have confidence that it will do so for the remainder of the flight.

Collins concluded by thanking the manifold NASA personnel responsible for the crew's survival and success; like the periscope of a submarine, Apollo 11's crewmembers were only the most visible part of an effort much larger than themselves, but a part combining extreme danger with almost unimaginable responsibilities, aided by checklists that had guided them through every stage of their flight (National Aeronautics and Space Administration, 1969a: 588–89).

Conclusion

In the late 1950s, a group of American test pilots confronted a tremendous threat to their professional identity: a new flight regime in which the role of the human was far from secure (Mindell, 2006: 148–49). Already skilled as aviators, pilots adjusted to new flying machines that demanded more than quick reflexes, manual dexterity, or even good judgment. Rather, piloting increasingly required technical sophistication and the management of huge of amounts of information. The arrival of new workplace technologies can empower a professional group or undermine it (Sandelowski, 2000): pilots, leveraging their skills and status as elite aviators mastered the new information technologies and retained control of their machines. Space technology emerged as a complex socio-technological system, and a technology that appeared to rob the pilots of some of their autonomy – the checklist – actually offered America's astronauts a way to demonstrate their technical and managerial skill.

In space, memory took a back seat to documentation. The tension between explicit, written information and tacit knowledge is a feature of scientific practice: seldom, as Harry Collins and others have written, has a published scientific paper alone enabled a scientist to reproduce the experiment of another (eg, H. M. Collins, 1992: 51, *et seq*.). For astronauts, though, personal knowledge of how to do things became a flawed, untrustworthy resource better replaced by strict procedures and detailed instruction manuals. NASA's astronauts of the 1960s, in turn, experienced a workplace little different from that of other white-collar workers of the period, in which procedures for the organization of information trumped individual initiative as the key to successful operations. Often, Apollo spacecraft became workspaces in which life and death were determined by how quickly information – the status of a guidance computer or propulsion system – could be recorded, read, and moved from place to place according to highly choreographed procedures.

Indeed, one of the lasting images of Apollo is of the engineers in MCC assenting in series to mission milestones with a crisp utterance of 'go': human checklists. To Norman Mailer, whose 1970 book *Of A Fire on the Moon* skewered NASA's efforts to drive spontaneity out of Apollo 11's flight, the Moon landing's textual regimentation was just another example of how NASA made the landing utterly predictable and its astronauts creepy automatons (Mailer, 1970). Yet for the astronauts, the checklist was a mark of distinction rather than a badge of servitude. Rather than obliterating the human, David Mindell writes, Apollo's LM checklists bound 'human and machine into a single integrated mechanism' that seemed to work better than either alone (Mindell, 2008: 197). Often, the rise of industrial mass production has been seen as detrimental to the autonomy of the worker, replacing craft practice with the mechanical inflexibility of the jig and the assembly line (eg, Braverman, 1975). In spaceflight, though, the difficulties entailed in preparing a practical checklist suggested the continued need for an astronaut as a professional manager, and a new kind of knowledge worker for the Space Age.[5]

Notes

1 One might have imagined the profusion of paper aboard Apollo to have been a potential fire hazard. Checklists, though, were not the cause of the launch pad fire that killed three Apollo astronauts in 1967. While the spacecraft had contained an 'extensive distribution of combustible materials,' far more dangerous than paper was the Velcro used to affix the manuals to the spacecraft interior. The checklists escaped blame; in fact, the investigators wondered whether more

timely revision and distribution of checklists might have informed personnel of potentially unsafe conditions and lessened the danger posed by 'plugs-out' test that triggered the fire (National Aeronautics and Space Administration 1967: 5.2, 5.9, 5.12).

2 Bean, an enthusiast of checklists, had asked Gibson and NASA engineer Bob Roberts to create a more portable system of documentation to accompany him on Moon walks. Attending to lunar experiments on Apollo 12, Conrad and Bean praised the cuff checklists, singling out Gibson for his efforts (National Aeronautics and Space Administration 2006: 134:05:43–56).

3 Gibson later appeared to take credit for these additions (Gibson, 2000: 21).

4 'Service Propulsion System,' the large rocket engine on the Apollo Service Module that would blast the crew out of lunar orbit and back to Earth.

5 The author would like to thank the University of Pennsylvania's Department of History and Sociology of Science, the Smithsonian's National Air and Space Museum, and the archivists and librarians of the National Aeronautics and Space Administration for their support of this project. Chris Jones, Eric Hintz, Allan Needell, Emily Pawley, and Roger Turner provided useful feedback on early drafts; Greg Bryant, Daniel Berry, Paul Ceruzzi, Ruth Schwartz Cohen, David DeVorkin, Robert Kohler, Walter Licht, Valerie Neal, Harrison Schmitt, Margaret Weitekamp. Michael Chesnes, Martin Collins, Colin Fries, Dittmar Geiger, Richard Hallion, Kate Igoe, Roger Launius, Michael Neufeld, Jane Odom, Richard Spencer, and Elizabeth Suckow provided advice, encouragement, and access to sources.

References

Braverman, H., (1975), *Labor and Monopoly Capital; the Degradation of Work in the Twentieth Century*, New York: Monthly Review Press.

Brooks, C. G., Grimwood, J. M. and Swenson, Jr, Loyd, S., (1979), *Chariots for Apollo: A History of Manned Lunar Spacecraft*, Washington: National Aeronautics and Space Administration.

Campbell-Kelly, M., (1994), 'The Railway Clearing House and Victorian Data Processing' in Lisa Bud-Frierman (ed.), *Information Acumen: The Understanding and Use of Knowledge in Modern Business*, New York: Routledge.

Chandler, A. D., (1977), *The Visible Hand: The Managerial Revolution in American Business*, Cambridge: Belknap Press.

Collins, H. M., (1992), *Changing Order: Replication and Induction in Scientific Practice*, Chicago: University of Chicago Press.

Collins, M., (1974), *Carrying the Fire: An Astronaut's Journeys*, New York: Farrar.

David, G. H., (1976), 'The History of Apollo on-Board Guidance, Navigation & Control' in Ernst A. Steinhoff (ed.), *The Eagle Has Returned: Proceedings of the Dedication Conference of the International Space Hall of Fame, Held at Alamogordo, New Mexico, from 5 through 9 October 1976*, San Diego: American Astronautical Society: 270–300.

Degani, A. and Weiner, E. L., (1991), *Human Factors of Flight-Deck Checklists: The Normal Checklist*, Moffett Field: NASA Ames Research Center.

Dick, S. J., (2004), 'The Fisher Space Pen', *NASA History Division*, National Aeronautics and Space Administration ⟨http://history.nasa.gov/spacepen.html⟩ [accessed 6 May 2008].

Faber, S. and Johnson, H. I., (1964), 'Simulators and Training for Manned Space Flight' in P. E. Purser (ed.), *Manned Spacecraft: Engineering Design and Operation*, New York: Fairchild Publications: 477–90.

French, F. and Burgess, C., (2007), *In the Shadow of the Moon: A Challenging Journey to Tranquility, 1965–1969*, Lincoln: University of Nebraska Press.

Fullerton, C. G., (2002), *Oral History Transcript, Rebecca Wright, interviewer*, NASA Johnson Space Center Oral History Project; NASA Dryden Flight Research Center: National Aeronautics and Space Administration.

Gawande, A., (2007), 'The Checklist: If Something So Simple Can Transform Intensive Care, What Else Can It Do?', *The New Yorker*, December 10.

Gerovitch, S., (2007), 'New Soviet Man' inside the Machine: Human Engineering, Spacecraft Design, and the Construction of Communism', *Osiris* 22: 135–57.

Gibson, E. G., (2000), *Oral History Transcript, Carol Butler, interviewer*, NASA Johnson Space Center Oral History Project; Houston: National Aeronautics and Space Administration.

Guidance & Control Procedures Section, Systems Procedures Branch, Crew Procedures Division, Manned Spacecraft Center, (1971), 'CSM Launch Checklist (Apollo 15)' Houston: National Aeronautics and Space Administration.

Hallion, R., (1981), *Test Pilots: The Frontiersmen of Flight*, Garden City: Doubleday.

Hoag, David G., (1976), 'The history of Apollo on-board guidance, navigation and control', in *The Eagle Has Returned: Proceedings of the Dedication Conference of the International Space Hall of Fame*, held at Alamogordo, New Mexico, from 5 though 9 October 1976, edited by Ernst A. Steinhoff: 270–300, San Diego: American Astronautical Society.

Johnson, S. B., (2002), *The Secret of Apollo: Systems Management in American and European Space Programs*, Baltimore: Johns Hopkins University Press.

Jones, E. M. and Glover, K., (eds.), (2007), *'Apollo 12, Cuff Checklists'*, Apollo Lunar Surface Journal.

Jones, T. D., (2006), *Sky Walking: An Astronaut's Memoir*, New York: Smithsonian Books.

Kuehnel, H. A., (1964), 'Inflight Crew Activities' in P. E. Purser (ed.), *Manned Spacecraft: Engineering Design and Operation*, New York: Fairchild Publications: 457–66.

Lewis, C. R. and Lockhard, D. T., (1964), 'Inflight Systems Monitoring' in P. E. Purser (ed.), *Manned Spacecraft: Engineering Design and Operation*, New York: Fairchild Publications: 451–56.

Mailer, N., (1970), *Of a Fire on the Moon*, Boston: Little, Brown.

Manned Operations Branch, Flight Crew Support Division (1969a), *Apollo 11 Technical Crew Debriefing (U)*, Vol. 2, Manned Spacecraft Center, National Aeronautics and Space Administration.

Manned Operations Branch, Flight Crew Suppport Division (1969b), *Apollo 11 Technical Crew Debriefing (U)*, Vol. 1 (Manned Spacecraft Center, National Aeronautics and Space Administration).

Mindell, D. A., (2006), 'Human and Machine in the History of Spaceflight' in S. J. Dick and Roger D. Launius (eds), *Critical Issues in the History of Spaceflight*, Washington, DC: National Aeronautics and Space Administration, Office of External Relations, History Division: 141–68.

Mindell, D. A., (2008), *Digital Apollo: Human and Machine in Spaceflight*, Cambridge: MIT Press.

National Aeronautics and Space Administration (1967), 'Part V: Investigation and Analyses' in *Report of Apollo 204 Review Board*, Washington, DC.

National Aeronautics and Space Administration (1969a), *Apollo 11 Technical Air-to-Ground Voice Transcription, GOSS NET 1*, Houston: Manned Spacecraft Center.

National Aeronautics and Space Administration (1969b), *Apollo Stowage List Mission as 506 CM 107/LM-5 Apollo 11* Houston: Manned Spacecraft Center.

National Aeronautics and Space Administration (1969c), 'Notebook, Checklist, Command Module Operations, Apollo 11, Michael Collins'.

National Aeronautics and Space Administration (1969d), 'Notebook, Checklist, Launch Operations, Apollo 11, Michael Collins'.

National Aeronautics and Space Administration (1972), 'Apollo 17 CDR EVA-2 Flown Cuff Checklist', *Apollo Lunar Surface Journal* ⟨http://www.hq.nasa.gov/alsj/⟩ [accessed December 17 2007].

National Aeronautics and Space Administration (2006), 'Apollo 12 Lunar Surface Journal: Surveyor Crater and Surveyor III', *Apollo Lunar Surface Journal* ⟨http://www.hq.nasa.gov/alsj/a12/a12.html⟩ [accessed January 2 2008].

O'Neill, J. W., Cotter, J. B. and Holloway, T. W., (1972), *Apollo Experience Report: Flight Planning for Manned Space Operations*, Houston: NASA Manned Spacecraft Center.

Reyes, R. E., (1992), *Oral History Transcript, Aaron Gillette, interviewer*, NASA Kennedy Space Center: National Aeronautics and Space Administration.

Reyes, R. E., 'Ernie' (1998), *Oral History Transcript, Carol L. Butler, interviewer*, NASA Johnson Space Center Oral History Project; Titusville: National Aeronautics and Space Administration.

Rowe, C., (2007), 'On Buckeyes, Nanotechnology and Playmates in Space', *Playboy.com* ⟨http://www.playboy.com/blog/2007/01/on-buckeyes-nanotechnology-and-playmates-in-space.html⟩ [accessed March 3 2008].

Sandelowski, M., (2000), *Devices and Desires: Gender, Technology, and American Nursing*, Chapel Hill: University of North Carolina Press.

Schefter, J. L., (1999), *The Race: The Uncensored Story of How America Beat Russia to the Moon*, New York: Doubleday.

Schmitt, H. H., (2000), *Oral History Transcript #2, Carol Butler, interviewer*, NASA Johnson Space Center Oral History Project; Houston: National Aeronautics and Space Administration.

Secord, J. A., (2000), *Victorian Sensation: The Extraordinary Publication, Reception, and Secret Authorship of Vestiges of the Natural History of Creation*, Chicago: University of Chicago Press.

Smith, M. R., (1977), *Harpers Ferry Armory and the New Technology: The Challenge of Change*, Ithaca: Cornell University Press.

Society of Experimental Test Pilots (1978), *History of the First 20 Years*, Covina: Taylor Pub. Co.

Training Office, Crew Training and Procedures Division (1974), 'Crew Training Summaries: Mercury, Gemini, Apollo & Skylab Programs', Houston: NASA Johnson Space Center.

Wells, R., (1961), *What Does an Astronaut Do?* New York: Dodd.

Yates, J., (1989), *Control Through Communication: The Rise of System in American Management*, Baltimore: Johns Hopkins University Press.

A political history of NASA's space shuttle: the development years, 1972–1982

Brian Woods

Introduction

To assert that the Space Shuttle was influenced by politics is perhaps neither remarkable, nor controversial. Roland (1985), Logsdon (1986) and Heppenheimer (1999), among many others, have all documented how the Shuttle's design is the result of political compromise born out of a series of lengthy debates that raged both between and within NASA, the White House, Congress, the Department of Defense (DOD) and other branches of the Federal bureaucracy from 1968 to the end of 1971. In the main, these debates have served as the foci for analysis on the politics of the Shuttle. Yet the politics that result in the construction of the Shuttle (both as a thing and as a representation) go far beyond the 1968–1971 design phase and in many respects continue today. In this account, I concentrate on some aspects of Shuttle politics during what might loosely be called the development phase (1972–1982).

While Diane Vaughn's (1996) seminal work has done much to dispel the idea that the Challenger accident was the result of organizational deviance, with the loss of Columbia there was a re-emergence of the idea that both accidents were the result of flawed design, which resulted from political interference during 1969–71. At best, such commentary assumed that the technological and the political become separated once development of the technology begins – that the project embarks on a *natural technological trajectory* (Dosi, 1982) – at worse, this mode of thinking places politics on the outside where it is seen to impinge on and is deemed detrimental to technological progress. Thus, technological failure is often articulated in terms of the dichotomy between technical and political decisions, between objectivity and interests, where political compromise diverts value-free technological progress. The history and sociology of technology has long shown that interests, dispute, controversy, negotiation, and compromise (ie politics) are a normal part of technology building (eg MacKenzie, 1993). Political interests are never absent from technological production, but intrinsic to it (Barnes, 1977). Technology can thus be seen as a negotiated space where actors play out their own agendas. Technological projects require assemblages of people and things to bring them into existence, to negotiate their meaning, purpose and functioning. In this chapter I will survey a gathering of particular actions, affiliations, events, decisions and discourses that were leading to the militarization and the marketization of Shuttle and with it NASA. After the Challenger accident in 1986, both these processes came to a virtual halt (at least temporarily), but up to that event, both were emerging forcefully.

Akin to Noble (1984), this account will primarily explore politics at a macro level. This is not to say that micro-politics is less important. Indeed, I have dealt with aspects of interconnectedness of politics and technology across the social scale elsewhere (eg Woods, 2003). Here, however, my concentration is on the limits of NASA's transformative capabilities – how the ambitions of the Shuttle builders were interwoven with, shaped, and reshaped by different power relations and how those who wielded political power defined to a considerable extent what was and what was not technically possible. The quest for space arose from the post-war economic boom, the escalation of the Cold War, and the growth of the technocratic state. NASA and its Shuttle were products of these conditions, but the Shuttle itself emerged during a period of transition. The history of the twenty years after 1973 is that of instability, crisis and the formation of a different role for government and state. The argument then is that to some extent, the form, function and purpose of the Shuttle and NASA arose in part from the wider social, economic and political conditions within which they were made.

While this style of analysis obviously contravenes Latour's (2005) thesis in that I am guilty of using shortcuts to differentiate the landscape, I do not wish to depart entirely from what Latour calls a sociology of associations. Accordingly, the account surveys the traces left by the formations of advocates and adversary, of actor's work to mobilize and enrol a variety of different actors in an endeavour to convince them to commit to their project in particular ways and thus persuade them to redraw the boundaries around the object in question. Consistent with Latour, this chapter endeavours (within the space provided) to present a descriptive account, albeit with a somewhat restricted focus.

Revolution

On 5 January 1972, President Richard Nixon announced that the United States would invest in a multi-billion dollar enterprise to develop 'an entirely new type of space transportation system'. In a statement that was, inherently, technologically determinist, Nixon proclaimed the Shuttle as the 'next logical step' from the Apollo Moon landing programme and a technology that would 'transform the space frontier and *revolutionize*' space transportation (Nixon, 1972: my emphasis). The Shuttle symbolized the maturation of the space age. The plans formulated under the guidance of NASA's Office of Manned Space Flight promised technology that would precipitate a revolution akin to those thought to have been engendered by the ship, the train and the aeroplane that preceded it. Routine space travel meant the increased exploitation of this off-world environment – space would be open to the inventors and entrepreneurs of tomorrow who would forge new industries and new communities high above the Earth's surface. It was a vision that was bright and technically led: a progeny of an era of technological enthusiasm, when human progress was firmly tethered to advancements in science and technology.

Despite the rhetoric, Nixon was not a NASA fan. Even though NASA was established under his Vice Presidency during the Eisenhower Administration, he essentially saw the civilian space programme as a Kennedy project. Moreover, Nixon had formed the opinion that scientists and academics were against him, a view that contributed to his decision to abolish the President's Science Advisory Committee and Federal Council on Science and Technology (Killian, 1982; McDougall, 1985). Since his inauguration in 1969, therefore, Nixon endeavoured to rein in NASA's expectations, demands, and ambitions. Towards the end of 1971, however, the Office of Management and Budget (OMB) advised, unsurprisingly, that rapid economic growth and falling unemployment in 1972 benefited an incumbent president seeking re-election (Tufte, 1978). Nixon thus decided to plunge ahead with increased federal spending to produce boom conditions in the election year (Reichley, 1981). The approval of the shuttle programme may well have been part of that agenda. NASA came to believe that Nixon was persuaded to go ahead with the shuttle because the continuing depression in the aerospace industry and the relatively high rate of unemployment among the national pool of scientists and engineers might become election issues (Hoban, 1995).

On the day that Nixon announced the Shuttle programme, he also sent a letter to the chair of his New Hampshire campaign committee announcing his candidacy for re-election. Overwhelming support in all the Republican primaries ensured his nomination to stand again (Nixon, 1978). The Democratic primaries had furnished a sufficient majority for Senator George McGovern to stand as Nixon's opponent, a nomination that had surprised many because of McGovern's radical manifesto for a 'peace economy.' For the aerospace industry in particular, McGovern's plan was for the 'conversion' of military production into civilian production (McGovern, 1974). As in 1968, the continued involvement of the US in Vietnam dominated the 1972 election, clouding most other issues including Watergate (Ambrose, 1981). Nevertheless, the award of a multi-billion dollar project during an election year did not go unchallenged. Although NASA was a civilian agency and prided itself on its civilian status, McGovern believed the Shuttle to be primarily a military programme. Two weeks after Nixon's announcement to develop the Shuttle, McGovern told a Florida campaign audience that if elected he 'wouldn't manufacture a foolish project like the Space Shuttle to provide jobs' and that furthermore he considered the programme to be 'an enormous waste of money' (quoted in Hechler, 1980: 289). The Shuttle thus became part of the divide between McGovern and Nixon. An early campaign speech from Vice President Spiro Agnew launched a vicious attack on the Shuttle's critics, labelling them 'reactionaries, utopians and unrealistic' in arguing that spending on space technology should be redirected to social problems. Such policies he argued would 'bring to a virtual halt this country's technological progress' (Agnew, 1972: 1, 2). The advancement of science and technology, the accumulation of new knowledge, spin-off technology and investment in high skilled employment, were all well rehearsed compositions of promotional rhetoric for the space programme and Agnew cited them all as examples of the 'benefits from the space program that will improve the quality of life for all mankind' (ibid, 5, 6). Support for Nixon came from large portions of the aerospace industry. The Shuttle's relationship to jobs in that sector and its embodiment of scientific and technical progress meant that McGovern's intentions received a hostile reaction from many in the industry, who feared that he planned to 'strip' America's 'technology to the bare bones.' In their view, 'for an aerospace worker to vote for Sen. McGovern would be to vote for self-destruction' (Hotz, 1972: 7).

Conservative politics also prevailed within the executives of the aerospace unions long after Vietnam had shattered the cold war consensus. The American Federation of Labour (AFL) and the Congress of Industrial Organizations (CIO) were so vexed by McGovern's nomination that for the first time in its history the executive council adjourned without voting for any presidential endorsement (Brody, 1980). The AFL-CIO's declaration of neutrality, however, did not prevent considerable labour support for McGovern (Machinist, 1972). Nixon, nonetheless, had the support of his 'silent majority' (Nixon, 1978) and despite McGovern's plea to not 'let this man fool you again', 60 per cent of the voters chose Nixon in what was then the largest election victory in modern American history (Ambrose, 1981). Although Nixon was not an ardent champion of NASA, a Republican triumph assured continued support for the Shuttle programme. Presumably, under McGovern, the Shuttle would have been a symbolic peace economy casualty. Even assuming that McGovern could not have forced through all of his radical policies it is conceivable that a Democrat win would have resulted in the programme's cancellation.

The shape and direction of the NASA revolution however, fed as much upon reflections from the past as it did on a vision of the future. Its burgeoning nature, form and function were witnessed with some trepidation as Adelbert Tischler (1995) NASA Director of Chemical Propulsion within the Office of Advanced Research and Technology, recollected:

When the Shuttle program was approved . . . NASA officials and many other people in NASA, plus a great number of the contractors said this is the Apollo substitute. The Centers rushed to get their people piled onto this program – a drastic mistake because everyone wasn't competent to do that kind of thing. The contractors that were accepted by the Centers were identically the same contractors used in the Apollo program. In many respects . . . right there the program was starting to go wrong.

Nevertheless, as the Shuttle progressed towards fabrication, the politics first gravitated towards the building blocks of NASA's claims to economic and routine access to space.

Paragons of demand

In the first half of 1970, the Office of Manned Space Flight envisaged an operational Shuttle fleet conducting 75 flights per year (OMSF, 1970), but as NASA faced delays to their development plans during the politics of 1970 and 1971, these predictions fluctuated widely to settle eventually in 1974 to a predicted 60 flights per year (Myers, 1971a; OMSF, 1974). Disagreement about NASA's claims of inexpensive access to space tended to converge on NASA's proclamation made in 1971 that with the Shuttle the cost of sending payloads into space would reduce to $100 per pound (Myers, 1971b). In 1972, the eminent physicist, senate committee consultant and senior member of the Quadri-Science Incorporation, Ralph Lapp, told the Senate that the 'true price' of Shuttle operations would be $5100 per pound (Lapp, 1972), while the GAO reported to Congress in 1973, that costs per pound would be closer to $3500 (GAO, 1973). In that same year, George Rathjens, a professor of political science at the Massachusetts Institute of Technology, advised Congress that NASA's traffic models were 'overstated' and that the agency were proposing 'at least twice as many flights as can be justified' (Space Business Daily, 1973a). NASA rebutted much of what the GAO reported (Fletcher, 1973a), but in an attempt to manage the debate, NASA shifted away from cost-per-pound as a measurement of efficiency and instead introduced cost per flight as the basis upon which to gauge the Shuttle's economic advantage (NASA, 1972). As Charles Donlan (1995), Deputy Associate Administrator for Manned Space Flight, recalled:

> [Cost per pound was] an elusive criteria, a siren, it attracted people, but when you analyzed it cost per pound [was not] all that great. It was the cost-per-flight that was important.

Intertwined with the contested issue of launch costs were two other related and equally contestable issues: first, how often NASA/DOD were going to launch the Shuttle; and second, how sizable was the demand for a Shuttle service going to be? The higher the demand the more flights – the more flights, the lower the cost.

Although NASA's higher echelons fought off criticism, there was growing doubt within the agency itself over the predictions of how many flights per year the Shuttle would make, as Space Shuttle Manager, Robert Thompson (1995) recalled:

> There was some things that came out early . . . that may have misled some people. We talked about . . . 55 flights a year, something like that. I never felt we would ever get up to anything like that. I mean 55 Shuttle flights a year would put more stuff in orbit than you could even think about doing. No one has got that kind of funding or that kind of need, so we never configured any of the logistics or the infrastructure behind the Shuttle for much more than about twenty-something flights per year.

George English (1995), a chief bureaucrat at Kennedy, also recollected:

> Nobody here [Kennedy] really believed that we would do 40 or 50 flights per year, that was totally unrealistic. That was guys trying to sell the program, that's exactly

what that was. . . . The work involved in preparing a vehicle for launch, particularly a reusable vehicle, is pretty horrendous. So there was never any of our knowledgeable people . . . who ever thought we would be able to launch 40, 50 Shuttles a year. We used to talk about that and without a serious purpose, a serious goal, there was no need for it. People were talking about communication satellites, but how many do you think we would put up?

Hans Mark (1995) then Director at NASA's Ames Center, reflected:

The whole cost-effectiveness argument, I believe, was fraudulent from the start . . . and I said so in the private councils at the time, but I didn't want to get thrown out so I never went public with it.

NASA's actual launch rate with expendable rockets had peaked at 31 in 1966 and by 1973 it was down to 13 (NASA, 1995: B4).

Despite these internal misgivings, the uncertainty of what a future space programme would look like tended to favour NASA's position. The debate on economic questions had become extraneous because NASA's predictions stretched as far as 30 to 40 years into the future so neither side could really prove its case (Space Business Daily, 1973c). NASA and its supporters had successfully shifted the debate temporarily away from economics. Unpredictability meant flexibility. The Shuttle, touted as a flexible technology, promised an adaptable new space transportation system that could meet the needs of an uncertain future in space. George Low's (Associate Administrator) original premise that the importance of the Shuttle lay in its new capabilities had permeated enough for one Senator to comment that he saw: 'merit in the argument that the Space Shuttle represents *the next logical step* in space' (Congressional Record, 1973).

Debates about the necessity of spending taxpayers' money on the Shuttle and its place within a host of national priorities, had failed to terminate the programme in 1970 and 1971, and although they circulated Congress once more during 1973 and 1974, they had minimum political impact. The justification that the Shuttle would ease the aerospace depression, which had taken more than 250,000 jobs since 1969, swayed the arguments in NASA's favour (Space Business Daily, 1973b; Cranston, 1973; Machinist, 1973). Moreover, the aftermath of the Watergate scandal silenced most other politics at this time. Between 1973 and 1974, the Nixon Administration fell from one political crisis into another. Vice President Spiro Agnew resigned in October 1973 on State corruption charges and Nixon himself, with impeachment pending, finally became the first president to resign from office on the 8 August 1974. The affair marked the end of the imperial presidency and resurgence in the power of Congress. President Gerald Ford attempted to restore confidence in the office of the presidency, but he experienced unprecedented opposition from Congress and a growing cynicism from the American public with public institutions (Schell, 1975).

Enterprise rolls out

NASA produced its first shuttle, Enterprise on schedule in 1976. Although Enterprise was only a test shuttle to be used solely for atmospheric test flights at relatively low altitudes, for NASA it was an important milestone in the Shuttle's development. For many members of the American public it was an opportunity to escape political cynicism and marvel at the technological sublime. Following aerospace tradition, the *Enterprise* was unveiled to a public extravaganza at the Palmdale assembly plant in California on 17 September 1976. Over 2000 guests, three major television networks, two senators, two congressional representatives and six cast members from the television series *Star Trek* attended the ceremony. As Enterprise emerged from its hanger, the Golden West Air Force band rolled drums and played the *Star Trek* theme tune. The reason *Star Trek* played such a prominent role was the result of a concerted write-in campaign to the White House by fans demanding that NASA change the name of the first shuttle from its original *Constitution* to the name of the fictitious star-ship *Enterprise*. During a 45-minute meeting on 8 September 1976, President Gerald Ford notified NASA Administrator, James Fletcher, of the campaign and made it known that *Enterprise* was his preferred choice. It is not clear why Ford intervened in such a minor part of the Shuttle programme, since for most of his presidency he left the project to its own devices. Coming at the end of an election year, Ford may have considered that this populist manoeuvre would win him some critical votes, at least from the *Star Trek* fan club. Fletcher's agreement with Ford over the naming of the first shuttle caused some concern within NASA, because of the commercial and marketing activities associated with the series, but senior agency officials saw the name as giving the Shuttle ready recognition. The mythology of an American-led multinational corps of missionaries spreading peace by enterprise suited the post-lunar propaganda and served to justify the continuing exploitation of space (O'Toole, 1976; *Aviation Week*, 1976a; Carter, 1988).

A crisis of confidence

In the spring of 1979, a second oil shock struck at the heart of the US economy. Petrol lines (which had not been seen since 1973) reappeared, but this time accompanied by panic, hoarding and even violence. After a ten-day summit at Camp David, President Jimmy Carter returned to Washington DC to deliver a long awaited speech on the energy crisis. Carter (1982) perceived the problems facing America as stemming from what he deemed an invisible threat – a 'crisis of confidence.' Confidence, declared Carter, defined the course of America and was the foundation of America's belief in progress. His speech was thus a declaration in the faith of the technological capabilities of America to solve any problem, or any obstacle that lay in its path. Carter upheld the Lunar landings as a powerful symbol of America's progress and as a sign of the nation's confidence and world leadership. Yet, those same people that had placed an American on the Moon were experiencing their very own crisis of confidence.

Carter's victory in 1976 came at a time when the US was still suffering from the 'humiliation' of Watergate and Vietnam. Carter's apparent youth, confidence and integrity attracted popular support, whereas President Ford by contrast appeared uninspiring, hesitant and offering only a second-rate leadership of a country that was becoming a second-rate power (Derbyshire, 1988). To NASA however, Carter was an enigma. He was an engineer by training but many at NASA did not think of him as a space programme supporter (Kraft, 1995; Mark, 1995; Yardley, 1995). Despite pre-election statements supporting both the agency and the Shuttle, NASA officials remained cautious (Kozicharow, 1976; Aviation Week, 1976b).

Size of the fleet

The key issue for NASA at the start of the new Administration was procurement of the Shuttle fleet, although attempts by NASA to secure a five-shuttle fleet had actually begun before the election. The debate intensified in 1976 because NASA was uncertain about the political terrain. Many at the agency were concerned that if approval on the fleet budget was not made before the election, then NASA would have to go through a completely new justification procedure for the entire programme and there was a real sense of trepidation about the outcome (Fletcher, 1977). Back in 1971, the Office of Manned Space Flight pictured a future in which five shuttles, launching out of two launch sites, would hold monopoly over US space flight (Preston, 1971; NASA/DOD, 1973; Malkin, 1973). Indeed, NASA's justification for inexpensive space flight was predicated on a Shuttle monopoly. The politics of the size of the Shuttle fleet was thus interconnected with the politics of the presumed demand for space flight.

In 1976, NASA had a development budget that provided funding for production of the first two shuttles and a production budget that included funding for a third. Beyond that, there was no budget for a fourth or fifth shuttle. The additional shuttles were excluded because both the White House and the Congress had perceived shuttles four and five as an Air Force procurement responsibility. During the early 1970s, both NASA and the DOD embraced the idea of a partnership and a perception that each partner would share the funding of building the shuttle fleet persisted into the mid-1970s. By 1975, however, it became clear to NASA that the DOD had shifted position (Low and Currie, 1976a and b; NASA, 1976). As Lieutenant General, Forrest McCartney (1995) reflected:

> There was some talk about the Air Force buying some [shuttles], where they would become what we called blue Shuttles; Air Force blue Shuttles. That just became too expensive at the time, so our . . . plan in the Air Force was to use the NASA fleet.

The DOD's role evolved from partner to major user as it became more sceptical about NASA claims and concerned about NASA's drive towards monopolization:

> We in the Air Force felt that NASA had overstated the capability and need for the Shuttle. . . . So I think, in those days the Air Force could see in the early 70s [that the Shuttle] would become the only launch vehicle that the country [would have]. The Air Force always had reservations about that, always opposed that and always felt that they did not want to be confined or dedicated to one vehicle (McCartney, 1995).

Confirmation of the DOD's intentions came during an informal meeting between NASA and the DOD in May 1976. Malcolm Currie (Pentagon Director of Research and Engineering) indicated that he personally would support a five-shuttle fleet, but warned NASA that if Congress directed the DOD to fund two of them then 'its support for the Shuttle would vanish' (Low, 1976a). Indeed, the Pentagon hinted at this before the Senate, when it confirmed that if the Air Force paid for the additional shuttles it would mean that they would no longer see the programme as cost-effective (McElheny, 1976). George Low (Associate Administrator for Space Flight), forced by the DOD's changed position, set in motion a campaign to convince Congress during 1976 that NASA should fund shuttles four and five (Low, 1976b). Arguments in favour of a five-shuttle fleet were nonetheless on weak ground, so Low and Currie assumed the political position of claiming a need for six shuttles all to be NASA built (Low and Currie, 1976a and b). To camouflage fractures in the argument, the five-shuttle fleet, described as *sufficient* in 1973, was presented in 1976 as the *minimum* fleet size (Fletcher, 1976b). However, NASA failed in its attempt to secure additional shuttle production funding before the presidential election and the debate on fleet size continued into the Carter Administration.

James Fletcher's resignation as NASA Administrator became effective on 1 May 1977. Frank Press, President Carter's science advisor, pushed to have Robert Frosch as the fifth NASA Administrator. Frosch, a weapons scientist with a background in physics, was a friend of Press, so presumed loyal to the Carter Administration. During his first meeting with the President, Carter asked Frosch to examine the Shuttle programme closely to determine whether he should shut it down. Frosch found out very quickly that he was working with a White House that was trying to free itself from the past, that would examine every programme with the view that if it was not cost-effective it should be eliminated. Frosch eventually decided that the Shuttle programme was a valuable asset if only because it was the sole means by which the US could maintain a human space programme. Meanwhile, the new OMB, under the guidance of Vice President Walter Mondale (a long-time critic of NASA) was examining methods of reducing the Shuttle fleet (OMB, 1977).

On 29 November 1977, the OMB called a high-level meeting to discuss the Shuttle's future. The OMB presented three options to the meeting. First, continue with the current plan, a five-shuttle fleet operating out of two launch sites.

Second, cut the programme back to three shuttles operating from Kennedy only, which involved breaking the Shuttle's monopoly. Third, a compromise position of constructing four shuttles and leaving the question of a second launch site open for future review. The OMB made a strong argument for the second option. Secretary of the Air Force, Hans Mark (also a former NASA employee), and Secretary of Defence, Harold Brown refused to accept the OMB's proposal, so no decision was made (Mark, 1995). The OMB continued to push for some sort of a decision in that year and another meeting took place on 16 December 1977 to reach a final settlement. At this meeting, Harold Brown took a very strong position against the OMB's proposal. He argued that a three-shuttle fleet was unacceptable from a national security standpoint because NASA's first two shuttles (Columbia and Challenger) would be heavier than the following vehicles (Discovery and Atlantis) and so unable to lift the DOD's heaviest payloads. He also argued that at least two of the lighter shuttles would be required because the DOD would need a backup in case one of them was lost. Brown's arguments eventually swung Carter's decision over to the compromise position and he reduced the fleet to four shuttles (Ibid). However, NASA Administrator, Robert Frosch told Congress that Carter's decision was an indication that his Administration had misgivings over whether the Shuttle would be capable of conducting all the missions forecast and that he interpreted the deferment of the fifth shuttle as a policy of caution (Covault, 1978a; *Aviation Week*, 1978a, b and c; *Aerospace Daily*, 1978).

Financial and management crisis

The seeds of NASA's financial problems had actually been sown soon after Nixon's re-election in 1972. Following the boom conditions initiated by an increase in government spending from 1971, the OMB sought to reverse policy and work towards a reduction of the budget deficit through an austere economic programme (Reichley, 1981). As part of this policy, the OMB told NASA that it had to take a major cut in its funding. NASA Administrator, James Fletcher, advised Nixon that OMB action could result in a pending crisis that might ultimately result in the Shuttle having to be cancelled; but despite numerous petitions, NASA lost its argument for the need for a 'constant' annual budget of $3.4 billion in 1971 dollars ($28.7 billion in 2007 dollars) (Shapely, 1972; Fletcher, 1973a and b). This defeat then fused with a larger, more pervasive dynamic, rising inflation, which presented NASA with the onset of acute financial difficulties.

Sustained economic growth in the US had been based primarily on the reliance of the cheap flow of oil and raw materials from the Developing World. By 1973, the Developing economies sought to redress the terms of trade and the prices of raw materials began to rise, culminating in the Organization of Petroleum Exporting Countries quadrupling the price of crude oil. The rising prices of primary products, together with rising wages, squeezed US profits substantially and the profit rate plummeted (Makoto, 1990; Hobsbawm, 1994). With rising costs, many of the Shuttle's contractors argued that it was difficult to continue. The prime contractor, Rockwell, went back to NASA to seek more money; but NASA told them to absorb their losses (Covault, 1974; Johnsen, 1974).

By the end of 1977, a myriad of technical problems were having a cumulative effect on the Shuttle programme's finances. The Shuttle had consumed over $1.2 billion ($5.9 billion in 2007 dollars) during 1976/77; but additional testing, major redesigns of both hardware and software, and the need for the employment of additional labour in the fabrication of Columbia, had drained the programme's reserves and placed pressure on the agency's overall resources (Frosch, 1977b). To save the programme and remain on target for a first launch in March 1979, NASA Administrator Robert Frosch proposed a plan to Congress to shift $100 million from the production budget to the design, development and testing budget. The plan, although approved, did not go without some criticism (Frosch, 1977a). In January 1979, however, NASA officials went before Congress again to request an additional $185 million to keep the Shuttle programme on schedule for a 1979 launch date. Congress approved the request based on Frosch's testimony that the budget now fully supported the development programme (*Aviation Week*, 1979a; *Defense Daily*, 1979a). Yet as the year progressed, it became apparent that Frosch's guarantee was empty.

NASA's first space flight shuttle, Columbia, arrived at Kennedy in late March 1979. With the first launch due some months later, President Carter announced that, 'The first great era of space is over. The second is about to begin' (Carter, quoted in NASA, 1979). The statement, largely based on the assurances coming from NASA, was, nonetheless, premature. The shipment of Columbia to Kennedy was a political manœuvre, as former NASA employee, Herb Yarbrough (1995), recalled: NASA knew that 'it was not ready for delivery, but the program had a milestone and we had budget problems and not delivering on time wouldn't have helped that.' March 1979 had been the predicted launch date for a number of years and getting the Columbia to Kennedy by that date had become a key objective. Yet, it soon became apparent to those at Kennedy that the vehicle was nowhere near ready to fly, as Rockwell engineer, John Tribe (1995), remembered: 'When the vehicle got here it wasn't finished. . . . So, we had a lot of work to do down here, it was almost like we had to finish building it'.

In a tremendous effort to complete the work on Columbia in time for a November 1979 launch, NASA moved over 2000 workers from Palmdale, California, to Kennedy at a cost of over $1.8 million ($7.2 million in 2007 dollars). A huge complex of temporary accommodation and facilities was established at Kennedy to house all the workers, who were working seven days a week, three shifts a day, to finish building Columbia. In addition, NASA also hired every man and women in Bravade County that wanted to work on the Shuttle, to work with the application of the thermal protection tiles, because it was such a labour-intensive operation. Included in that workforce were over 320 high school graduates and college students on their summer vacation (Tribe, 1995; Jeffrey Smith, 1979). But technical problems continued to plague the programme through 1979 and 1980. John Tribe (1995) recalled how he 'wondered if we'd ever fly. It just seem like that every time we started to put things back together there would be another [modification], or another crisis would occur, so that we had to go and start taking it apart again'.

By March 1979, it had become clear to NASA that their budget could not sustain the development programme and in April, NASA went back to Congress and the White House again to inform them that the programme required an additional $500 million ($2 billion in 2007 dollars) over the next two financial years (O'Toole, 1979; Noble Wilford, 1979). As former Director of Johnson Space Center Christopher Kraft (1995) recalled, it was a request Congress did not receive well:

> NASA finally confessed up to the problems they had. They had been sort of keeping them undercover and accepting the fact that they had to live with the smaller budgets that [the Carter] administration was placing on the Shuttle. That got us in trouble with the Congress because two weeks before . . . we had been up in the Congress testifying that we really didn't need any more money. . . . When they found that we needed more money then that's when . . . the shit hit the fan and the Congress became very, very upset with NASA.

Indeed, the disclosure of funding problems led to a general crisis of confidence over NASA's ability to manage the Shuttle programme. Despite NASA Administrator, Robert Frosch claiming that NASA's top management did not know about the enormity of the increases sooner because of 'institutional pride,' both the Congress and the White House insisted on investigations into NASA Shuttle management (Frosch, 1979a; Lovelace, 1979).

Recovery

NASA's profile on Capitol Hill plummeted after its request for additional funding and there was a growing concern within the agency about the rise in opposition to the Shuttle. As Kraft (1995) remembered, it was a dangerous time for the programme:

> It was about the period [when] . . . we began to recognize that we had a large financial problem on our hands [that] NASA was almost in the position where they had to turn the program into an R&D program, as opposed to an operating vehicle. And go to just producing one vehicle and finding out what we could do with it, as opposed to producing a number of vehicles and making it the work horse of the space program, which was what it was originally designed to be.

NASA considered that without support from the White House it would not be able to get the increases through Congress (Lovelace, n.d.). Paradoxically, given Carter's election rhetoric, it was the military potentials of the Shuttle and of space in general, that had become significant to the White House. In mid-1977,

Carter established an Inter-agency Space Program Coordinating Committee to draw up various space policy options. Its conclusion caused some controversy, as it emphasized the military and intelligence utilization of space and greater DOD control over the civilian space programme. Nevertheless, in October 1978, Carter authorized the space policy directive and established a number of inter-agency committees to ensure both civilian and military exploitation of the Shuttle (White House Press Office, 1978; Covault, 1978b; 1979a and b). Hence, the Shuttle became further embroiled with a military agenda and when the request for additional funding reached the highest echelons of power, the density of this entanglement intensified.

Late in 1979, Carter declared his support for NASA's request for extra funding (Covault, 1979c and d). NASA claimed surprise over Carter's decision, but as Kraft (1995) recalled, it soon became clear that Carter was using the 'Shuttle as a political tool, an international political tool, to threaten the Russians with the capabilities the Shuttle would have to intervene in a hot war and as a spy tool.' Sources within the Pentagon professed that the key issue that convinced Carter to push Congress for the extra funding was the availability of the Shuttle to launch intelligence missions needed to verify Soviet compliance with the second round of the Strategic Arms Limitation Talks (SALT II), which Senate was debating at the time (Marsh, 1979; *Aerospace Daily*, 1979). NASA had maintained that they were unaware of the implications of SALT II on the delay of shuttle production, but by end of 1979, the agency had no problem with using SALT II to reinforce its position (Frosch, 1979b). On 14 November 1979, Frosch and Carter had a private meeting to discuss the status of the Shuttle. At this meeting, Carter reiterated his support for the programme and confirmed that the driving force behind keeping the Shuttle on schedule was the SALT II agreement (Carter, 1979; Frosch, 1979c).

Transitions

Columbia's first launch, which eventually took place in April 1981, marked the end of the long process of design, development and fabrication. The technology had taken on physical form. It existed as an object and was ready to make the transition from conditions of construction to conditions of use. The boundary between creation and operation was, nonetheless, more opaque. Conditions of use were as significant during construction, as conditions of construction were during use.

Axioms from the Airliner Lexicon

On 4 July 1982, (American Independence Day) President Ronald Reagan welcomed Columbia home from its fourth test flight. From a flag-decked rostrum, Reagan announced that the Shuttle was ready for its transition from development to operations. He was reading straight from a NASA policy document (Hoban, 1995). But, as NASA Associate Administrator, James Abrahamson, remembered, 'nobody knew what that meant, because every flight after that time was anything but operational, so that was quite arbitrary.' The biggest issue for NASA's upper management in the early 1980s was transforming the culture of the agency, from one that treated every flight as unique to one that conformed to routine operations (Beggs, 1995).

Based on the premise of a mass space market, the essence of the Shuttle revolution was economies of scale. What this meant in operational terms was a radical shift in the way NASA was organized and the way in which that organization had worked. Conceived as a routine operational vehicle, the Shuttle was to compel parts of NASA to face a new environment; an environment geared to providing a regular service. Yet regular, routine, or mundane work was not part of the perceived practice of NASA's space divisions (Yarbrough, 1995). Before 1970, NASA had built a reputation for being an innovative organization, working largely in realms of the unknown and pushing forward the boundaries of both knowledge and machinery. Assimilated into this image after 1970, was a NASA-speak that voiced idioms from the airliner lexicon. Customer service, customer demand, the marketplace, load factors, and frequent turnaround, all became part of a discourse exhorting the Shuttle revolution (Yardley, 1979; Gregory, 1976). In the new politics of space, analogies with the airlines were often used to accentuate the shape of things to come as Kennedy Management Systems Officer, George English recollected:

> George Low [NASA Associate Administrator]... left us a terrible heritage.... He said we have to take a Frontier Airlines approach to Shuttle operations. Now, Frontier Airlines was a little airline out west that had cheap rates. . . . Well it gave the public the impression that flying the Shuttle was like flying an airline (1995).

Unlike NASA's previous human space programmes, where the agency designed the requirements, developed the vehicle and served as the customer, with the Shuttle, NASA would have to provide a flexible, on-going service, for people other than itself (Yardley, 1979). NASA expressed a preference for turning the management of virtually all Shuttle operations over to private hands, allowing the agency to remain a research and development organization. In the short term at least, however, NASA knew it would be responsible for Shuttle operations. In the early to mid-1970s, NASA contacted some of the major US airlines in an effort to accumulate expertise in operational procedures, but NASA was unable to gain much experience or knowledge from them that it found applicable (Hoban, 1995; English, 1995). Nevertheless, the idea that NASA could run the Shuttle along similar lines to a commercial airline had become ingrained as Rockwell engineer, John Tribe (1995) remembered:

> If you look back at the pictures, at the artist's styling of what it was going to be like, [they] showed [a shuttle] sitting in this sterile [processing facility], glistening floors, one little access stand and about two technicians wandering around. It was totally unreal, but unfortunately we believed the propaganda.

Once the design, development test and engineering was essentially completed and the shuttle moved into routine operations, the NASA penchant for invention surfaced anew. NASA's engineers wanted to begin work on the next project, but since the political climate was not amenable to committing funds for a space station at that time, NASA's engineers tended to find things on the Shuttle. As Johnson engineer, Norman Chaffee (1995) recalled:

> We started focusing on every little anomaly that would occur on a shuttle flight [and] . . . it would get almost humorous, because when missions went well and there were no anomalies the managers would invent anomalies, things that they normally weren't interested in knowing about or didn't care about. . . . I think NASA is a problem-solving organization . . . and if NASA doesn't have a real problem to work on, NASA will make up a problem to work on, and that's just part of the culture.

For NASA Administrator, James Beggs (1995) and Johnson Director, Christopher Kraft (1995), continuous miniscule changes in design were becoming a major hindrance to the transition to operations. In particular, it fed into production resulting in design changes to the shuttles rolling off the production line, so that no shuttle was identical. Prior to the Shuttle, everything NASA built was unique so there was an inherent difficulty within the organization with standardizing the technology. Standardization is an important part of operational technologies and without commonality, the procedures and logistics of service and repair all became more complicated.

The consequence of these difficulties was a shuttle flight rate that was far lower than predicted in the 1970s. In 1979, the new Office of Space Transportation Systems had attempted to lay down a concrete traffic model in the face of confusion between different sections of NASA and the contractors (Lee, 1979), but soon after Columbia's first flight, NASA's predicted flight manifest just kept on falling (Lee, 1995). The falling flight rate, of course, had a severe impact on the cost-per-flight – an issue that had been politically sensitive since the shuttle's conception. NASA Deputy Administrator, George Low had established a pricing policy in 1976, which averaged the Shuttle's cost-per-flight at around $18 million in 1975 dollars. By 1984 however, the Associate Administrator for the Office of Space Flight, Jesse Moore, indicated that the total average cost of operating the shuttle has grown to an average of $60 million per flight in 1975 dollars, or just shy of $132 million in 1984 dollars (Low, 1976c; Congressional Record, 1984). NASA management blamed the reduced flight activity, but NASA's Acting Administrator, Alan Lovelace admitted in 1981 that the Shuttle's operational costs would not meet the projected figures drawn up in the 1970s, because those projected costs were overly optimistic and 'partially designed to defend a program on the basis of its cost effectiveness' (Lovelace, 1981).

In 1982, the GAO had released a report claiming that the shuttle could cost $116 million per flight in 1975 dollars ($214 million in 1982 dollars), which they argued effectively meant NASA would be subsidizing non-government users (GAO, 1982). Members of Congress were incensed by the idea of government subsidizing commercial users and they pushed for a policy whereby non-government users would pay a share of the fixed costs. NASA, however, argued that government had to pay for the fixed costs regardless, so marginal costs, which would be all the expenses of a particular flight, did not constitute a subsidy (Congressional Record, 1984). Capturing the commercial market was of utmost importance to NASA. The political arguments for the Shuttle had long rested on the technology monopolizing the space market, so winning the debate on marginal costs became a crucial element of justifying both the Shuttle and NASA operating it. A NASA Advisory Council study had found that many commercial users would be willing to use the shuttle, but only if it was competitive with expendable launch vehicles. Nonetheless, commercial users were also apprehensive about NASA's preoccupation with R&D and its 'fascination' with the role of astronauts, rather than with improving customer service (NAC, 1983; Fink, 1983). Delays and schedule problems had instilled a lack of confidence in the shuttle on the part of the commercial world. In addition, because humans were flying the Shuttle, the interface and safety documentation required by NASA for the shuttle vastly exceeded what commercial users had become accustomed to with expendable launch vehicles.

During 1983 and 1984 the Shuttle's flight rate climbed slowly, reaching a peak of nine in 1985. The agency was still on a very steep learning curve, but NASA was optimistic about increasing its flight rate further in 1986 (Yarbrough, 1995). Then, on 28 January 1986, Challenger exploded 73 seconds into its flight with the loss of life of all her crew.

Conclusion

After the Moon landing, NASA's interests involved both retaining the perception of its indispensability within its field of operation through the monopolization of space capabilities and the procurement of greater resources through the adoption of new goals – processes that represent classic organizational behaviour (see, Blau, 1963). The decade that followed the Moon landing was very different from the one that preceded it. The old socio-technical order built up around getting an American in the Moon was dismantling and NASA entered the new world of post-Apollo with no concrete identity. NASA also experienced a pivotal shift in the locus of control over its activities. After 1969, the agency no longer occupied the role of technical expert dictating the direction of space technology to a lay audience on Capitol Hill. Instead, NASA had to be more aware of and become more responsive to key actors in the political system (McCurdy, 1993). Two processes can thus be seen at work during the 1970s, what Bruno Latour called a translation of interests and what Langdon Winner termed reverse adaptation (Latour, 2005; Winner, 1978). Essentially, NASA had to tailor the utility of the Shuttle to cater not only for its own interests but also for the interests of others. It had to ally with those who had long fought for a consensus based on the *exploitation* of space (its marketization and militarization) as opposed to the old consensus of exploration and scientific advancement.

These various shifts emerged in part out of different states of indeterminacy. After the initial instability of the politics of 1968–1971, the Shuttle programme entered into a period of *fragile stabilization* during 1972–1982. Scattered throughout the tangled fabric of the development years were various states of indeterminacy: different paths of technological development, numerous points of intervention, and the ever-present possibility of retrenchment. In essence, this account has attempted to show that things could always have been otherwise – that there were many moments in the Shuttle's development where its function, purpose or even existence could have been (and in some cases was) different. For NASA, the Shuttle was always a stepping-stone to the project upon which they really wanted to embark after Apollo, the space station; but within the turmoil of the 1970s, representations of what the Shuttle was going to be drew from a complex nexus of ideas about space travel, the fortunes of human history, and the role of (space) technology in the economy and in society. The Shuttle was simultaneously high-tech and utilitarian – a fleet of space work-horses and a research and development project that would push forward the frontiers of scientific and technological progress. It had difficulty being both and it is debatable whether it achieved either.

According to Roland (1989), Challenger marked a watershed in NASA's history, symbolizing the end of the romantic era of space flight. With hindsight, however, Challenger marked the end of the militarization and marketization of the Shuttle and a shift for NASA back towards its original sphere of activity, with these functions largely conducted by other organizations using traditional expendable rockets. Although it is evident now that the Shuttle could never fulfil all the promises made of it, this failure of purpose is a not simply a story about flawed design or overstated ambition; it is primarily a story about complexities in relations between the machine, its makers, its financers, and all the associations they encountered and crafted along the way.

References

Abrahamson, J., (1995), NASA Associate Administrator, Lieutenant General US Air Force, interview with the author, 5 July 1995, Washington DC.

Agnew, S., (1972), address by the Vice President of the United States at the Florida Jaycees State Convention, Daytona Beach, Florida, January 29, 1972, Kennedy Space Center Archive, Florida.

Ambrose, S., (1981), *Rise to Globalism: American Foreign Policy, 1938–1980*, Middlesex, England: Penguin Books, second revised edition.

Aerospace Daily (1978), 'GAO Sticks To Its Guns On Shuttle Fleet Sites,' *Aerospace Daily*, 8 August 1978: 161–162.

Aerospace Daily (1979), 'Administration Vetoed NASA Plan to Slip Shuttle Further,' *Aerospace Daily*, 20 September 1979: 36.

Aviation Week (1976a), 'Shuttle Orbiter Named,' *Aviation Week and Space Technology*, 13 September 1976: 26.

Aviation Week (1976b), 'Space Agency Readies Carter's Briefing,' *Aviation Week and Space Technology*, 15 November 1976: 22.

Aviation Week (1978a), 'Fifth Orbiter, Stereostat Voted Funding by House Committee', *Aviation Week and Space Technology*, 6 March 1978: 13–14.

Aviation Week (1978b), 'Senate Unit, House Vote Fifth Orbiter,' *Aviation Week and Space Technology*, 1 May 1978: 22–23.

Aviation Week (1978c), 'Senate Unit to Consider Funds for Fifth Orbiter,' *Aviation Week and Space Technology*, 31 July 1978: 21.

Aviation Week (1979a), 'NASA Budget Provides No Real Growth,' *Aviation Week and Space Technology*, 22 January 1979: 16.

Barnes, B., (1977), *Interests and the Growth of Knowledge*, London: Routledge & Kegan Paul.

Beggs, J., (1995), NASA Administrator, interview with the author, 6 June 1995, Washington DC.

Blau, P., (1963), *The Dynamics of Bureaucracy: A Study of Interpersonal Relations in Two Government Agencies*, Chicago: University of Chicago Press, revised edition.

Brody, D., (1980), *Workers in Industrial America: Essays on the Twentieth Century Struggle*, New York, Oxford: Oxford University Press.

Carter, D., (1988), *The Final Frontier: The Rise and Fall of the American Rocket State*, New York: Verso.

Carter, President J., (1979), letter to Robert Frosch, 26 November 1979, NASA Washington DC: History Office Archive.

Carter, President J., (1982), 'Crisis of Confidence Address, July 15, 1979,' In R. Hofstadter and B. Hofstadter (eds), *Great Issues in American History: From Reconstruction to the Present Day, 1864–1981*, New York: Vintage Books: 522–524.

Chaffee, N., (1995), Johnson Space Center, Chemical Engineer, interview with the author, 6 September 1995, Houston, Texas.

Congressional Record (1973), 'The National Space Programme', cutting from the Congressional Record, the Senate, 30 May 1973, Washington DC: NASA History Office Archive.

Congressional Record (1984), 'Space Shuttle Requirements, Operations, and Future Plans,' Hearings before the Subcommittee on Space Science and Applications, US House of Representative, Washington DC: US Government Printing Office.

Covault, C., (1974), 'Inflation Forcing Shuttle Changes,' *Aviation Week and Space Technology*, 23 September 1974: 20–22.

Covault, C., (1978a), 'Fifth Orbiter Support Rises in Congress,' *Aviation Week and Space Technology*, 27 February 1978: 20–21.

Covault, C., (1978b), 'Space Policy Mandates US Leadership,' *Aviation Week and Space Technology*, 16 October 1978: 24–26.

Covault, C., (1979a), 'Debate on Space Policy Heats', *Aviation Week and Space Technology* (5 February 1979): 12–13.

Covault, C., (1979b), 'Space Policy Discussion Stresses Solid Goal Need,' *Aviation Week and Space Technology* (19 February 1979): 52–54.

Covault, C., (1979c), 'Administration Backs Shuttle Fund Rise,' *Aviation Week and Space Technology* (17 September 1979): 22–23.

Covault, C., (1979d), 'Carter Backs Shuttle Fund Rise', *Aviation Week and Space Technology* (19 November 1979): 16–18.

Cranston, A., (1973), Press release from the Office of US Senator Alan Cranston, 10 April 1973, Washington DC: Smithsonian Air and Space Museum.

Derbyshire, I., (1988), *Politics in the United States: From Carter to Bush*, Edinburgh: W & R Chambers Ltd.

Defense Daily (1979), 'House Unit Okays $185 million FY '79 Supplement For Shuttle', *Defense/Space Daily* (7 March 1979): 34.

Donlan, C., (1995), NASA Deputy Associate Administrator for Manned Space Flight, interview with the author, 7 June 1995, Washington DC.

Dosi, G., (1982), 'Technological paradigms and technological trajectories: A suggested interpretation of the determinants and directions of technical change,' *Research Policy* 11: 147–162.

English, G., (1995), NASA bureaucrat at Kennedy, interview with the author, 26 July 1995, Kennedy, Florida.

Fink, D., (1983), Chairman NASA Advisory Council, letter to James Beggs, 17 November 1983, Washington DC: NASA History Office Archive.

Fletcher, J., (1973a), letter to Richard Nixon, 13 July 1973, Washington DC: NASA History Office Archive.

Fletcher, J., (1973b), letter to Roy Ash, Director of OMB, 13 July 1973, Washington DC: NASA History Office Archive.

Fletcher, J., (1976a), letter to President Ford, 4 June 1976, Washington DC: NASA History Office Archive,

Fletcher, J., (1976b), Letter to James Lynn, Director Office of Management and Budget, 22 October 1976, Washington DC: NASA History Office Archive.

Fletcher, J., (1977), Memorandum to John Yardley, 28 March 1977, Washington DC: NASA History Office Archive.

Frosch, R., (1977a), Letter to Representative Edward Boland, Democrat, Massachusetts, 9 November 1977, Washington DC: NASA History Office Archives.

Frosch, R., (1977b), statement before the Senate Appropriations Committee, HUD – Independent Agencies Committee, draft version, 29 November 1977, Washington DC: NASA History Office Archives.

Frosch, R., (1979a), letter to Senator Howard Cannon, reprinted in *Aerospace Daily*, 14 May 1979: 68.

Frosch, R., (1979b), Memorandum to President Carter, 11 September 1979, Washington DC: NASA History Office Archive.

Frosch, R., (1979c), press briefing on Robert Frosch's conversation with President Carter regarding the space Shuttle, 14 November 1979, Washington DC: NASA History Office Archive.

GAO, (1973), *Analysis of Cost Estimates for the Space Shuttle and Two Alternate Programs*, report to the Congress, 1 June 1973, Washington DC: General Accounting Office Distribution Center.

GAO, (1982), *NASA Must Reconsider Operations Pricing Policy to Compensate for Cost Growth on the Space Transportation System*, report to the Congress, 23 February 1982, Washington DC: General Accounting Office Distribution Center.

Gregory, W., (1976), 'Shuttle Opens Door to New Space Era,' *Aviation Week and Space Technology*, 8 November 1976: 39–43.

Hechler, K., (1980), *Towards the Endless Frontier: History of the Committee on Science and Technology, 1959–79*, Washington DC: US Government Printing Office.

Heppenheimer, T. A., (1999), *The Space Shuttle Decision: NASA's Search for a Reusable Space Vehicle*, Washington DC: NASA History Series.

Hoban, F., (1995), Executive Assistant to the NASA Deputy Administrator, interview with the author, 15 May 1995, Virginia: Fairfax.

Hobsbawm, E., (1994), *The Age of Extremes: The Short Twentieth Century 1914–91*, London: Michael Joseph Ltd.

Hotz, R., (1972), 'Editorial,' *Aviation Week and Space Technology*, July 31, 1972: 7.

Jeffrey Smith, R., (1979), 'Shuttle Problems Compromise Space Program,' *Science* 206, 23 November 1979: 910–914

Johnsen, K., (1974), 'Inflation Boosts Labor Demands', *Aviation Week and Space Technology*, 23 July 1974: 12–13.

Killian, J. R., (1982), *Sputnik, Scientists, and Eisenhower*, Cambridge Mass: MIT Press.

Kozicharow, E., (1976), 'Shuttle Support Seems Assured,' *Aviation Week and Space Technology*, 8 November 1976: 14–15.

Kraft, C., (1995), Director of Johnson Space Center, interview with the author, 1 September 1995, Houston, Texas.

Lapp, R., (1972), 'Testimony to the Committee on Aeronautical and Space Science,' in *NASA Authorization for Fiscal Year 1973*, Washington DC: US Government Printing Office.

Latour, B., (2005), *Reassembling the Social: An Introduction to Actor-Network-Theory*, Oxford: Oxford University Press.

Law, J. and Mol, A., (2002), *Complexities: Social Studies of Knowledge Practice,* Durham NC: Duke University Press.

Lee, C., (1979), letter to John Yardley, 30 March 1979, Washington DC: NASA History Office Archive.

Lee, C., (1995), Director of STS Operations, interview with the author 2 May 1995, Arlington, Virginia.

Logsdon, J. M., (1986), 'The Space Shuttle Program: A Policy Failure?' *Science* 232, 30 May 1986.

Lovelace, A., (n.d.), Memorandum to Curt Hessler, Associate Director OMB, no date, Washington DC: NASA History Office Archives.

Lovelace, A., (1979), Memorandum to Robert Frosch, reprinted in *Aerospace Daily*, 14 May 1979: 69.

Lovelace, A., (1981) quoted in, 'Lovelace sees Fewer Flights, Increased Costs Likely For Shuttle,' *Aerospace Daily*, May 6, 1981: 25–26.

Low, G., (1976a), Memorandum for the record, meeting with Malcolm Currie on orbiter procurement and reimbursement policy, 19 May 1976, Washington DC: NASA History Office Archive.

Low, G., (1976b), Memorandum to Associate Administrator for Space Flight, 19 April 1976, Washington DC: NASA History Office Archive.

Low, G., (1976c), Memorandum to James Fletcher, 28 May 1976, Washington DC: NASA History Office Archive.

Low, G. and Currie, M., (1976a), Memorandum to the Secretary of Defense and the NASA Administrator, 8 May 1976, Washington DC: NASA History Office Archive.

Low, G. and Currie, M., (1976b), proposed memorandum to be signed by NASA Administrator, James Fletcher and Secretary of Defense, Donald Rumsford, and sent to the President or the director of the OMB, 8 May 1976, Washington DC: NASA History Office Archive.

Machinist (1972), 'Convention Backs McGovern, No Support at all for Nixon' *The Machinist*, 14 September 1972: 1: 7.

Machinist (1973), 'UAW + IAM = Shuttle', *The Machinist*, 12 April 1973: 1.

MacKenzie, D., (1993), *Inventing Accuracy: A Historical Sociology of Nuclear Missile Guidance*, Cambridge, Mass: MIT Press.

Makoto, I., (1990), *The World Crisis and Japanese Capitalism*, London, MacMillan Press.

Malkin, M., (1973), Memorandum to Associate Administrator for Manned Space Flight, 30 May 1973, Washington DC: NASA History Office Archive.

Mark, H., (1995), Director NASA Ames Center and Secretary of the US Air Force, interview with the author, 8 September 1995, Austin, Texas.

Marsh, A., (1979), 'SALT Support Tied to Defense Gains,' *Aviation Week and Space Technology*, 6 August 1979: 20.

McCartney, F., (1995) NASA Kennedy Space Center Director, Lieutenant General US Air Force, interview with the author, 28 July 1995, Kennedy, Florida.

McCurdy, H., (1993), *Inside NASA: High Technology and Organizational Change in the US Space Program*, Baltimore: Johns Hopkins University Press.

McDougall, W. A., (1985), *The Heavens and the Earth: A Political History of the Space Age*, New York: Basic Books.

McElheny, V., (1976), 'Aerospace Contracts, Put at $1 Billion, Hinge on Debate Over Space Shuttles', *The New York Times*, 24 August 1976: 37.

McGovern, G., (1974), *An American Journey: The Presidential Campaign Speeches of George McGovern*, New York: Random House.

Myers, D., (1971a), Memorandum to Deputy Associate Administrator, Planning, 17 June 1971, Washington DC: NASA History Office Archives.

Myers, D., (1971b), 'Statement at the hearings before The Committee on Science and Astronautics,' in *1972 NASA Authorization*, Washington DC: US Government Printing Office.

NAC (1983), NASA Advisory Council study of effective shuttle utilization, conducted by a NAC Task Force, 1983, Washington DC: NASA History Office Archive.

NASA (1972), 'Comments on the Statement of Dr Ralph Lapp on the Space Shuttle', in *NASA Authorization for Fiscal Year 1973*, Washington DC: US Government Printing Office.

NASA (1976), draft issue paper on orbiter procurement, 8 May 1976, Washington DC: NASA History Office Archive.

NASA (1979), *NASA Activities*, May 1979, Washington DC: NASA History Office Archive.

NASA (1995), *Pocket Statistics*, Washington DC: NASA History Office.

NASA/DOD (1973), Space Shuttle Orbiter Fleet Size Analysis, prepared by the Office of Manned Space Flight and US Air Force Systems Command, 15 May 1973, Washington DC: NASA History Office Archive.

Nixon, R., (1972), Press Release from the Office of the White House Press Secretary, 5 January 1972, Washington DC: National Air and Space Museum.

Nixon, R., (1978), *The Memoirs of Richard Nixon*, London: Sidgwick & Jackson Ltd.

Noble, D., (1984), *Forces of Production: A Social History of Industrial Automation*, New York: Alfred Knopf.

Noble Wilford, J., (1979), 'Delay in Space Shuttle Facing Carter Review; Funds May be Raised,' *New York Times,* 11 May 1979.

OMB (1977), Space Shuttle: Office of Management and Budget Production Options February 2, 1977, Washington DC: NASA History Office Archives.

OMSF (1970), Office of Manned Space Flight, Space Shuttle Program Requirements Document Level 1, 1 July 1970, Washington DC: NASA History Office Archive.

OMSF (1974), Office of Manned Space Flight, Space Shuttle Program Requirements Document Level 1, Revision No. 4, 12 March 1970, Washington DC: NASA History Office Archive.

O'Toole, T., (1976), 'Space Shuttle Orbiter Shown for First Time in California', *Washington Post*, 18 September 1976.

O'Toole, T., (1979), 'Space Shuttle Money Pinch May Force Science to Back Seat,' *The Washington Post*, 6 May 1979.

Preston, M., (1971), Memorandum, 4 June 1971, Florida: Kennedy Space Center Archive.

Reichley, J., (1981), *Conservatives in an Age of Change: The Nixon and Ford Administrations*, Washington DC: The Brookings Institute.

Roland, A., (1985), 'The Shuttle: Triumph or Turkey', *Discover*, November 1985.

Roland, A., (1989), 'Barnstorming in Space: The Rise and Fall of the Romantic Era of Spaceflight, 1957–1986,' in Radford Byerly (ed.) *Space Policy Reconsidered*, San Francisco: Westview Press.

Schell, J., (1975), *The Time of Illusions*, New York: Vantage.

Shapely, W., (1972), memorandum to George Low, 26 July 1972, Washington DC: NASA History Office Archive.

Space Business Daily (1973a), 'Mondale Hoping New GAO Report will Help Kill Shuttle', *Space Business Daily*, 11 April 1973: 230.

Space Business Daily (1973b), 'Proxmire "Frustrated" by Capable Defense of Shuttle' *Space Business Daily*, 12 April 1973: 236–238.

Space Business Daily (1973c), 'Ranking GOP Committee Member Opposes Proxmire on Shuttle', *Space Business Daily*, 4 June 1973: 188.

Thompson, R., (1995), Space Shuttle Manager, interview with the author, 9 September 1995, Houston, Texas.

Tischler, A., (1995), NASA Director of Chemical Propulsion within the Office of Advanced Research and Technology, interview with the author, 3 May 1995, Washington DC.

Tribe, J., (1995), Rockwell Chief Engineer at Kennedy Space Center, interview with the author, 28 July 1995, Kennedy, Florida.

Tufte, E., (1978), *Political Control of the Economy*, New Jersey: Princeton University Press

Vaughn, D., (1996), *Challenger Launch Decision: Risky Technology, Culture, and Deviance at NASA*, University of Chicago Press.

White House Press Office (1978), press release from the Office of the White House Press Secretary on the Presidents Space Policy, 18 October 1978, Marshall Space Flight Center Archive, Huntsville, Alabama.

Winner, L., (1978), *Autonomous Technology: Technics-out-of-Control as a Theme in Political Thought*, Cambridge: Massachusetts, MIT Press.

Woods, B., (2003), 'Heated Debates: A History of the Space Shuttle's Thermal Protection System 1970–1981,' *Quest: The History of Spaceflight Quarterly*, 10, 3: 39–55.

Yarbrough, H., (1995), NASA, Johnson Space Centre, Interview with the author, 5 September 1995, Huston, Texas.

Yardley, J., (1979), 'To the First Launch,' *Aeronautics & Astronautics*, February, 1979: 28–34.

Yardley, J., (1995), NASA Associate Administrator for Space Transportation System, President of McDonnell Douglas Aeronautics, interview with the author, 9 August 1995, St Louis, Missouri.

The geostationary orbit: a critical legal geography of space's most valuable real estate

Christy Collis

This chapter begins 35,786 km above the Earth's equator, where a satellite drifts eastward at 11,100 km per hour. The satellite receives information from Earth and bounces it back. The satellite is an average one: about 3.8 meters high, and, with its solar panel 'wings' extended, about 26 meters wide. It weighs 1,727 kilograms, including its fuel, which it will use to maintain its precise orbital position over the course of its operational lifespan of about 15 years (Boeing, 2001). Two aspects of this satellite make it particularly important, neither of which has to do with the satellite itself. Its importance rests instead on its location, its geography. At this precise height over the equator, the satellite moves at exactly the same speed as the Earth beneath it: it forever stays in the sky above a single fixed point on the Earth. Second, because it is above the equator, the satellite can 'see' 42 per cent of the Earth's surface at once, from 81 degrees north to 81 degrees south (Kelso, 1998: 76). What is called its terrestrial footprint is larger than that which could be achieved by a satellite in any other orbit around the Earth. As such, it's a particularly powerful communications tool: the receiving stations on Earth below it do not need to be adjusted or calibrated because the satellite never moves from its position above them, and its data can be broadcast to 40 per cent of the Earth's surface at once. What makes this satellite so powerful, and so valuable, is that it is located in the geostationary orbit (GEO):[1] the single orbital belt, 35,786 km above the equator and a relatively miniscule 30 km wide, in which satellites orbit at the same speed as the ground below them. Because of its special properties, the GEO is Space's[2] most valuable position. With a satellite in GEO, a communications provider does not have to pay the massive costs associated with maintaining several satellites to provide full-time coverage, or construct multiple Earth stations or moving receivers. With only three satellites in GEO, a communications provider can cover almost the entire Earth. For satellites, which currently carry much of the world's communication data, as well as its navigation and meteorological information, the GEO is *the* place to be. But, as the above citations of the GEO's size indicate, the GEO is not infinite: satellites have to be positioned apart from each other so that they don't interfere with each others' transmissions; they are strung along the GEO's thin belt 'like pearls on a string' (Wiessner, 1983: 225). Only so many pearls can fit on a string, particularly when they have to be spaced at prescribed intervals. This chapter addresses two key questions about the valuable GEO: who, if anyone, owns it; and what kind of a cultural space is it?

The chapter is grounded in two theoretical approaches: cultural geography, and critical legal geography. The chapter is framed by the cultural geographical concept of 'spatiality', a term which signals the multiple and dynamic nature of geographical space. As spatial theorists such as Henri Lefebvre assert, a space is never simply physical; rather, any space is always a jostling composite of material, imagined, and practiced geographies (Lefebvre, 1991). The ways in which cultures perceive, represent, and legislate that space are as constitutive of its identity – its spatiality – as the physical topography of the ground itself. The second theoretical field in which this chapter is situated – critical legal geography – derives from cultural geography's focus on the cultural construction of spatiality. In his *Law, Space and the Geographies of Power* (1994), Nicholas Blomley asserts that analyses of territorial law largely neglect the spatial dimension of their investigations; rather than seeing the law as a force that produces specific kinds of spaces, they tend to position space as a neutral, universally-legible entity which is neatly governed by the equally neutral 'external variable' of territorial law (Blomley, 1994: 28). 'In the hegemonic conception of the law,' Pue (1990: 568) similarly argues, 'the entire world is transmuted into one vast isotropic surface' on which law simply acts. But as the emerging field of critical legal geography demonstrates, law is not a neutral organizer of space, but is instead a powerful cultural technology of spatial production. 'Rather than seeking to bridge the gap between law and space, the argument here is that there is no gap to bridge,' Blomley explains (Blomley, 1994: 37). Or as Delaney (2001: 494) states, legal debates are 'episodes in the social production of space'. International territorial law, in other words, makes space, and does not simply govern it. Drawing on these tenets of critical legal geography, as well as on the Lefebvrian concept of multipartite spatiality, this chapter does two things. First, it extends the field of critical legal geography into Space, a domain with which the field has yet to substantially engage. Second, it demonstrates that the legal spatiality of the GEO is both complex and contested, and argues that it is crucial that humanities scholars understand this dynamic legal space on which the Earth's communications systems rely.

Thinking carefully and critically about the legal geography of the GEO is important, and increasingly urgent. One aspect of this importance is entirely practical: most of our communications, meteorological, and navigational systems depend upon satellites in the GEO: it is no understatement to say that global communication and navigation now depends on the GEO. As Warf (2007: 385) notes, 'satellites and earth stations comprise a critical, often over-looked, part of the global telecommunications infrastructure'. Castells's (2007: 394) 'space of flows,' he continues, 'would be impossible without the skein of earth stations and orbital platforms that lie at the heart of the [satellite] industry'. In an article on the astropolitical environment, MacDonald (2007: 594) similarly notes that 'our lives already extend to the Outer-Earth in ways that we entirely take for granted'. Parks (2005: 7) describes satellites as 'moving persistently through orbit, structuring the global imaginary, the socioeconomic order, and the tissue of everyday experience across the planet'. Accordingly, the satellite industry – one which is largely centred in the desirable GEO – has become an increasingly powerful component of global economies: satellite world revenues in 2004 were $103US billion, and were predicted to exceed $158US billion by 2010 (Jakhu, 2007: 176). Understanding the GEO – and in particular its legal geography – is thus critical to understanding how the very infrastructure of world communication works.

Understanding the legal geography of the GEO is also of particular importance to cultural theorists. As the previous paragraph indicates, for media and communication scholars – or for anyone with an interest in communication – understanding the legal geography of the GEO is fundamental: the GEO is *the* space – physical and legal – which allows contemporary communication practices to exist. For cultural theorists concerned with the creation of social spaces, with the ways in which ideological forces produce the social and material world, or with the ways in which cultures interact with and shape their environments, the GEO is of profound salience. Yet disturbingly little scholarship on Space exists inside what can roughly be called the humanities: despite the demonstrated ability of humanities scholars – cultural geographers, critical legal geographers, media and communication scholars, cultural studies scholars in particular – to understand and explain cultural, historical, and political phenomena, when it comes to Space, there is a curious critical silence (see Parker and Bell, this volume). As Parks (2005: 5) notes, 'Despite the global significance of satellite technologies, cultural theorists have been relatively silent about their ramifications.' MacDonald (2007: 610) makes a similar argument, noting that for many humanities scholars, Space seems too absurd, odd, and abstract a subject with which to engage: this assumption, however, is a direct result of lack of understanding of the centrality of Space – and in particular the GEO – to everyday life. My experience as a Space cultural theorist demonstrates that this lack of understanding at times leads to condemnation of Space scholarship: when people are starving on Earth, I've been scolded, how can you morally justify sitting around thinking about Outer Space? Yet as this chapter – and this book – signal, Space is imbricated into our lives, our social organization, our cultures, and the power politics of the world: 'what is at stake – politically and geopolitically – in the contemporary struggle over outer space is too serious to pass without critical comment' (MacDonald, 2007: 593), and is too serious to be left to engineering, scientific, and legal scholars alone. 'In cultural theory the satellite has been missing in action, lying at the threshold of everyday visibility and critical attention' (Parks, 2005: 7): it is time then for cultural theorists to extend their analytical skills, their attention, and their distinct critical perspectives beyond the surface of the Earth.

This is not a chapter about what kind of a space I think the GEO should be, or how I think it should be created as a legal geography. Similarly, this chapter is not a recondite philosophical argument about the nature of spatiality. Instead, this chapter provides an anatomy of the legal geography of the GEO, a spatial history (Carter 1987) of this valuable and contested site on which we now rely. It is expository rather than argumentative for one key reason: few humanities and social science scholars are aware of the existence of the GEO itself, let alone its complex cultural history and constitution. Before debates about the GEO can be initiated, and before humanities scholars can lend their critical thoughts and insights to the struggle for the GEO, the GEO first needs to be understood and anatomized. To do so is the purpose of this chapter.

1957–1967: 'A lawless environment'

It is a common assumption that when the Soviet Sputnik satellite launched as part of the 1957 International Geophysical Year blasted into orbit, it entered an entirely lawless environment, a space which simply did not exist as a legal geography (Wassenbergh, 1991: 15). To some extent, this is true: laws specifically pertaining to Space did not yet exist in 1957. Space was not entirely lawless, however. From as early as 450BC, Roman law asserted that the airspace over crops belonged to the crops' owners, and that if a neighbour's tree intruded into this airspace and impeded the crop's growth, the crop's owner could have the right to remove the overhanging branches. Legal space, in other words, was not solely terrestrial; it reached up into the air (Klein, 1959) and extended the legal geography of possession beyond the surface of the Earth. In 1587, English law similarly constructed airspace as a legal geography: adapting the Roman legal principle of *cujus est solum ejus est usque ad coelum* (he who owns the land owns up into the sky) (Schick, 1961: 681) so that private property owners owned the airspace superjacent to their land. The legal geography of the air became a particularly pressing issue during the World War One period, as aerial bombing emerged as a key aspect of war for the first time. The Paris Peace Conference of 1919 formalized the legal status of the air, giving each state 'complete and exclusive sovereignty over the air space above its territory' (in Latchford, 1959: 403): for the first time, airspace became the legal possession of states. Any state that wished to fly into the airspace of another state would have to seek permission first, thus legally recognizing that airspace as a legal possession. Airspace as property, it was assumed, extended upwards from the coastal boundaries of the subjacent state: the legal geography of state possession reached indefinitely into the sky.

But as far as Space was concerned, this legal geography was entirely abstract until 1957, when Sputnik, the first satellite, achieved Earth orbit. Sputnik overflew various states, including the USA, but no state protested that its legal airspace had been violated by the satellite (Lissitzyn, 1962: 138). In international law, a state's territorial possession is created not only by physical acts – the planting of a flag, the visiting of unvisited land, or the construction of a government base – but also by other states' recognition of it (Triggs, 1986: 33). When the Soviet Union's Sputnik, launched as part of the 1957–58 International Geophysical Year, travelled through Space without official protest, Space became an entirely new legal geography: a space beyond state possession, a vast space owned by no one at all. It was not yet clear what kind of a legal geography Space was, but one thing became clear: Space was not a state possession. The fact of satellites' physical presence in Space meant that what had hitherto been an abstract and theoretical legal geography suddenly became an occupied one. A legal geography which accommodated this development was clearly required. In 1961 and 1963, the General Assembly of the UN passed two resolutions on Space,[3] suggesting that 'the exploration and use of outer space and celestial bodies shall be carried out in accordance with international law' (1961) and that Space was not subject to national appropriation (1963) (Cheng, 1997: 71 & 85). Although these resolutions were non-binding, and although there were not yet any specific international laws for Space, they marked a beginning of the legal geography of Space: the laws of the Earth, according to the UN, encompassed Space; Space was, albeit vaguely, a legal geography. The US, seeing this legal geography of non-possession as an opportunity to keep Space open for its own spy satellites, and seeing it as a way to avoid a costly extraterrestrial war, quickly endorsed this new spatiality (Stone, 2006). Yet already in the two UN resolutions, a deep contradiction regarding the legal geography of Space arose: customary law, which the first resolution suggests should be applied to Space, allows states to claim territory; indeed, the management of states' territorial possessions is one of the cornerstones of international law (Jennings, 1963: 2). Yet the second resolution suggested that Space was unavailable to states; that it was a new kind of legal geography, akin only to the high seas and the unclaimed sector of Antarctica (Peterson, 1997). At this point, the fundamental bifurcation in the legal geography of Space – a split which continues to characterize the GEO today – emerged: was Space just another area to enfold into the Earth's standard legal geographies – particularly those which create the Earth as a series of state territorial possessions – or was it a different kind of space altogether, a shared space in which Earth's standard legal geographies did not apply? Was the legal production of Space simply a matter of extending Earth's legal geographies upwards, or was it a matter of creating an entirely new kind of legal geography?

Throughout the 1960s an increasing number of satellites achieved orbit, entering this unstable legal space. The first satellite to achieve geostationary orbit was NASA's 71 cm by 39 cm Syncom 3, in 1964: as of this date, the GEO became an occupied space. The bar-fridge-sized Syncom 3 broadcast the 1964 Olympics in Japan to the US, beaming the first TV content ever across the Pacific (Jasentuliyana, 1999: 281). Not only did Syncom 3 integrate East Asia into the expanding global media and communication system (Parks, 2005: 21), but it also proved the value of the GEO: unlike earlier satellites, Syncom 3 never disappeared from 'sight' of its US Earth receivers. In 1965, the US corporation COMSAT's Early Bird, the first privately-owned satellite, entered the GEO: with this, the legal geography of the GEO was suddenly no longer a matter of state-state competition, adding a complication to existing legal frameworks. Early Bird began to highlight the economic value of the GEO: it could carry 240 telephone calls, almost ten times the maximum available on the trans-Atlantic analog line (Chartrand, 2004: 6). As more satellites entered GEO, a second fundamental split in its legal geography emerged. The 1961 UN Resolution stated that satellite communications should be made available to all states: the GEO, in other words, should be readily available to any state which wished to use it, rather than monopolized by the states or corporations with the economic and technological power to get there first. But as the numbers of satellites increased, and with them the volume of radio signals on Earth and in Space, concern emerged that satellites' radio waves would interfere with existing radio signals on Earth, and with each others' signals in Space. In 1963, the UN's International Telecommunication Union (ITU), which is in charge of allocating and organizing international radio and communication frequencies, held its first Space conference, or World Administrative Radio Conference (WARC). The 1963 Space-WARC allocated specific and limited radio frequencies and frequency locations to Space in general, and to the GEO in particular, to ensure that satellite transmissions from GEO did not interfere with Earth signals, or with transmissions from other GEO satellites.[4] This seems logical and reasonable, but the legal geography it established for the GEO was far from universally accepted.

Under the ITU process, to secure a GEO position, or 'slot', and its associated radio frequency, a satellite's owner must register first with the ITU, which then checks that the slot positioning is acceptable in relation to other satellites, and then assigns that slot and its frequency to the satellite (Soroos, 1982: 229). Developing states argued that this effectively meant that states with economic and technological power could, and would, help themselves to the GEO in a first-come-first-served rush of satellites, and that states with less money would effectively find themselves locked out of the GEO (Jaysentuliyana, 1999: 288). They argued that a different kind of legal geography, one which favoured developing states, was required. This second division between visions of the GEO's legal geography is based in two contradictory ontologies of law. In one ontological approach, the civil law approach, law creates geographies based on specific principles; in this vision, legal geographies are produced first, shaping and governing all future activity within them. This chapter uses the term *a priori* for this legal ontology and its resultant geographies. In the other ontological approach, one based in the Anglo-American tradition of common law, legal geographies are generated in response to activities and practical issues as they happen; they are based on cases and activities rather than on abstract principles (Jaysentuliyana, 1999: 292). This chapter uses the term *a posteriori* for this legal onotology and its resultant geographies.[5] These are fundamental questions about the relationship between law and geography, and about the purpose of legal geography. Foucault (1980) notes that places never simply 'are'; rather places are always constructed as 'places for' certain people or activities. Creating 'places for' is precisely the role of legal geography: for what and for whom the GEO was constructed was the question.

In 1965, Space in general and the GEO in particular, became a legal geography of *a posteriori* common law: the developed world's satellites which were beginning to populate it created GEO as a *res nullius*, or land owned by no one, available to whoever could get there first.[6] As such, by 1967, the GEO was a space for the developed world, and particularly for the US: at the end of 1966 only the US and the Soviet Union had launched satellites and all 11 of the satellites in the GEO were American (UN Office for Outer Space Affairs, 2008). With the ITU's first-come-first-served approach to GEO slot and frequency allocation, and Space's apparent lack of ownership, it seemed as if the GEO was becoming a familiar type of legal geography: one in which the wealthiest and most powerful states – and in particular the US – rushed in and claimed 'squatters' rights' (Soroos, 1982: 666) to the most valuable real estate, the 'geostationary gold' (Warf, 2006: 388). As Warf (2006: 385) notes, access to satellites, and in particular to satellites in the GEO, 'reinforces . . . terrestrial power-geometries of states in the world-system.' 'Space exploration, then, from its earliest origins to the present day, has been about familiar terrestrial and ideological struggles here on Earth' (MacDonald, 2007: 597): the geo-power politics of the Earth had begun to incorporate and inform the GEO.

1967–1975: Space transformed

The legal geography of Space – and of its most valuable real estate, the GEO – did not remain static, however: in 1967, it was radically transformed. In the 1960s, numerous new states emerged as a result of global decolonization, many of them determined that legal geographies should no longer reflect the power and property imbalances of the colonial era.[7] One way in which this could be achieved, they argued, was the legal creation of specific spaces as the Common Heritage of Mankind [sic] (CHP).[8] In 1967, Arvid Parvo, the Maltese ambassador to the UN, famously proposed that the high seas should become a CHP;[9] in the same year, the Argentine ambassador Aldo Cocca similarly proposed to the UN's Committee on the Peaceful Uses of Outer Space that Space should be created as a legal geography based on CHP principles. In the vision of legal geography of the CHP, areas such as Space, the high seas, and Antarctica: should not be available to state possession, should be jointly managed by all states, should be used for peaceful purposes only, and – most controversially – any economic benefits from their exploitation should be shared equitably among all states (Jasentuliyana, 1999: 139). This was a radical new legal geography, one which proposed to supplant the dominance of the legal geography which had defined the Earth since the 1648 Peace of Westphalia: that is, the partitioning of the Earth into states' possessions (O'Tuathail, 1996: 4). It also proposed to transform Space and the GEO from their then-current legal status as a *res nullius* to a variety of *res communis*: the developing states proposed to transform the legal geography of Space, radically and entirely.[10]

In 1967, these proposals partially succeeded, and Space became an entirely new legal geography. In 1967, the 'Treaty on Principles Governing the Activities of States in the Exploration and Use of Outer Space, Including the Moon and Other Celestial Bodies' (The Outer Space Treaty, or OST) was adopted by the UN General Assembly to transform Space legally. The US, USSR, and the UK immediately ratified the Treaty, giving it significant international power. The OST produced Space – including the GEO – as a space of international parity and justice, stipulating that 'the exploration and use of outer space shall be carried out for the benefit and in the interests of all countries irrespective of their degree of economic or scientific development' (OST Article I). No longer was the GEO simply another *res nullius* space 'out there' awaiting national claimants; after the OST, the GEO became a shared international space – a *res communis* – in which state claims, weapons testing, and scientific secrecy were banned (United Nations Office for Outer Space Affairs, 1967). Galloway (2000) suggests that the fact that the Soviets beat the US into Space impacted profoundly on the ensuing legal geography of Space: suddenly aware that the USSR had the potential to conduct Space warfare and to potentially occupy prime GEO slots, the US quickly agreed that Space should be a space of peace and international cooperation. The OST bans military activity from Space, making Space 'exclusively for peaceful purposes' (OST, Article IV); it also makes all of Space open to 'free use' and exploration (OST, Article I). Article II of the OST is the most powerful in terms of spatial construction: according to this Article, 'Outer Space, including the Moon and other celestial bodies, is not subject to national appropriation by claim of sovereignty, by means of use or occupation or any other means.' With this Article, Space became a legal geography of non-possession, a *res communis*; although the exact height at which sovereign airspace ends and Space begins remained under debate – with this Article, Earth's legal geographies of state sovereignty were given a ceiling. While developed states lauded the OST's prevention of Space warfare, developing states celebrated its new legal geographical regime: the OST, as India argued, would prevent 'extraterrestrial colonialism' (Jasentuliyana, 1999: 142). State territorial sovereignty and *res nullius* were confined to the Earth; the GEO had become a unique legal geography of international peace and sharing.

While the OST, however, was a legally-binding treaty (at least for the states who ratified it), it did not instantly solve the problems of the GEO. In fact, it appeared to exacerbate them. If the GEO was available for 'free use' by anyone, developed states and organizations argued that they were entirely within their rights to continue to populate it as quickly and as thoroughly as they wanted: it was, after all, a legal geography of open access (Cahill, 2000–1: 236). In the early 1970s, India and Indonesia began to plan satellite systems for the GEO slots above their terrestrial territories, but developed states and the US-dominated international satellite consortium INTELSAT[11] refused to adjust their satellites to accommodate them (Jasentuliyana, 1999: 152): while the OST prevented state claims to possession of the GEO, it apparently did not prevent the 'squatters' rights' *a posteriori* spatiality of the ITU. Because the ITU is a regulatory body, which lacks enforcement powers, it could not compel the existing satellites' owners to accommodate India and Indonesia (Jakhu, 2007: 181). The question of the legal geography of the GEO was thus back on the agenda at the 1971 WARC, which passed 'Resolution Spa 2-1' declaring that ITU slot allocations 'should not provide any permanent priority for any individual country . . . and should not present an obstacle to the establishment of space systems by other countries' (Thompson, 1996: 62).[12] But this aspirational spatiality did not override the *a posteriori* legal geography of the GEO: satellites have a limited operational lifespan, so stating that they were not allowed to occupy slots permanently was not particularly powerful. The *a posteriori* spatiality of the GEO emerged largely unchanged from the 1971 WARC but not unchallenged: France, the UK, and Latin America all argued that a new legal geography for the GEO was required. In 1973, the ITU declared the GEO a 'limited natural resource,' akin to Amazonian rainforests or the aquifers of the Sahel: with this, the GEO was for the first time legally differentiated from Space in general; it became a finite new legal geography within the infinity of Space. No longer was the GEO simply a space to be managed equitably; it was now a 'resource' necessary to human life, and a limited resource at that. If all states, as the 1971 WARC resolved, should be able to establish space systems in the GEO, and if the GEO was officially limited, then *a posteriori* spatiality was no longer legitimate: although the *a posteriori* spatiality remained in place in 1974, it was beginning to erode (Thompson, 1996: 293). Once again, the legal geography of the GEO became unstable.

1975–82: Bogota, and the moon

Until 1975, the general argument of the developing states was that some kind of *a priori* system should characterize the legal geography of the GEO so that the 'limited resource' would be available to all states, no matter what their current level of technological capability. In 1975, however, frustrated that this legal geography was not evolving at the same speed at which developed states were putting new satellites into the GEO, Colombia made a radical move: in 1975, Colombia asserted sovereignty over a section of the GEO. In 1976, at the 31st UN General Assembly, Panama did the same; and in 1976, Colombia, Brazil, Congo, Ecuador, Indonesia, Kenya, Uganda, and Zaire together created and signed the Bogota Declaration, in which they collectively claimed sovereignty of the sections of the GEO superjacent to their terrestrial territories. This was a radical move because it was the first ever claim to Space sovereignty: to date, the GEO remains the only area of Space which has been subject to formal state claim. It was also a radical moment in the legal geography of the GEO: according to the Bogota Declaration, the GEO was not part of Space, and was therefore not a part of the legal geography of the OST. Although it seems audacious, excising the GEO from Space had a legal basis: in 1975 – and indeed still today – there was no legal agreement as to exactly where airspace ended, and

Space began (Harris and Harris, 2006): Bogota simply asserted that Space began beyond the GEO (Weissner, 1982/3: 237). The Bogota Declaration applied the legal principle of contiguity – the same principle through which states claim sovereignty to areas of the continental shelf off their shores (Triggs, 1986: 90) – to the GEO (Jasentuliyana, 1999: 153), firmly placing the GEO within the Earth's legal geography of state sovereignty. The Declaration argued that the signatories' national appropriation of the GEO was hardly radical or novel: 'under the name of a so-called non-national appropriation,' they argued, 'what was actually developed was technological partition of the orbit, which is simply a national appropriation' by the developed states, and in particular by the US (in Weissner, 1983: 238). The GEO was subject to de facto national claims based on the *a posteriori* legal geography in place. Maintaining their proposed legal geography of the GEO, the eight Bogota signatories, as well as Gabon, refused to sign off on satellites assigned at WARC 1977 and 1979 into 'their' slots. The Declaration treated existing satellites as earlier European empires had treated the residents of 'new' territories they 'discovered' and claimed: it stated that 'Equatorial countries do not condone the existing satellites or the positions they occupy on their segments of the Geostationary Orbit nor does the existence of said satellites or use of the segment unless expressly authorized by the state exercising sovereignty over this segment' (in Weissner, 1983: 237). With the Bogota Declaration, the legal geography of the GEO became yet more complex and contested, and the geopolitical nature of its contours became more visible.

Almost all states and space organizations rejected the Bogota Declaration outright: some developing states argued that it would effectively lock them out of access, the UK stated that the GEO was a part of Space and therefore unavailable for claim under the OST, and Belgium insisted that the equatorial states were unable to 'effectively occupy' their GEO claims and were therefore unable to 'perfect' those claims at law (Gorove, 1979: 452). The majority of counter-arguments rested on the GEO's being a part of Space, even in the absence of a clear legal definition of Space. The legal production of geography is particularly visible in these exchanges: not only were they concerned with what kind of a space the GEO should be, they also sought to establish what and where, exactly, Space was. The Bogota Declaration was particularly productive in its stimulation of new debates about the legal geography of the GEO. The GEO, responses to Bogota affirmed, was part of Space, and not part of Earth's legal geographies of possession. While Bogota did not succeed in transforming the GEO into the property of equatorial states, it did firmly situate developing states on the agenda of GEO spatial considerations: that developing states should have equitable access was now largely accepted; that transforming the GEO into Earth-bound sovereign territory was the way to accomplish this was refused.

Throughout the 1970s, increasing numbers of satellites claimed slots, particularly as international organizations such as INTELSAT, Intersputnik (established 1974 to service the USSR, Eastern Bloc states, Iraq, and Syria), Immarsat (non-profit cooperative of 28 countries which provides maritime satellite services, established 1973), Eutelsat (European organization, established 1977 to service European communication, first satellite launched 1983), and Arabsat (established 1976, first satellite launched 1986 to service members of the Arab Laegue of states) emerged. In competition with these large, state-based organizations, in 1972 the US's Federal Communication Commission proclaimed its 'open skies' policy, 'allowing any party to apply for orbital slots, effectively initiating the era of privately-owned domestic commercial satellites' (Warf, 2007: 392). While physically, the GEO continued to fill – it remained a *res communis* governed by *a posteriori* spatiality – legally, it assumed yet another character in 1979. The 1979 UN Agreement Governing the Activities of States on the Moon and Other Celestial Bodies ('The Moon Treaty') attempted to transform Space again: it constructed Space as not only *res communis*, but as a CHP area (Gruner, 2004: 327). Unlike the earlier OST, which created Space as a space beyond state sovereignty, the Moon Treaty created Space as a very specific form of economic geography. The Moon Treaty stipulated that any wealth derived from Space had to be shared equally with the Earth's less-developed, poorer states, thus preventing Space from becoming a site for increased economic power for already wealthy states: developing nations should benefit equally from any proceeds of Space exploration, particularly from resource extraction (Herber, 1991: 393). The Moon Treaty transformed the vague *res communis* of the OST into a codified economic geography. No space-faring state has ever signed the Moon Treaty, rendering it largely impotent. Space, they assert, may be a geography of spatial sharing, but not of revenue sharing.

In this way, in the 1970s, the proposed spatialities of the GEO swung from one extreme of legal geography – state sovereignty – to the other – a CHP economic geography of non-sovereignty and enforced revenue sharing. Yet at the same time as these *a priori* geographies hovered over the GEO, seeking traction, the growing numbers of satellites entering it maintained its status as an *a posteriori* legal geography, dominated by the developed world.

1980–1988: Space WARCs and a combined legal geography

In 1979, the ITU convened the first General WARC since 1959: its aim was to finalize, once and for all, the allocation of all frequencies, particularly those associated with specific slots in the GEO. Marked inequality continued to govern the legal geography of the GEO: 90 per cent of the world's radio spectrum was, at the time, allocated to countries with only 10 per cent of the world's population; of the 74 satellites in the GEO in 1982, only four belonged to developing states (Weissner, 1983: 239). The 1979 WARC resolved that all states have equal rights to the limited natural resource of the GEO, but failed to effect this aspirational moral geography (Park, 2006: 877) into the more powerful domain of established legal geography (Waite and Rowan, 1986: 357). The 1982 Plenipotentiary Conference of the ITU injected a similar resolution, stating that 'the special needs of developing countries and the geographical situation of particular countries' should be taken into account in GEO frequency/slot allocation procedures (Thompson, 1996: 289), a resolution which remained similarly aspirational to the 1979 proposal. How these ideals might be activated into law was the agenda for the 1985 & 1988 'ITU WARC on the Use of the Geostationary Satellite Orbit and the Planning of Space Services Using It'. Arguments were heated, and ontological: the developed world's proponents of the *a posteriori* legal geography characterized the ITU's consideration of the developing world as an egregious 'intrusion of political pressures into an ostensibly objective, technical engineering issue' (Waite and Rowan, 1986: 356). Reserving specific slots for developing states, they argued, ran counter to the OST, which stipulated that no area of Space could be appropriated (Waite and Rowan, 1986: 363). Developing states, on the other hand, continued to argue that the GEO, like other non-sovereign spaces such as the deep seabed and Antarctica, should be an *a priori* domain in which economic and power inequalities were balanced. Debate revolved around semantics: did the 'equitable access' of the 1973 Convention mean 'equal access' to the GEO, or did it mean in proportion to expenditure (Thompson, 1996: 294)? In terms of legal geography, WARC 85/88 generated a compromise.

The 1988 Implementation Session of the WARC finally generated a new, combined legal geography of the GEO. It guaranteed every state one 'predetermined arc' (PDA) in the GEO's Fixed Satellite Service expansion bands (Waite and Rowan, 1986: 364). In other words, every state gained the right of occupancy to a PDA of the GEO closest to its territory. For the first time, the GEO became an *a priori* geography, clearly tethered to the terrestrial geographies of the Earth's states. But only a very limited one. As Thompson points out, the Fixed Satellite Service expansion bands legislated into PDAs constituted only one per cent of the Space spectrum, and further, the ruling did not apply to most telecommunication slots (1996: 295). Existing satellites were grandfathered, or exempted from the rule (Cahill, 2000–1: 233). Additionally, although each state gained a PDA, the WARC regulations allowed that PDA to be shifted without that state's consent in order to accommodate other satellites (Thompson, 1996: 296). In order to maximize use of the GEO, 'additional use provisions' allowed anyone to place a satellite into another state's PDA, but only for a maximum of 15 years (Jasentuliyana, 1999: 75). The 1980s WARCs also confirmed the GEO as a space dominated by states, rather than by private organizations: it stipulated that private satellites had to provide service for any state whose PDA they occupied, and assigned PDAs only to states (Cahill, 2000–1: 234). While some commentators argue that the WARC changes of the 1980s did not go far enough in re-inventing the GEO as an equitable one, others argued with equal vigour that the changes would retard GEO development and use. Despite these entrenched oppositional positions about the ontological nature of the GEO's legal geography, with the 1980s WARCs, became a space of combined *a priori* and *a posteriori* spatialities; the GEO had become a new legal geography.

Tonga and the GEO, 1988–1995

Responding swiftly to this new spatiality, in 1988, the tiny Pacific nation of Tonga rocked the legal geography of the GEO. In 1987, Mats Nilson, a US satellite entrepreneur, approached Tonga's King Taufa'ahua Tupou IV with an idea for the PDA of the GEO Tonga had received as a result of the 1980s WARCs. Tonga's PDA comprised the last remaining 16 slots which link Asia, the Pacific, and the US: given that the market for telecommunications traffic between the US and Asia totalled $2.5US billion in 1989, and was growing at 21 per cent per year, these slots were particularly valuable (Andrews, 1990: A1). Nilson proposed that he and Tonga form a national satellite organization, Tongasat, which would claim all of these slots, and then lease them to anyone who could pay for them at $2US million per slot per year (Levin, 1991: 42). From Nilson's perspective, Tonga was an ideal partner for him in this plan. Tonga was not a member of INTELSAT, so was not constrained by INTEL-SAT's regulation which blocks member states from launching their own satel-lites; Tonga had no national communications regulatory board to slow down satellite plans; and Tonga now had the legal basis to claim its PDA in a valuable area of the GEO. The plan also appealed to Tonga: it would provide Tonga with the telecommunication infrastructure it lacked, it would give Tongans access to global telecommunications and thereby 'create or reinforce a notion of their country as one part of the world community' (Ezor, 1992/3: 919), and it would increase the national budget by 20 per cent (Andrews, 1990: A1). Thus, between 1988 and 1990, the newly-formed Tongasat – in which Nilson had a 20 per cent stake – formally filed a claim with the ITU for the last 16 slots in the Pacific sector of the GEO.

Tonga's move was in keeping with the legal geography of the GEO estab-lished by the 1980s WARCs: it mobilized the *a priori* spatiality according states the right to priority of claims in their assigned PDAs, as well as the *a posteriori* spatiality of first-claimed-first served. But this was the first time a developing nation had claimed GEO for largely commercial, rather than simply domestic telecommunications, purposes. INTELSAT reacted furiously. INTELSAT dominated the GEO: most states claimed slots in their PDAs on behalf of INTELSAT, which had the finances to populate them with satellites which would then provide telecommunications to the claiming state. Ezor (1992/3: 939) observes that INTELSAT had become complacent about its dominance of the GEO: not imagining that developing states such as Tonga might attempt to configure the GEO for their own, competitive, purposes, INTELSAT had not claimed the remaining Pacific slots, simply assuming that 'it had a lock' on them. Seeing its monopoly eroded, INTELSAT rushed to the ITU, arguing that the Tongan GEO claims broke with the legal geography of the GEO (Cahill, 2000/1: 244) by transforming PDAs into property. INTELSAT stated that Tonga was setting a dangerous precedent for 'claimstaking' and 'hoarding' of GEO slots by developing states, as well as creating 'financial speculation in the GEO'

(Thompson, 1996: 281) in contravention of the 'spirit' of the new legal geography of the GEO. While US satellite corporation Columbia Communications demanded that the US FCC deny Earth reception to any satellites in Tonga's PDA, INTELSAT went further and insisted that the ITU must change its regulations at the 1992 WARC, and therefore again change the legal geography of the GEO itself (Ezor, 1992/3: 927).

INTELSAT's challenges, and Tonga's actions, revolved around interpretations of the nature of the GEO's legal geography: who, and what was the GEO for? For Tonga, the OST and the 1980s WARCs produced the GEO as a place for developing states to gain some degree of economic competitiveness with developed economies, a space for the creation of global economic parity. For INTELSAT, the OST and the *a posteriori* aspects of the WARCs produced the GEO as a place for the continuation and further development of the existing economic order, a place for the Earth's major powers. In adjudicating this dispute, the ITU would be creating the legal geography of the GEO. If it sided with Tonga, it could be creating the GEO as a form of private property, which ran counter to the geography established by the OST (Ezor, 1992/3: 935). In siding with INTELSAT, the ITU would override its own legal geography of compromise, one which made the GEO a site for equalizing the global economy for developing states. It would mean admitting that PDAs could be overridden by states or organizations with superior Space capacities and bargaining power: it would mean once again transforming the GEO into a solely *a posteriori* legal geography. Once again, the ITU created a compromise geography: Tonga was granted six of its claimed 16 slots, and was allowed to auction these off as planned; it dropped its claim to the other ten. In 1991, then, the GEO became a legal geography of *a priori/a posteriori* compromise, which also comprised some private property – insofar as states could auction or lease 'their' PDAs.

Conclusion: a tangled geography, the GEO 1993–2008

The GEO remains a space of conflict, compromise, and instability, all results of its complex and evolving legal geography. Although fibre optics now carry some of the communication data once solely carried by satellites (Warf, 2006), the GEO is under increasing pressure, particularly as the markets for satellite TV, telephony, and broadband grow. 'The existing spacefaring nations are increasing the number of their satellites. At the same time, more nations want to launch and own their own satellites' (Jakhu, 2007: 178). Further, militaries around the world rely heavily on satellites for communication, remote sensing, and navigation, putting substantial pressure on the GEO: although warfare in Space is prohibited by the OST, the GEO is highly militarized (Park, 2006), as Galace (2006: 20) states, 'the wars in Iraq and Afghanistan are eating up massive satellite bandwidth to support coalition military operations . . . military use will generate 46 per cent of all satellite service revenues from 2002 to 2007'.

Elsewhere in this book, Peter Dickens argues that Space is on the cusp of being incorporated into capitalism: that the geography of capitalism is expanding to incorporate Space, and the geography of Space will soon be transformed by capitalism. As this chapter has demonstrated, at least one area of Space – the GEO – has been geographically redefined, and literally occupied, by capitalism since 1964. As this chapter has indicated, this capitalization of Space, and debates about whether or not Space should be incorporated into Earth's organising structures – particularly capitalism and state territorial possession – have shaped the legal geographies of the GEO for over forty years, and will continue to do so. The case for creating the GEO as a legal geography outside of capitalism and outside of state possession has been made, and debated vigorously, for decades: understanding the history of these debates, and of the GEO, is key to understanding the ways in which capitalism and state expansionism have – and more importantly have not – shaped the legal geography of Space.

The current legal geography of the GEO is unlikely to hold. As demand for limited GEO slots increases, the ITU's ability to maintain its legal geography of compromise is diminishing. The ITU's legal geography faces two key problems. First, the ITU is now inundated by 'paper satellites': because the right to a slot is determined by registration with the ITU rather than by the existence of an actual satellite, states with no capacity for launching satellites are pre-emptively claiming slots which they may never occupy. Of 1,300 applications for slots submitted to the ITU in the early 2000s, 1,200 were for paper satellites: processing this glut of claims means that the ITU now needs three years just to catch up with existing claims filed (Jakhu, 2007: 182). The ITU is attempting to deal with this by charging a filing fee – thus transforming the GEO into a form of purchasable property – and by insisting that a state must occupy any slot it has been granted within seven years. Second, it is increasingly apparent that the ITU might have been able to play a major role in the creation of the legal geography of the GEO to date, but it has no power to enforce that geography (Park, 2006: 871). In 1993, for example, Indonesia complicated the Tongasat situation further by simply launching its PALAPA-B1 satellite into one of the slots claimed by Tonga: it did this without registering with the ITU, arguing that the GEO was an *a posteriori res nullius* rather than an *a priori* space (Thompson, 1996: 282), and that Tonga's claims to the GEO were illegitimate. The ITU could do nothing: only the collapse of the Indonesian satellite project resolved the conflict over this slot. Similarly, when Japan and Tonga's occupation of Vietnam's PDA blocked Vietnam's VINASAT-1's entry, the ITU could not compel them to shift.[13] Many private space development organizations and legal scholars now argue that the OST only applies to states, and that Space is therefore available to claim by non-state actors (see for example Marko, 1992/3; Reynolds, 1998; Wiles, 1998). 'It is impossible to deny,' argues Park (2006: 878), 'that space is the next strategic frontier, both militarily and economically speaking. Unfortunately, the creators of the current legal regime for space failed to forsee the rate at which these advancements would take place.' In other words, the legal geography of the GEO must, again, change.

35,786 km above the Earth, a legal geography upon which the global communications infrastructure depends remains riven and unstable, characterized by power struggles and ideological challenges. In this, it is no different from any of Earth's historical resource frontiers: creating the GEO's legal geography is little different from when, at the dawn of European imperialism, legal scholars debated who and what the lands of the 'new world' were for. Creating the legal geography of the GEO both reflects and will shape terrestrial power relations, communication infrastructures, and global economics far into the future. It is well past time for humanities and social science scholars to attend to this geography critically and thoroughly. As MacDonald (2007: 593) argues, 'a critical geography of Space is long overdue.' When it comes to Space's most valuable real estate, the GEO, this need is particularly urgent.

Notes

1 Geostationary Earth Orbit. The GEO is also sometimes referred to as the GSO and sometimes as The Clarke Orbit, after Arthur C. Clarke, who proposed its existence in 1945. The GEO should not be confused with geosynchronous orbits, which do not remain in place over a single terrestrial point. Satellites in geosynchronous orbit circle the Earth once a day, but unlike satellites in the GEO, they do not remain in place over a single terrestrial point. Satellites in geosynchronous orbits will pass north and south of the Equator in the course of a day; satellites in the GEO will remain directly above the Equator at all times (Kelso, 1998: 77). Maintaining coverage of a specific terrestrial area using satellites in a geosynchronous orbit requires two expensive solutions: terrestrial Earth stations which can move in order to track the mobile satellite; and multiple satellites so that one satellite is always over the terrestrial area (Soroos, 1982: 667). More than one satellite means multiple launch costs, multiple satellite purchases, and multiple satellites to maintain. Geosynchronous orbits are thus less valuable as real estate than the GEO.
2 To differentiate between the physical place, Space, and the general concept of space, the former will be capitalized in this chapter.
3 Declaration of Legal Principles Governing the Activities of States in the Exploration and Use of Outer Space. Resolution 1721A (XVI) was adopted by the UN 20 December 1961; resolution 1962 (XVIII) was adopted by the UN 13 Dec. 1963.
4 Once approved by member states, the results of WARCs have the legal status of international treaties.
5 This chapter also uses these terms because they are the terms generally used in legal discussions of GEO spatiality.
6 At international law, *terra nullius* is defined as land belonging to no one, and is thus available for possession through 'discovery', claiming, and 'effective occupation'. *Res nullius* is the term used when this legal geographical term is applied to Space, as technically, Space is not 'land'.
7 This movement is referred to as the New International Economic Order, and was led by developing states, particularly in the UN, whose one-state-one-vote system granted them structural force (Gorman, 2001: 16).
8 Recent usage is 'Common Heritage Principle' rather than 'Common Heritage of Mankind' to reflect the legal status of the idea, and the existence of women.
9 This bid was largely successful: in the 1982 UN Law of the Sea Convention, the deep sea-bed was declared a CHP area: under the Convention, revenues earned from deep-sea mineral extraction must be shared with developing countries through the International Seabed Authority (Joyner, 1986: 196).

10 On the CHP, see Herber (1991) and Joyner (1986).
11 From 1964 to 2001 the US-based INTELSAT was a cooperative international satellite organisation. States can become members/shareholders of INTELSAT; voting power is determined by share ownership. In 2007, the US owned nearly 25 per cent of INTELSAT shares (Warf, 2007: 390). In 2001, INTELSAT became a private company. INTELSAT dominates the satellite industry, and the GEO, although this dominance is being eroded by the increasing emergence of national satellite systems.
12 The Resolution was adopted as Article 33 at the 1973 ITU Plenipotentiary Conference.
13 VINASAT-1 finally launched in 2008.

References

Andrews, E., (1990), 'Tiny Tonga seeks satellite empire in space', *New York Times*, 28th August, A1.
Blomley, N., (1994), *Law, Space and the Geographies of Power*, New York: Guilford.
Boeing Satellite Systems (2001), 'What is a satellite?' http://www.sia.org/industry_overview/sat101.pdf [Accessed June 2008].
Cahill, S., (2000–1), 'Give me my space: implications for permitting national appropriation of the geostationary orbit', *Wisconsin International Law Journal*, 19: 231–48.
Carter, P., (1987), *The Road to Botany Bay: An Essay in Spatial History*, London: Faber.
Chartrand, M., (2004), *Satellite Communications for the Nonspecialist*. Bellingham, Washington: SPIE Press.
Cheng, B., (1997), *Studies in International Space Law*, Oxford: Clarendon.
Delaney, D., (2001), 'Running with the land: legal-historical imagination and the spaces of modernity', *Journal of Historical Geography*, 27(4): 493–506.
Ezor, J., (1992/3), 'Costs overhead: Tonga's claiming of sixteen geostationary orbital sites and the implications for U.S. space policy', *Law and Policy in International Business*, 24: 915–42.
Foucault, M., (1980), *Power/Knowledge: Selected Interviews and Other Writings, 1972–1977*, Brighton: Harvester.
Galace, D., (2006), 'Asia's satellite industry: winning by the numbers.' Satmagazine.com, 4(3), 20–25, available at: http://www.satmagazine.com/june2006/june2006.pdf [Accessed June 2008].
Galloway, E., (2000), 'Organizing the United States government for outer space: 1957–1958', in R. Launius, J. Logsdon and R. Smith (eds), *Reconsidering Sputnik: Forty Years Since the Soviet Satellite*, London: Routledge: 309–26.
Gorman, R., (2001), *Great Debates at the United Nations: An encyclopedia of fifty key issues, 1945–2000*, Connecticut, USA and London: Greenwood.
Gorove, S., (1979), 'The geostationary orbit: issues of law and policy', *American Journal of International Law*, 73: 444–61.
Gruner, B., (2004), 'A new hope for international space law: incorporating nineteenth century first possession principles into the 1967 space treaty for the colonization of space in the twentieth century', *Seton Hall Law Review*, 35: 299–357.
Harris, A. and Harris, R., (2006), 'The need for air space and outer space demarcation', *Space Policy*, 22: 3–7.
Herber, C., (1991), 'The common heritage principle: Antarctica and the developing nations', *American Journal of Economics and Sociology*, 50(4): 392–406.
Jakhu, R., (2007), 'Legal issues of satellite telecommunications, the geostationary orbit, and space debris', *Astropolitics: the International Journal of Space Politics and Policy*, 5: 173–208.
Jasentuliyana, N., (1999), International space law and the United Nations. The Hague: Kluwer Law International.
Jennings, R., (1963), *The Acquisition of Territory in International Law*, Manchester: Manchester University Press.

63

Joyner, C., (1986), 'Legal implications of the concept of the Common Heritage of Mankind', *The International and Comparative Law Quarterly*, 35(1): 190–99.

Kelso, T., (1998), 'Basics of the geostationary orbit', *Satellite Times*, 4(7): 76–7.

Klein, H., (1959), 'Cujus est solum ejus est . . . quousque tandem?' *Journal of Air Law and Commerce*, 26: 237–54.

Latchford, S., (1959), 'The bearing of international air navigation conventions on the use of outer space', *The American Journal of International Law*, 53(2): 405–11.

Lefebvre, H., (1991), *The Production of Space*, translated by Donald Nicholson-Smith, Oxford: Blackwell.

Levin, H., (1991), 'Trading orbit spectrum assignments in the space satellite industry', *American Economic Review*, 81(2): 42–5.

Lissitzyn, O., (1962), 'Some legal implications of the U-2 and RB-47 incidents', *The American Journal of International Law*, 56(1): 135–42.

MacDonald, F., (2007), 'Anti-*Astropolitik*: outer space and the orbit of geography', *Progress in Human Geography*, 31(5): 592–615.

Marko, D., (1992/3), 'A kinder, gentler Moon Treaty: a critical review of the Moon Treaty and a proposed alternative', *Journal of Natural Resources and Environmental Law*, 8: 293–346.

O'Tuathail, G., (1996), *Critical Geopolitics: The Politics of Writing Global Space*, Minneapolis: Minneapolis University Press.

Park, A., (2006), 'Incremental steps for achieving space security: the need for a new way of thinking to enhance the legal regime for space', *Houston Journal of International Law*, 28(3): 871–911.

Parks, L., (2005), *Cultures in Orbit: Satellites and the Televisual*, Durham, NC: Duke University Press.

Peterson, M., (1997), 'The use of analogies in developing outer space law', *International Organization*, 51(2): 245–74.

Pue, W., (1990), 'Wrestling with Law: (Geographical) Specificity versus (Legal) Abstraction', *Urban Geography*, 11(6): 566–85.

Reynolds, G., (1998), 'Space property rights: an activist's approach', *To The Stars* (Sept/Oct): 19–21.

Schick, F., (1961), 'Space law and space politics', *The International and Comparative Law Quarterly*, 10(4): 681–706.

Soroos, M., (1982), 'The Commons in the Sky: the Radio Spectrum and Geosynchronous Orbit as Issues in Global Policy', *International Organization*, 36(3): 665–77.

Stone, C., (2006), 'Orbital strike constellations: the future of space supremacy and national defense', *The Space Review*, available at: http://www.thespacereview.com/article/628/1 [accessed 10th April 2007].

Thompson, J., (1996), 'Space for rent: the international telecommunications union, space law, and orbit/spectrum leasing', *Journal of Air Law and Commerce*, 62: 279–311.

Triggs, G., (1986), *International Law and Australian Sovereignty in Antarctica*, Sydney: Legal Books.

United Nations Office for Outer Space Affairs (1967), *Treaty on Principles Governing the Activities of States in the Exploration and Use of Outer Space, including the Moon and Other Celestial Bodies*, available at: http://www.unoosa.org/oosa/en/SpaceLaw/outerspt.html [accessed 10 June 2008].

United Nations Office for Outer Space Affairs (2008), 'Online Index of Objects Launched into Outer Space', available at: http://www.unoosa.org/oosa/osoindex.html [accessed: 3 October 2008].

Waite, B. and Rowan, F., (1986), 'International communications law, part two: satellite regulation and the space WARC', *International Law*, 20: 341–65.

Warf, B., (2006), 'International competition between satellite and fiber optic carriers: a geographic perspective', *The Professional Geographer*, 58(1): 1–11.

Warf, B., (2007), 'Geopolitics of the satellite industry', *Tijdschrift voor Economische en Sociale Geografie*, 98(3): 385–97.

Wassenbergh, H., (1991), *Principles of Outer Space Law in Hindsight*, The Hague: Martinus Nijhoff.

Wiessner, S., (1983), 'The public order of the geostationary orbit: blueprints for the future', *The Yale Journal of World Public Order*, 9(2): 217–74.

Wiles, G., (1998), 'The man on the Moon makes room for neighbors: an analysis of the existence of property rights on the Moon under a condominium-type ownership theory', *International Review of Law, Computers and Technology*, 12(3): 513–34.

The cosmos as capitalism's outside

Peter Dickens

Capitalism's 'outside'

Can capitalism go on expanding forever? It is a question many people have asked for many years. It is also a relevant question when considering the prospect of capitalism's potentially infinite expansion into the cosmos.

In the early decades of the 20th century, Rosa Luxemburg suggested that capitalism always needs an 'outside', a zone of non-capitalism in which people would buy goods made in capitalist societies (Luxemburg, 2004). To continue expanding, capitalism needs to continue placing a large part of its surplus into the means of production, machines and technology. Imperialism, according to Luxemburg, is the competitive struggle between capitalist nations for what remains of the non-capitalist 'outside'. And yet, Luxemburg also argued, there is a fundamental contradiction, one ultimately leading to capitalism's collapse. As it increasingly draws its 'outside' into itself, capitalism also destroys the very demand it needs for its products. The surplus value produced by capitalism simply cannot be absorbed.

This is not the place to assess in detail Luxemburg's arguments or the debates she has generated. Suffice to note that many Marxists now argue that, while crises of underconsumption are important, crises stemming from over-accumulation of capital and the need for 'outside' regions in which to invest are even more significant as regards the further expansion of capitalism (Brewer, 1990; Harvey, 2003). Luxemburg was nevertheless the first attempt explicitly to raise the question of how capitalism relates to a non-capitalist 'outside' and whether capitalism can, in principle, last forever as it colonizes its outside.

The question of capitalism's 'outside' is now being asked again, albeit in a rather different form. Hardt and Negri, in their influential text *Empire*, tell us that 'there is no more outside.' They state that 'in the passage from modern to postmodern, from Imperialism to Empire, there is progressively less distinction between inside and outside' (2000: 187). They make this case in relation to the economy, politics and militarism in today's form of globalization.

As regards economics, Hardt and Negri admit that the capitalist market has always run counter to any division between 'inside' and 'outside'. It has been constantly expanded globally and yet has encountered barriers. But at the same time it has also thrived on overcoming such barriers, reorganizing itself to overcome these limits. But now the global market is so dominant that it is even more difficult to envisage a distinction between an 'inside' and an 'outside' market waiting to be subjugated, made part of the capitalist market and in due course reorganized as a site of capitalist production. There is no 'outside' left and capital is reduced to re-engaging in a form of 'primitive accumulation'; privatizing publicly-owned assets, making them into commodities to be bought and sold.

As regards politics, Hardt and Negri argue that sovereignty has in the past invariably been conceived in terms of territory and its relation to an 'outside'. The Enlightenment ideal is one in which civil order and sovereignty are established within an inside region, while 'social disorder' and 'nature' are an outside still to be controlled and exploited. Such, according to Hardt and Negri, is the old model of empire, one in which there was a radical distinction between an imperializing inside and a dominated outside. But the old model has now gone, there being no 'outside' left in our globalized society and with opposition in its many forms as likely to be within the nation states it is opposing.

In military terms too there is no longer, according to Hardt and Negri, any distinction to be made between inside and outside. The 'enemy' is as likely to be 'within' a nation state as located in an outside, hostile, region or an outside state. 'The history of imperialist, inter-imperialist and anti-imperialist wars', Hardt and Negri assert, 'is over.' (2000: 189). This makes every war into an internal, domestic or civil strife. 'In the smooth space of Empire, there is no place of power – it is both everywhere and nowhere.' (2000: 190). At the same time, and as part of this incorporation of warfare into nation states, militarization has been made permanently integral to the whole of economic, social and political life. Hardt and Negri go on to argue that resistance to capitalism is everywhere and nowhere. A 'multitude' is emerging within the new 'smooth space of Empire', one capable of overturning the social system of which it is part (Hardt and Negri, 2006).

The cosmos as capitalism's outside

The imminent conquest of outer space raises the question of 'outside' and 'inside' yet again. Capitalism now has the cosmos in its sights, an outside which can be privately or publicly owned, made into a commodity, an entity for which nations and private companies can compete. As such the cosmos is a possible site of armed hostilities. This means, *contra* Hardt and Negri, that there is an outside after all, one into which the competitive market can now expand indefinitely. A new kind of imperialism is therefore underway, albeit not one attempting to conquer and exploit people 'outside' since there are no consumers or labour power to exploit in other parts of the solar system. Ferrying wealthy tourists into the cosmos is a first and perhaps most spectacular part of this process of capital's cosmic expansion. Especially important in the longer term is making outer space into a source of resources and materials. These will in due course be incorporated into production-processes, most of which will be still firmly lodged on earth.

Access to outer space is, potentially at least, access to an infinite outside array of resources. These apparently have the distinct advantage of not being owned or used by any pre-existing society and not requiring military force by an imperializing power gaining access to these resources.

Bringing this outside zone into capitalism may at first seem beneficial to everyone. But this scenario is almost certainly not so trouble-free as may at first seem. On the one hand, the investment of capital into outer space would be a huge diversion from the investments needed to address many urgent inequalities and crises on Earth. On the other hand, this same access is in practice likely to be conducted by a range of competing imperial powers. Hardt and Negri (2000) tell us that the history of imperializing wars is over. This may or may not be the case as regards imperialism on earth. But old-style imperialist, more particularly inter-imperialist, wars seem more likely than ever, as growing and competing power-blocs (the USA and China are currently amongst the most likely protagonists) compete for resources on earth and outer space.

Such, in rather general terms, is the prospect for a future, galactic, imperialism between competing powers. But what are the relations, processes and mechanisms underlying this new phenomenon? How should we understand the regional rivalries and ideologies involved and the likely implications of competing empires attempting to incorporate not only their share of resources on earth but on global society's 'outside'?

Social crises, outer spatial fixes and galactic imperialism

Explanatory primacy is given here to economic mechanisms driving this humanization of the universe. In the same way that they have driven imperializing societies in the past to expand their economic bases into their 'outsides', the social relations of capitalism and the processes of capital-accumulation are driving the new kind of outer space imperialisms. Such is the starting-point of this paper (See also Dickens and Ormrod, 2007). It is a position based on the work of the contemporary Marxist geographer David Harvey (2003) and his notion of 'spatial fixes'. Capitalism continually constructs what he calls 'outer transformations.' In the context of the over-accumulation of capital in the primary circuit of industrial capital, fresh geographic zones are constantly sought out which have not yet been fully invested in or, in the case of outer space, not yet been invested in at all.

'Outer spatial fixes' are investments in outer space intended to solve capitalism's many crises. At one level they may be simply described as crises of economic profitability. But 'economic' can cover a wide array of issues such as crises of resource-availability and potential social and political upheavals resulting from resource-shortages. Furthermore, there is certainly no guarantee that these investments will actually 'fix' these underlying economic, political and social crises. The 'fix' may well be of a temporary, sticking-plaster, variety.

Capital, crises and spatial fixes

At the centre of the imperialising process (cosmic and earthly) is 'the primary circuit of capital' in which value is made through the exploitation of labour-power. (See Figure 1.) Money buys labour-power and the means of production; raw materials and technology. A labour-process is then set in train and commodities are produced. These commodities are sold on the market, with some of the money-proceeds taking the form of wages paid to workers and some being recycled back to the investors of capital investing in new circuits. This primary circuit is no less than the underlying essence of capitalism.

This recycling takes place (usually via banks and other financial institutions) into what Harvey calls 'the secondary circuit', that in which 'fixed capital' is created as inputs to new rounds of production (Figure 2). In this way the productivity of labour is increased. Alternatively the secondary circuit takes the form of consumers' savings being circulated, again via banks and the capital market, into the creation of consumer durables, houses and the like. This circuit is important to Harvey as a geographer since it underlies urban and regional development, including the process of suburbanisation in previously sparsely-populated regions. And it is important for this study since we are specifically interested in the *spatial* implications of capital's 'fixes'.

Figure 1: *The primary circuit of capital.*

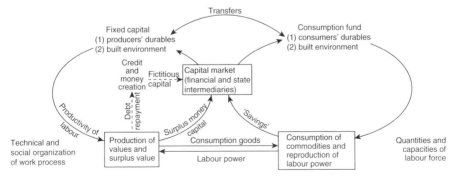

Figure 2: *The primary and secondary circuits of capital.*

Finally, Harvey identifies a 'tertiary circuit' in which states are mediators in the flow of capital into new investments (Figure 3). Surpluses are extracted (mainly by the device of government taxation) from the surpluses made in the primary circuit and reinvested in technology, science and administration. Similarly, they are extracted for other 'state functions' such as social expenditure; military expenditures, police, education and the like. Again, these flows generate new primary circuits of capital.

Figure 4 shows the three types of circuit of capital combined. The diagram looks rather mechanistic but circuits of capital are unstable and crisis-ridden. Indeed, crises often underlie the switching practices outlined above. One form of crisis develops when all those consumers inclined and able to consume a particular product at a particular price will have actually done so. A crisis of

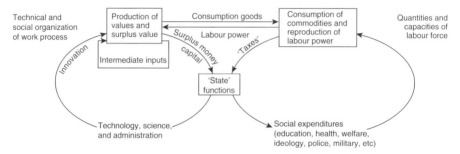

Figure 3: *The primary and tertiary circuits of capital.*

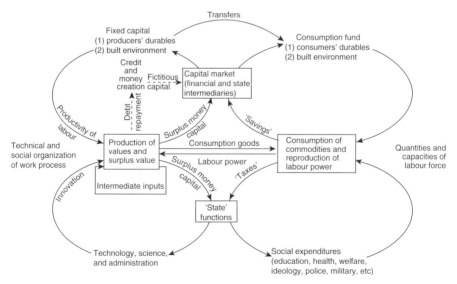

Figure 4: *The three circuits of capital combined.*

over-production ensues and rates of profit fall. There are a number of possible 'fixes' for this crisis, one of the most relevant to outer-space imperialism being the search for cheaper (usually meaning more plentiful) supplies of raw materials. Cheaper inputs should mean that commodities start reaching more consumers and, if this happens, new rounds of accumulation are underway.

Attempting to restore profitability through access to new raw materials therefore means that capitalism's fixes often involve geographical expansion. Capital, in Neil Smith's words 'stalks the Earth in search of material resources' (1984: 46). He goes on to say that 'no part of the Earth's surface, the atmosphere, the oceans, the geological substratum or the biological superstratum are immune from transformation by capital' (*op. cit.* p. 56). The galaxy can now be added to this list of resources being 'stalked' by capital.

Capital switches and outer space: space tourism

Perhaps the most obvious current switches of capital into outer space projects are those associated with the burgeoning space tourism industry. This is one of the most wasteful forms of conspicuous consumption imaginable though it does indicate how outer space might in due course be made the site of new production-processes.

The idea of putting hotels in space was first mentioned by Barron Hilton, president of Hilton Hotels, as long ago as 1967 (Spencer and Rugg, 2004: 160). In addressing the American Astronautical Society, he assured them that 'when space scientists make it physically feasible to establish hotels in space, the hotel industry will meet the challenge' (Billings, 2006: 162). Designs for hotels incorporate large viewing windows and, in an extended weightless stay, the space tourism visionaries can imagine even more fantastic leisure pursuits and games to be enjoyed in zero gravity. Ashford (2002) elaborates two of these ideas as he describes how orbital hotels will allow tourists to fly with wings and play in cylindrical zero-gravity swimming pools. In similar vein, Collins *et al.* (2000) have produced a design for an orbital sports stadium. These fantastic orbital hotels sound like something of the distant future, but again research and design work is already well under way. Bob Bigelow, the leading contender, is spending $500 million on a space hotel and has already built working 1:3 scale models. He is now planning a cruise ship designed to ferry tourists the moon.

Some of these visions are now coming to pass as a result of switches in Harvey's 'secondary circuit.' Richard Branson is currently switching capital from his other Virgin enterprises to set up the Virgin Galactic space tourism company. PayPal founder Elon Musk and Amazon.com entrepreneur Jeff Bezos have also drawn surplus capital from their other investments and ploughed it into developing the infrastructure and vehicles for space tourism.

Meanwhile, after a number of abortive attempts by American and Russian conglomerates, American company Space Adventures sold flights on board a Russian Soyuz rocket to three multimillionaire businessmen. Each flight cost $20 million, the first being that of Dennis Tito. Space Adventures have announced that by 2010 they expect to be offering tourist trips to the International Space Station (ISS) for $20 million and around the moon for $100 million. One thousand clients are said to be interested. It now seems possible, however, that the ambitions of these potential space travellers will be thwarted. The Russian Federal Space Agency has announced that the increasing number of nations involved in ISS, combined with popular criticism in Russia of this use of the ISS, mean that from 2010 this asset will only be used by trained crew-members (China Post, 2008).

Projections for the future of privately-financed space tourism nevertheless remain ambitious. Spencer and Rugg (2004) make the analogy between the growth of luxury cruising on the oceans and that in space. They argue that Tito's flight was a 'pioneering phase'. In ten years or so the International Space Station will have been converted into the first 'private orbital yacht' and around one thousand private citizens will have travelled 'off world'. In the next 'exclusive' phase, wealthy individuals and corporations will, it is projected, be engaging in orbital yacht racing and celebrities will be making outer space their preferred venue for weddings. The 'mature phase' will be one in which cruise ships seating one hundred persons and offering a range of recreational facilities will be available. By 2050, one million people will be touring off-world and 'the year 2075 could see 3,000 to 5,000 tourists and sports fans going every day' (Spencer and Rugg, 2004: 52).

Yet there are now also signs that the technology and expertise gained in the relatively benign space tourism industry are possibly being adopted for more sinister purposes. Northrop-Grumman, a leading US defence manufacturer, has recently bought outright Scaled Composites. The latter company has pioneered the use of lightweight materials for outer space vehicles, materials eventually used in the manufacture of Richard Branson's space vehicles. The reasons for this purchase are not clear at the time of writing. But Northrop-Grumman has for years made huge profits by the construction of satellite-guided Unmanned Air Vehicles. These are used by the USAF for surveillance and what their website terms 'precision strike missions.' This switch of capital into a company which has pioneered lightweight materials for space vehicles is creating another example of a familiar phenomenon. In a similar way to surveillance satellites being simultaneously used for military and civil purposes (see Collis, this volume), the technologies used for helping wealthy people to take vacations to increasingly exotic zones in space are also being used for observing, regulating and even eliminating warlords and other supposedly 'undesirable' populations scattered over the earth.

Humanizing the outside: outer spatial fixes and the secondary circuit

The resources to be incorporated within future circuits of capital will take a range of forms. As regards the secondary circuit, capital is now starting to flow into forms of outer space activity other than tourism. For example,

Declan O'Donnell and his United Societies in Space (an organisation of space lawyers) have attempted to establish an International Space Development Authority corporation (ISDAC) similar in function to the World Bank. This would operate as a space bank for investment in a future space colonization programme. Loans would be made to developing countries, assisting them to invest in outer space. On a more superficial level, companies such as Pizza Hut have paid (via intermediaries such as Space Marketing Inc.) to put their logos on space rockets.

With a much longer-term perspective, private companies are now working on research for lunar and asteroidal mines, these being actively supported by a number of pro-space organizations (Prado, 2008). The Moon might seem a more obvious target but asteroids are currently seen as a better bet due to their metallic density. Metals found on the Moon are, after all, just the dispersed debris of asteroids. Compared with an equal mass taken from the Moon, asteroids have about three hundred times as much free metal. In the 1990s the market value of metals in the small known asteroid, known as 3,554 Amun, was $20 trillion. This includes $8 trillion worth of iron and nickel, $6 trillion worth of cobalt and about $6 trillion in platinum-group metals (Lewis, 1996). The Moon, however, remains attractive from a different viewpoint. Millions of tons of Helium-3 could be obtained from there, one metric ton being currently worth about $3 million.

Caution is needed, however, regarding the prospects of all these materials as direct inputs into Earthly production-processes. The costs of returning materials to Earth would add so much to the cost of extracting them that it seems likely they will be unavailable for Earthly use in the foreseeable future. Advocates realizing this emphasize the use of space resources *in space* rather than bringing them down to Earth (Prado, 2008).

But all these fixes are some way from being realized, although they are under certainly active development. Their investors are those seeing space resources as an opportunity to realize profits out of crises stemming from increasingly scarce natural resources on earth. The ideology most frequently adopted is that of refuting the Club of Rome's famous 'Limits to Growth' thesis. This predicted that population growth would soon be limited by lack of resources. (Meadows *et al.*, 1972, 2005). The existence of space resources has also been used to criticize Marx's political economy (Thomas-Pellicer, 2004). James O'Connor (1994), coming from a Marxist perspective, argues that capitalism will eventually fall foul of its 'second contradiction' – that between the forces and relations of production on the one hand and the conditions of production (inputs like labour, natural resources and infrastructure) on the other. This would cause a crisis in supply rather than demand and potentially result in state ownership and control over the means of production. Yet O'Connor's second contradiction thesis, can according to advocates of space development and settlement, be easily refuted. Outer space represents resources for capitalism to continue *ad infinitum*, especially if unfettered by state intervention.

Further humanizing the outside: outer spatial fixes and the tertiary circuit

As regards investments connected with outer space, perhaps the most benign form of the tertiary circuit is a form of civic 'boosterism', whereby governments provide large outlays of capital in the hope of attracting investors to develop new primary circuits in a particular region. An example is 'Spaceport America', a planned $225 million development to attract Richard Branson's Virgin Galactic company.

Other outer-space investments being made in the 'tertiary circuit' include 'Paper NASA', a phrase used to refer to NASA's investments into research and the development of new technologies. State finances, siphoned off the primary circuit, are being used as a Keynesian regulator for the economy as a whole and as a means of keeping scientists in work. The somewhat vague hope is that some of their ideas will eventually bring financial returns. Similarly, much state expenditures goes (at least in the case of the USA) into the production of scientific equipment such as telescopes and computers. This, despite the fact that there may be few long-term prospects of these investments resulting into profits made in the private sector. Again, the tax-funded tertiary circuit (operated by government in a mediating role) is being used in a pump-priming way to keep the private sector profitable.

Meanwhile, other elements of the 'tertiary circuit' (those associated with military and surveillance activities) are a good deal less benign than spaceports but will also benefit some already very powerful private sector enterprises. What President Eisenhower famously called 'the military-industrial-complex' (or what is now often termed 'the military-industrial-*space*-complex') has experienced a remarkable revival in recent years, one spurred on by the attacks made on the US mainland on September 11th 2001. Since then an array of new enemies has been discovered. These are being used to justify yet further switches of capital by government into the tertiary circuit making military hardware of all kinds and increasingly sophisticated forms of visual and electronic surveillance (Dennis, 2008). Those companies making such hardware for government are amongst the largest bloc of industry in the United States and they have exceptionally strong connections in Washington. Table 1 shows their position relative to others in the world, Raytheon, General Dynamics being other US-based companies and the remainder being based in Europe.

Total revenues in 2006 for Lockheed Martin, Boeing and Northrop-Grumman were $37 billion, $54.8 billion and $30.7 billion respectively. Of these totals, $21 billion, $18.4 billion and $12 billion respectively came from government sources via the third circuit.

Imperialisms in outer space

Imperialism on earth and outer space should be seen within the above context of an ever-expanding capitalism, economic-cum-social-cum-resource crises and

Table 1: *Top ten arms producing companies in the world*

Company	Defence Revenues	% of Total Revenues
Lockheed Martin	30,097	94.6
Boeing	22,033	54.2
Northrop-Grumman	18,700	71.4
BAE Systems	17,159	76.7
Raytheon	16,896	93.3
General Dynamics	12,782	76.9
Thales	8,476	63.7
EADS	8,037	21.3
Finmeccanica	5,900	54.3
United Technologies	5,300	17.1

Source: Slijper (2005), based on 2003 data. Revenues in millions US$

new wars. Space tourism and the search for new materials are indicators of how capitalism and imperialism are now developing in outer space.

But imperialism involves more than the expansion of an economic structure. It entails a competitive struggle between capitalist states. This involves the constant upgrading of technologies and social relations and continuing conflict over ownership of territory and resources. These processes necessarily involve the political power of competing nation states. If we are adequately to understand the tensions and conflicts arising from imperialisms on Earth and in outer space, the notion of 'spatial fixes' therefore needs combining with an understanding of capitalist states (or in some cases, such as the European Union, a fusion of states) and their relationships with different social interests. This is one way in which Harvey's analysis can be taken forward.

Harvey's book *Limits to Capital* certainly concludes with a discussion of inter-imperialist rivalry and outright war as the most sinister means imaginable of destroying one set of spatial fixes prior to reinvestment in new fixes. And there are a number of allusions to competing capitalist states in his *The New Imperialism* (2003). The emphasis of Harvey's work is nevertheless on the purely economic and global level, when politically and culturally-orchestrated growth poles and regional coalitions are integral to processes of capital-accumulation and continuing social crises threaten to disrupt movements of capital within and between the three circuits. To use a phrase in Jessop's critique of Harvey, there is 'an inescapable political dimension to the historical materialist critique of capitalism' (2006: 162). We now further pursue this political dimension, and specifically its 'inter-imperialist rivalries'.

Outer spatial fixes and regional military-industrial-space-complexes

A number of coalitions at national level now have their own outer spatial fixes. These include Russia, China and South Korea. But perhaps most important, since they are the three dominant power-blocs in contemporary society, are the USA, Europe and China (Khanna, 2008). All three are competing for resources and military control, whether on earth or in outer space. All three are also caught up in a double-bind. On the one hand they are facilitating the operation of the three circuits of capital outlined above but on the other hand they are engaged in legitimating devices aimed at generating political support for these investments and switches of capital.

As regards the circuits of capital, all these societies have their own versions of the military-industrial-space complex, this being a network of contracts and money-flows between government agencies and defence contractors.

The military-industrial-space complex in the USA

The USA's version of the complex is particularly well-known, not least because it is currently much the largest. As mentioned earlier, the complex has greatly thrived, particularly since the attacks on the US mainland on September 11, 2001. The 'primary circuit' as represented by companies such as those listed in Table 1 has greatly benefitted from switches via the 'third circuit'. The binding purpose of the complex of which these companies are the dominant part is to exert social, military and political power over the globe and in outer space. As early as 1992 the then Undersecretary of Defence, Paul Wolfowitz, stated that the United States must 'prevent any hostile power from dominating a region whose resources would, under consolidated control, be sufficient to generate global power' (Wolfowitz, 1992). By 2001, and now as Deputy Secretary of Defense, Wolfowitz confirmed that this understanding of 'Pax Americana' had become mainstream strategic thinking. It is enshrined in the philosophy of what the US Department of Defence calls 'Full Spectrum Dominance'.

The European military-industrial-space-complex

The European military-industrial-space-complex, while considerably smaller than that of the US, also consists of close working connections between political and economic power. One of the largest 'primary circuit' groupings in Europe is the European Aeronautic Defence and Space Company (EADS), formed in 2000 as a merger between Daimler/Chrysler Aerospace, Aerospatiale and Construcciones Aeronauticas. Making both civil and military equipment including satellites and space vehicles, it has exercised considerable influence on the European Commission's thinking. As an EADS director put it in 2001, 'industry cannot put forward institutional or policy changes, of course, but it can give EU and national politicians new things to chew on.' (Slijper, 2005: 22). One of the 'new things to chew on', according to representatives of the European primary circuit, was the growing need for an aerospace industry focussed on defence and military programmes at the expense of the civil sector. While not aspiring to the outright militarism and 'Full Spectrum Dominance' of the US complex, European space policy has seen an increased emphasis on 'defence' since 2001 (Slijper, 2005). The European Commission's Galileo satellite navigation system, still in development, was intended to safeguard against the monopoly held by the US GPS system, but this threat has provoked suspicion and hostility from the US (Mean and Wilsdon, 2004).

The Chinese military-industrial-space complex

The imperializing tendencies of the United States and Russia were originally the chief generators of the state-driven Chinese space programme in the 1950s. Nuclear armed ballistic missiles were seen by the Chinese authorities as the way to counter both the American threat in Taiwan and the supposed threat from the Soviet Union (Dellios, 2005). The form of the military industrial complex now appears to be changing, largely as a result of broader attempts to marketize the Chinese economy, including its space and military sectors. On the one hand China possesses what one commentator calls 'one of the oldest, largest, and most diversified military industrial complexes in the world', consisting of some 300,000 engineers and technicians working in about 1,000 enterprises employing a total of three million workers (Bitzinger, 2005). These supply a complete range of weaponry from small arms to intercontinental ballistic missiles (Simons *et al.*, 2007). Yet these enterprises are widely seen by the Chinese authorities as inefficient, technologically-backward and too big a drain on public resources (Canadian Security, 2003). As an indication of ongoing reforms, ten new 'defence industry enterprise groups' have recently been made, these arguably being the first signs of a state-led 'tertiary circuit'. The eventual form of the Chinese military-industrial-space-complex is unclear but the fact that China recently destroyed one of its old weather satellites with a ground-based missile means it certainly cannot be dismissed as 'backward' from a purely military perspective.

Such are the key imperialist rivals, each seeking to make spatial fixes either on earth or in outer space. These rivalries are essential to the system as outlined by Harvey, each coalition responding in competitive military and economic fashion to the perceived challenges of others.

Economic and military overlaps

It is sometimes difficult to disentangle the 'military' from the 'economic' aspects of these rivalries. Chinese strategists, for example, are attempting to build a successful military-industrial-space-complex by focussing on technologies (such as satellite communications) serving both civil and military ends. (Simons, 2007). A similar example of military-cum-industrial example is Europe's Global Positioning System (GPS), due to be completed by 2010. This looks at first like a straightforward case of economic competition between the European and an older US system. The American system was, however, originally developed by the US military and can still be controlled by US military authorities. The European system, on the other hand, is intended to be run by a private consortium. The US military authorities have let it be known that they see the European system as a potential military threat to American interests.

Competing military-industrial-space complexes may, in the longer term, turn into outright armed wars, especially if US-style unilateralism returns along the lines represented by Paul Wolfowitz. A single industrial source could nevertheless easily finish up funding two or more states engaging in such wars. It is instructive to note that the industrial part of the 'US' complex is not averse to profiting from states supposedly in competition. Lockheed Martin and Boeing, the world's largest arms producers, are actively lobbying in Brussels for contracts, 'trying to reap the rewards afforded by Europe's military ambitions.'(Slijper, 2005: 28). Global capital, as Harvey and others point out, is incredibly fluid and flexible. It has seemingly few compunctions as to precisely which military-industrial-space-complex it invests in.

Legitimating outer spatial fixes

If regional coalitions of political, industrial and financial elites are responsible for promoting (via taxation and public spending) 'successful' circuits of capital, they are also responsible for legitimating the social and economic system they are supporting. How can massive public expenditures be couched in ways other than handouts to the shareholders of Boeing, EADS and the other major corporations outlined in Table 1? How can these shareholders' investments be seen as other than profiting from the labour of workers in Lockheed Martin, Boeing and the like?

As Marx pointed out in his early writings, capitalism survives because elites and capitalist states couch their practices in terms of general, universal values rather than the competing values of factional and warring interests (Marx, 1975) To varying extents all the regional rivals above, and the industrial elites with which they are associated, engage in a range of universalizing practices.

First, there is considerable emphasis on the 'pure', universal, scientific knowledge to be supposedly gained by outer space exploration. It is argued, for example, that NASA's $300 million Dawn Project will 'characterize the conditions and processes of the solar system's earliest epoch by investigating in detail two of the largest protoplanets remaining intact since their formations.' (NASA, 2007). (A similar rationale pervades the private space tourism industry, Space Adventurers assuring their wealthy clients that they will be able to conduct 'scientific experiments', thereby benefitting others besides themselves). Science is also used by NASA as a means of capturing the public imagination. The latest dramatic pictures of asteroids, the Moon and Mars are readily available on the NASA website.

Second, there is considerable stress on the benefits of outer spatial fixes to the global environment and to the world population. The European Space Agency, for example, emphasizes the 'multi-scale monitoring' of ecological conditions in the context of 'the challenge to the planetary environment.' This aspect of space-humanization also includes the proposed collection of solar energy for use by a globe fast running out of resources (ESA, 2000). Rather than developing countries receiving a share of the economic benefits of space exploitation as proposed in the UN Moon Agreement, these kinds of environment-saving projects supported by the UN Programme on Space Applications, were considered sufficient. The massive military investments benefiting the large military corporations as shown in Table 1 are meanwhile also couched in universalizing, non-military, 'defence' terms. And, by the same token, arms lobbyists have recently been recommended by the European Space Agency to use 'civil society language'. 'Protecting civil society and the freedom of citizens' is deemed a better alternative to 'macho ads with missiles and fighter planes' (Slijper, 2005: 78).

Third is the insistence that outer space exploration realizes the supposed innate need of humanity to explore. In 1961, for example, NASA asserted 'man's questing spirit' as a rationale for human visitation and exploration of the Moon. The notion of a biologically-engrained need of humans to conquer new horizons is also appealed to by the European Space Agency. They assert 'the timeless thirst for exploration and discovery' as a rationale for space exploration by the European Union (ESA, 2000: 18). Outer space exploration, according to this argument, releases human potential, specifically the rugged individualism which enabled earlier earthbound forms of colonialism to be so 'successful'. Similarly, it is suggested that human beings' adaptability makes them better than robots when it comes to exploration and colonization (Zubrin, 1999).

The counter-argument is that there is actually little or no scientific rationale for putting humans into the solar system. 'Humans' as Steve Weinberg (a Nobel Prize winning particle physicist) puts it 'don't serve any useful function in space. They radiate heat, they're very expensive to keep alive and desire to come back, so that anything involving human beings is enormously expensive' (2007, see also Rees, 2008).

Many nation-states, including relatively minor countries such as Korea as well as the USA, Russia and China nevertheless insist on projecting one or more of their citizens into the cosmos. In the end, the explanation of this phenomenon may have much more to do with governments generating public support for space programmes rather than any purely 'economic' rationale. Projecting citizens into the cosmos helps legitimate the huge amounts of public money involved. As the slogan often used to promote manned space flight puts it, 'no bucks without Buck Rogers'. Most older people actually have no desire to travel into outer space themselves (Dickens and Ormrod, 2007). But it may be that space programmes using humans in the cosmos appeal to a narcissistic streak in the human personality, perhaps most amongst younger people. The humanization of the cosmos is arguably creating a new kind of galactic personality, one taking possessive individualism to new extremes, by conquering, controlling and consuming not only the Earth but now the Universe. Yet separating the narcissistic self from society as a whole and treating the cosmos as a mere object creates an ultimately unsatisfying form of subjectivity. Perhaps older generations in particular recognise that disconnecting the self and objectifying the cosmos will result not in emancipation but enslavement (Slijper, 2005: 28).

Why humanize society's 'outside'?

If Rosa Luxemburg's theory of imperialism is correct, space-humanization will hasten the collapse of capitalism. The competitive struggle for the non-capitalist environment will only lead to the erosion of this 'outside'. War and social upheaval will ensue, the alternative to capitalism being global resistance and the creation of a new, socialist, society. If Harvey's theory is correct the cosmos might at best offer a series of temporary 'fixes' to the central crisis of capital's over-accumulation. But, meanwhile, growing social injustice, conflict and environmental degradation can be expected to worsen, especially under current neo-liberal regimes. In the meantime elites will make their way from Earth into the nearby cosmos to create yet another 'outer spatial fix' or to relax from their endeavours in one of Richard Branson's spaceships.

Over forty years ago Amitai Etzioni roundly criticized the space race as a 'monumental misdecision' (1964). On the one hand, he argued, resources had been switched away from pressing Earthly needs such as much-improved healthcare, education and civil rights. On the other hand, it had failed in virtually all of its promises. It had not stimulated economic growth in the United States. Productivity was not raised 'since orbiting objects or miniature atomic warheads do not have an automatic stimulant effect on consumers' (1964: 73–4). 'Spin-offs' to the economy in the form of, for example, miniaturization and new materials had been marginal and even trivial. 'Some are safely projected into a remote and dateless future, others should never have been made; still others are exaggerated out of proportion to their real value' (ibid.: 90). Another claim was that space exploration would help humanity to understand the evolution of the cosmos. But this too turned out to be a chimera; another grand promise to attract public funds but never delivered on.

Similar questions need asking now. Why is space travel happening? Who is benefiting? Whose problems is it solving? As things stand it is the already-powerful who stand to gain most. Shareholders investing in the military-industrial-space-complex remain largely content. Investors in companies extracting resources from the asteroids, the Moon and Mars will presumably be happy in the longer-term. But empire-making has always been a highly questionable process and the case for a future galactic imperialism has not been convincingly made. The arguments for stopping the humanization of outer space completely and focussing back on the relationships and crises on Planet Earth are becoming far more compelling.

Acknowledgements

Many thanks to James Ormrod and to the editors for their comments on an earlier version of this paper.

Illustrations reproduced from P. Dickens, J. Ormrod 2007, courtesy of Taylor and Francis Ltd. Reproduced with permission of Oxford University Press.

References

Ashford, D., (2002), *Spaceflight Revolution*, London: Imperial College Press.

Billings, L., (2006), 'Exploration for the masses? Or joyrides for the ultra rich? Prospects for space tourism', *Space Policy*, 22: 162–4.

Bitzinger, R., (2005), 'The PRC's Defense Industry: Reform Without Improvement', The Jamestown Foundation. http://www.jamestown.org/publications_details.php?volume_id=408&issue_id=3263. [accessed 12 May 08]

Brewer, A., (1990), *Marxist Theories of Imperialism. A Critical Survey*, 2nd edition, London: Routledge.

Canadian Security Intelligence Service (2003), 'Weapons Proliferation and the Military-Industrial Complex of the PRC', *Canadian Security Intelligence Service Commentary No.84*, http://www.fas.org/nuke/guide/china/com84.html [accessed 12 May 08]

China Post (2008), 'Russia Plans to Cease Space Tourism from 2010', April, 13. http://www.chinapost.com.tw/international/europe/2008/04/13/151669/Russia-plans.htm. [accessed 20 May 08].

Collins, P., Fukuoka, T. and Nishimura, T., (2000), 'Orbital sports stadium', in S.W. Johnson and K. Chua (eds), *Space 2000*, Reston, VA: American Society of Civil Engineers.

Dellios, R., (2005), 'China's Space Program: A Strategic and Political Analysis', *Culture Mandala*, Vol.7, 1. http://www.international-rekatuibs,cin/CM7-1WB/ChinasSpaceWB.htm [accessed 10 May 08]

Dennis, K., (2008), 'Global Gridlock: How the US Military-Industrial Complex Seeks to Contain and Control the Earth and Its Eco-System', Centre for Research on Globalization. http://www.globalresearch.ca/index.php?context=va&aid=8499, [accessed 12 May 08]

Dickens, P. and Ormrod, J., (2007), *Cosmic Society. Towards a Sociology of the Universe*, London: Routledge.

Etzioni, A., (1964), *The Moondoggle: Domestic and International Implications of the Space Race*, Garden City, NY: Doubleday.

European Space Agency (ESA) (2000), *Investing in Space. The Challenge for Europe*, report by Long-Term Space Policy Committee, http://www.esa.int/esapub/spf/sp2000/sp2000.pdf [accessed 08 May 08]

Hardt, M. and Negri, A., (2000), *Empire*, Cambridge, Mass: Harvard.

Hardt, M. and Negri, A., (2006), *Multitude*, Harmondsworth: Penguin.

Harvey. D., (1999), *Limits to Capital*, London: Verso.

Harvey, D., (2003), *The New Imperialism*, Oxford: Oxford University Press.

Harvey, D., (2006). *The Limits to Captial*, London: Verso.

Jessop, B., (2006), 'Spatial Fixes, Temporal Fixes and Spatio-Temporal Fixes' in N. Castree and D. Gregory (eds), *David Harvey. A Critical Reader*, Oxford: Blackwell.

Khanna, P., (2008), *The Second World*, Harmondsworth: Allen Lane.

Lewis, J., (1996), *Mining the Sky*, Reading, MA: Addison-Wesley.

Luxemburg, R., (2004), *The Accumulation of Capital*, London: Routledge, (1913).

Marx, K., (1975), 'Critique of Hegel's doctrine of the state', in L. Colletti (ed.) *Marx: Early Writings*, Harmondsworth: Pelican.

Meadows, D., Radners, J. and Meadows, D., (1972), *The Limits to Growth: A Report for the Club of Rome's Project on the Predicament of Mankind*, New York: Earth Island.

Meadows, D., Randers, J. and Meadows, D., (2005), *Limits to Growth: The 30-year Update*, London: Earthscan.

Mean, M. and Wilsdon, (2004), *Masters of the Universe: Science Politics and the New Space Race*, London: Demos.

NASA (1961), http://history.nasa.gov/SP214/Ch1-3.html/. [accessed 20 May, 2008]

NASA (2007), cited in http://en.wikipedia.org/wiki/Dawn_(spacecraft), [accessed 10 May 2008].

O'Connor, J., (1994), 'Is capitalism sustainable?' in M. O'Connor (ed.) *Is Capitalism Sustainable?: Political Economy and the Politics of Ecology*, New York: Guilford.

Prado, M., (2008), 'Introduction to "Permanent"', http://www.permanent.com/intro.htm. [accessed 21.10.08].

Rees, M., (2008), 'Let's forget NASA's fancy ideas', www.timesonline.co.uk/tol/comment/columnists/guest_contributions/article3365566.cce [accessed 12.05.08].

Simons, B., Lartey, E. and Cudjoe, F., (2007), 'One thing China can't offer Africa', *Asia Times* February 1st.

Slijper, F., (2005), *The Emerging EU Military-Industrial Complex. Arms industry lobbying in Brussels*, Transnational Institute Briefing Series 2005/1.

Smith, N., (1984), *Uneven Development: Nature, Capital and the Production of Space*, Oxford: Blackwell.

Spencer, J. with Rugg, K., (2004), *Space Tourism: Do You Want To Go?* Burlington, Ontario: Apogee.

Thomas-Pellicer, R., (2004), 'Facing our historical ontology today: the world social forum as an instance of the first and second contradictions of capitalism', paper presented at the Imaging Social Movements Conference, Edgehill College, Ormskirk, July.

Weinberg, S., (2007), 'Nobel Laureate Disses NASA's Manned Space 'Flight' www.space.com/news/070918_weinberg_critique_html [accessed 09.05.08].

Wolfowitz, P., (1992), *New York Times*, February 18, [accessed 12.05.08].

Zubrin, R., (1999), *Entering Space: Creating a Spacefaring Civilisation*, New York: Jeremy P. Tarcher.

Capitalists in space

Martin Parker

On the 12th of June 2008, an advert for 'Doritos', a flavoured corn chip snack, was broadcast from the EISCAT Space Centre in Svalbard, in the Arctic Ocean. Doritos are manufactured by the Frito-Lay Company of Plano, Texas, which is owned by PepsiCo Incorporated. In 2007, PepsiCo and its various subsidiaries delivered an operating profit of $8,025 million on a turnover of $39,474 million. The advert was aimed at a solar system 42 light years away orbiting the star 47 Ursae Majoris, in the constellation of the Plough. Dr Darren Wright, of the School of Physics and Astronomy at the University of Leicester claimed that:

> There could be potential commercial interest in enterprises like this. Imagine one day that companies on Earth might wish to advertise to other planetary colonies within our solar system – for example if man ever moves to colonise Mars! (Press Release 2008)

Imagine, one day . . .

Stage one

This chapter explores a paradox.[1] I want to believe that the ends of space exploration rest on a certain orientation to the future, a possibility that what comes next might be substantially different from what happens at the present time. This, I believe, is a sort of utopian projection that lies at the heart of any radical politics. At the same time, the means for space exploration currently appear to require that certain rather everyday desires are projected outwards to a star as if it were a new market segment. So we imagine 42 light years, and see PepsiCo in space. But I do not think that this is merely reducible to a matter of means or ends, as if the two never met. At the beginning of the 20th century Max Weber made a nice distinction between technical rationality (*zweckrational*) and value rationality (*wertrational*). The former refers to the sort of efficiency and organization that it is rational to adopt once you have decided on a particular course of action, and he claims that this is epitomised by the bureaucratic organizational form. Bureaucracy connects means to means, without hatred or passion, in order that ramified chains of cause and effect can be built that would otherwise stumble and evaporate. Without bureaucratic reason, we would not be able to administer a state, or manufacture a corn chip, or a Saturn V rocket. But states, corn chips and Saturn V rockets are insufficient to explain themselves, so Weber suggests that values must be the ultimate ends of action. Values, desires, are not 'rational' in themselves, but provide a target for technique. But, he says, there is a sense in which his age was becoming an age in which means were becoming ends in themselves, and notions of 'calling', of value, were fading away.

> 'Where the fulfilment of the calling cannot be directly related to the highest spiritual and cultural values, or when, on the other hand, it need not be felt simply as economic compulsion, the individual generally abandons the attempt to justify it at all. In the field of its highest development, in the United States, the pursuit of wealth, stripped of its religious and ethical meaning, tends to become associated with purely mundane passions, which often actually give it the character of sport.' (Weber, 1930: 182)

So the means become the end. The end is the playing of the game, and finds no justification beyond itself, and questions about ends, about values, are no longer asked.

This, it seems to me, is the paradox of having capitalists in space. As if the distance between the Earth and 47 Ursae Majoris is a problem for marketing, and the sublime evaporates in the exhaust fumes of managerialism. But, at the same time, it is naïve to imagine that Apollo and the rest have been free from such earthly entanglements. In the context, it doesn't matter that much whether we articulate these entanglements as nation building; party political interest; hidden subsidy of the military industrial complex, or research institutes; career and identity projects; needing to pay the mortgage; or compensating for small penis size. All these, and many more, have undoubtedly driven human beings to work on space exploration projects. But now, in an era of globalising capitalism, it seems that matters of profit and loss are becoming more relevant than ever in driving human beings to such work. Commercial space tourist flights will be the first clear example of what has, so far, been a tendency partly concealed by state and state agency operations. But now, it seems, NASA is being pushed out of the way, in order that enterprise can be launched.

Astronauts seem to spend much of their free time looking back at Earth, photographing it, talking about it, recognising it. In this chapter, in order to see capitalism more clearly, I will try to see what it looks like from space, and perhaps what it could look like from the future.

Space Money

When David Scott went to the moon on Apollo 15 he took with him some first-day postal covers in his Personal Preference Kit (PPK). Taking items into space as souvenirs had been common since the Mercury programme, the idea being that the astronauts handed them out to friends and family. However, the practice had commercial aspects. Astronauts were not particularly well paid, and space objects sold well. But matters were getting out of hand with the PPKs. Even before Apollo 14 launched, the Franklin Mint (a company manufacturing commemorative memorabilia) was advertising medallions containing silver from the flight. Some members of Congress asked questions, the deal was never done, and Deke Slayton (Director of Flight Crew Operations) halved the number of medallions allowed in PPKs. But Scott, Irwin and Worden were later persuaded, with Slayton's knowledge, to take 400 first day covers with them, 100 each, and 100 for a dealer in Germany. After the flight, the deal was exposed, and the three astronauts were formally reprimanded. NASA also had to admit that many other astronauts had been profiting in similar ways for many years (Scott and Leonov, 2004: 328–331; Hansen, 2005: 524).

This is not simply a story about corrupt astronauts, or poor auditing, but an everyday account of personal economics. Scott says he did the deal because he was promised that the money would go into a trust fund for his children. But do Scott's actions make his account of standing on the moon, blotting out the entire earth with his gloved thumb, any the less chilling (Scott and Leonov, 2004: 378)? Probably not. So it might be that exploring the implications of Weber's problem cannot stay at the level of the individual, as if (in some Kantian sense) the purity of your heart could determine the purity of your motive. Buzz Aldrin did a commercial for Volkswagen in 1972, and Armstrong one for Chrysler in 1979, but does that mean that the 'one small step' was demeaned?[2] We must, at the start here, acknowledge that motives are complex, and that this is an enquiry into generalities, or ideal types. What happens when profit becomes the institutional motive?

Nostalgia is a problem in any framing of such a question. NASA, in its Golden Age, was not an institution that relied on saintly scientists, dedicated administrators and heroic astronauts who had been commanded on a mission by a young and idealistic president. Even in general terms, the foundation of NASA represented something of an unholy alliance between military hawks, big research institutions, 'defence' contractors and politicians wanting the reflected sparkle of a little space dust or jobs for their state (DeGroot, 2007). There was a lot of money involved. According to Jones and Benson (2002: 22), in the 1960s, the US spent more than four per cent of Federal expenditures on space exploration. Wachhorst (2000: 130) translates this into $24 billion for Apollo. NASA's budget peaked in 1965 at what was 5.3 percent of the total federal budget for that year. In 1966 NASA directly employed thirty-six thousand people, and close to half a million others via roughly 500 main contractors and around 20 thousand sub-contractors (Klerkx, 2004: 165–6; Pyle, 2005: 8). Most of the money went to the big aerospace companies. Stage one was built by Boeing; stage two by North American Rockwell; stage three by McDonnell Douglas, and the rocket motors by Rocketdyne. The prime contractor for the Apollo Command and Service modules was North American Rockwell, the Lunar Module was built by Grumman, and the Lunar Roving Vehicle by Boeing.

It should be clear enough that NASA, for a while, was a very effective way for a whole host of organizations to get secure contracts from the state. The politics of this were clear enough to the participants, as a speech by Werner Von Braun to a banquet for what he called 'the leaders and captains of the mainstream of American industry and life' the day before Apollo 11 lifted off suggests.

> Without your success in building the economic foundations of this nation, the resources for mounting tomorrow's expedition to the moon would have never been committed. (in Mailer, 1971: 73)

Norman Mailer's beautiful analysis of the contradictions of Apollo, 'of the real and true tasty beef of capitalism (. . .) the grease and guts of it' makes the clear point that Apollo would not have been possible without 'a capitalist who risks all the moral future of his soul on the gamble that God believes in capitalism and wants each man to enrich himself as part of God's design' (*op. cit.* p. 158). For Mailer, the sublime strangeness and mystery of Apollo – the fire on the moon – was only possible because of this combination of scientific rationalism and corporate greed. It was a sacred effort, held together by the most profane of motives. In addition, the high end research and development that Big Defence were being paid to do could also feed into the manufacture and sales of many other products. It was, effectively, an extra 'civilian' funding stream in addition to the general budget for military hardware. By the late 1960s, as the Vietnam war became more and more expensive, the state gradually shrunk NASA's budget, though this did not damage the profitability of many of the aerospace and defence contractors because they were now selling more jets, bombers and missiles for the killing fields of South-East Asia.

There was lots of money in space for many other manufacturers too. The vogue for newness, science and streamlined technology meant that fabrics, wallpaper and furniture were often designed with a space theme. Clothing used whites, blues and new synthetic materials, often with metallic finishes, and innumerable children's toys were manufactured (DeGroot, 2007: 184). Food became space food. 'Tang', the powdered orange drink used by John Glenn on the third Mercury flight;[3] 'Space Food Sticks' and so on. And, of course, people bought books, magazines, newspapers and watched TV to find out about Mercury, Gemini, and Apollo. Copies of the post-mission dinner invitation from the White House vied with pop singles and swimming pool inflatables for consumer spending. Even some products that had already been developed, such as Teflon, Velcro, the Fisher Space Pen and WD40,[4] gained a huge boost from stories concerning their use on the space programme. Smith (1983) argues that 'selling the moon' was part of the project of 'commodity scientism', a conjunction of nation building and consumption. The shareholders of all of these organizations must have been grateful that the US economy allowed such generous state intervention, despite free market rhetoric. Space was, in an important sense, part of the general economy, even if NASA never 'officially' endorsed anything.[5]

As NASA's budgets declined, so was there an increasing pressure to find something that the agency could sell. However, during the 1970s and 80s NASA was still almost entirely funded by the US state, and was hence usually the purchaser of goods and services. The first sign that a commercial organization might buy something from NASA was a deal to explore space based pharmaceutical manufacturing signed by McDonnell-Douglas, Ortho Pharmaceuticals and NASA in 1975. This never materialized, but mutated into a series of suggestions about an Industrial Space Facility in the early1980s, backed by Boeing and Westinghouse (Klerkx, 2004: 81). At roughly the same time, the space shuttle was beginning to deliver commercial satellites into orbit, sometimes together with the first non-NASA or services personnel on board. Partly as an inducement to use the already heavily subsidized service, NASA took payload specialists from various companies on the shuttle in order to operate the cargo, and also gave 'free' flights to foreign nationals in return for launching their satellites. But these were attempts at marketing, and not commercial transactions.[6] So Prince Sultan Salman Al-Saud (who flew with a Saudi communications satellite), was not a paying space tourist, but an advertisement for NASA. The same was true of the two Congressmen who flew into space, presumably as a reward and incentive for continued support for NASA budget requests. In any case, the Challenger disaster of 1986 ended flights for a while, as well as slowing their pace and increasing their cost.

The massive historical irony is that it was the space programme that grew from state control that embraced the market first. After the collapse of the Soviet Union a 'rockets for roubles' policy was all that could keep the Russian programme going. Just keeping Mir, the Russian space station, in orbit required large amounts of cash. The first clearly commercial traveller seems to have been Toyohiro Akiyama, a Japanese broadcaster who spent a week on Mir in 1990 for $12 million, paid for by the Tokyo Broadcasting System. The following year Glavkosmos, the Russian space administration, charged around $10 million to take the first UK astronaut, Helen Sharman, to Mir. The money was to be raised by industrial sponsorship and underwritten by the UK subsidiary of the Narodny Bank (Sharman, 1993). Later Mir was being kept aloft by a deal with NASA for International Space Station training, and there was even a proposal by an organization called MirCorp to buy and run the ailing station as a commercial project. However, according to Klerkx (2004: 44), this deal was eventually killed by NASA and Big Aerospace, partly because neither wanted any competition for the new International Space Station.

The commercialization of the state space agencies continued during the 1990s, but with Russia very much in the lead. NASA took a generally more conservative position, and often acted to protect its monopoly, rather than breaking the alliances it had with both the US state and Big Aerospace. So it was the Russians who took the money on offer. In 1999 Pizza Hut paid one million dollars in order that a Russian Proton rocket would launch with a forty foot high 'Pizza Hut' logo emblazoned on its side. Two years later, the Soyuz that took Dennis Tito (the first of five paying astrotourists so far) to the International Space Station also delivered a salami Pizza Hut pizza, copies of *Popular Mechanics* magazine, talking picture frames and Lego toys that became prizes in a competition (Klerkx, 2004: 233–4). Tito paid between $12 and $20 million for his trip, which worked out at around 7 per cent of the budget of the entire Russian space programme that year. In comparison, 7 per cent of NASA's budget that year would have been about a billion dollars (Klerkx, 2004: 184). No wonder that a Pepsi commercial was filmed in Mir, whilst Radio Shack commercials have been filmed in the Russian part of the ISS. The Russians even signed an agreement with the creator of the TV show 'Survivor' for a reality TV show entitled 'Destination Space'. Contestants would train at Star City, with the winner going for a trip to the ISS (Commercial Alert, 2003).

From the mid 1990s onwards, NASA Administrator Daniel Goldin was arguing that financial and efficiency targets could be achieved by commercializing the programme. He mandated that 30% of the space on the new International Space Station should be used by private companies, and held talks with McDonald's and Coca-Cola about providing food for the station. Few deals actually happened though, unless you count existing relationships being renamed. Lockheed and Boeing formed a joint company called the United Space Alliance, which sells shuttle services, mainly maintenance, to NASA. In 2000, this contract was worth $1.6 billion (Klerkx, 2004: 100). There were some small, and perhaps symbolic, 'partnerships' such as the contract with Lego to name the two Mars rovers, or with Dreamtime to produce high definition broadcasts from space. The shuttles were also beginning to carry (again heavily subsidized) commercial payloads. For example, the shuttle Columbia contained an experiment for International Flowers and Fragrances Inc. concerning the effects of low gravity on flower scent, as well as seven other experiments (Commercial Alert, 2003).[7] The collapse of the stock market in 2001, combined with Columbia's 2003 disintegration over Texas, again put paid to NASA's ambitions for a while. According to Dickens and Ormrod, space-related capitalism had generated nearly $1 trillion in the decade up to 2004 (2007: 1). This is a lot of money, and there is every reason to imagine that NASA would like some of it. However, there is an even more compelling reason to expect NASA to behave more like a corporation in future – the beginnings of space tourism.

At the time of writing, in mid 2008, a host of companies are lining up to offer space tourist experiences to those with money to spend (Spencer with Rugg, 2004; Kemp, 2007). Most are small, despite their website hyperbole. The largest, and probably the first to succeed, is Virgin Galactic, which is intending to begin sending passengers up for four to five minutes of weightlessness for $200,000 by 2009. They have Richard Branson's money behind them, as well as the only current private sector re-useable vehicle. Thanks in part to Philippe Starck and celebrity endorsements, their marketing and corporate image is slick, even to the extent of claiming to be 'greener' than NASA. Their business plan suggests that they will be taking 3,000 people into space per year by their fifth year of operation (Kemp, 2007: 58). Their language articulates space as the exciting new destination of choice for affluent tourists, and not the old place where nationalism and bureaucracy culminated in repressed white men collecting rocks.

Space has become interesting again. And so much more fun. The Cold War rivalry of NASA and the Soviet cosmonauts was highly political and intensely serious. What is happening now is a space renaissance – and any renaissance is characterized by more colour and flair and a flowing of fresh thinking and activities (Kemp, 2007: 5).

Kemp's book, perhaps better described as a book length advert, has a foreword by Richard Branson and is published by Virgin. Virgin's competitors include companies with exciting names like Project Enterprise, EADS Astrium, SpaceX, Constellation Services International, Space Adventures Ltd and so on. Collectively they propose a future in which 'ordinary people' will be able to go into space, and break the stranglehold that the state has on this area of human endeavour.

Sharing this vision of deregulation are a series of companies who wish to take capitalism further into space. There are now commercial proposals for flying capsules with ash or mementoes to the moon or out into space, orbital rides around the moon, moon tourism, space hotels (including a proposal from Hilton International), new methods of collecting solar energy, and even mining on the moon. Companies such as Bigelow Aerospace, Excalibur Almaz, Rocketplane, SpaceDev and Venturer Aerospace are involved in various speculative projects, most of them proposed or 'under development'. At least eleven places are also vying to become 'spaceports', seven of them in the USA. It seems that, forty years after the first man on the moon, the state-industrial monopoly that put him there can no longer protect its territory. In 2007, a congressman on the Space and Aeronautics subcommittee even introduced a bill proposing that the agency could, like racing cars, sell advertising space on its vehicles, equipment and suits (Associated Content, 2007). Imagine Armstrong with a Doritos sticker on his helmet, intoning a script written by a PepsiCo marketing executive.

Frontiers and markets

In 1862, in an essay titled 'Walking' the American essayist Henry Thoreau said 'Eastward I go only by force; but westward I go free.' For Thoreau, the East was the site of the city, of civilization and constraint, whilst walking towards the setting sun signified 'wildness and freedom'. In 1893, Frederick Jackson Turner, the US historian, gave a talk entitled 'The Significance of the Frontier in American History'. According to Turner, the fact that the West had now been won augured badly for the future of the USA. American character was defined by novelty, adaptation and growth, so without this imaginative geography of a frontier, there was a danger of atrophy (Morton, 2002: 258; Dickens and Ormrod, 2007: 164).

> The existence of an area of free land, its continuous recession, and the advance of American settlement westward, explain American development. Behind institutions, behind constitutional forms and modifications, lie the vital forces that call these organs into life and shape them to meet changing conditions. (Turner, in Klerkx, 2004: 298)

For Turner, the wilderness, the edge of civilization, gave Americans their character as a nation who could tame the wild.

From the earliest days of NASA, frontiers have often been articulated, because it allowed these new pioneers to imagine national identity once more. 'Turnerism', as Benjamin (2004: 249) calls it, might not be unique to the USA of course,[8] but was certainly built into the NASA PR line from Mercury onwards (DeGroot, 2007: 109). But the call to the frontier, to the setting sun, has other resonances too. Wyn Wachhorst's eulogy to space flight contains a family of related metaphors – the child leaving the mother, the Renaissance, Columbus finding the new world, pilgrims leaving the homeland, and pioneers moving westwards (2000). Built into all these images is also the idea of escaping from a certain sort of repression – the mummy's boy, the closed mind, routine, those who would silence you, and the claustrophobia of the city. These are all ways of thinking about constraint, about some agency that prevents you from being what you might be. A space Turnerism now brings together ex-NASA employees, entrepreneurs and libertarian visionaries at annual conferences to bemoan the state bureaucrats who prevent 'citizen access' to space (Spencer, 2004). Groups such as ProSpace, the Space Frontier Foundation, L-5 Society, the Planetary Society, the Mars Underground and the Mars Society all trade (to a greater or lesser extent) on this idea of a radical off-earth freedom.

One of the early books that inspired this movement was Gerard O'Neill's *The High Frontier* (1989), elements of which have been borrowed by Robert Zubrin to justify his evangelical 'Mars Direct' project.

> the ongoing bureaucratization of daily life will make it ever harder for strong spirits to find adequate means for expressing their creative drive and initiative on Earth. A confined world will limit opportunity for all and seek to enforce behavioural and cultural norms that will be unacceptable to many. (Zubrin, in Klerkx, 2004: 285)

Similarly, for John Spencer, 'the founder, president and chief designer of Red Planet Ventures Inc', the conquest of space requires that enough people have the 'pioneering personality' (2004: 19).[9] Spencer, O'Neill, Zubrin *et al.* are also uniformly hostile to the state, to bureaucrats, and to NASA's attempt to regulate exploration and prevent competition (Klerkx, 2004; Morton, 2002: 254 *passim*). The fact that Virgin Galactic's vehicle, SpaceShipOne, was developed by the private sector, after the Ansari X Prize was offered by the private sector, serves as proof that big government doesn't work.

> Yes, we are right at the beginning of a space renaissance. And it is happening because we are finally getting it – that this renaissance is a private show. It is fuelled by you and me, not by mega-government agencies, not by skunk-black secret projects. (Spencer, 2004: 19)

Dickens and Ormrod summarize these economically and political libertarian arguments as generally falling into five broad themes – the freedom of the individual; the centrality of growth for humankind and the requirement for access to unlimited resources; the inspirational effects on the rest of mankind; the inherent nature of human curiosity; and the possibility of peace on earth as a result of all the above (2007: 165 *passim*). In other words, we have wars and conflict on earth because there are too many people competing for scarce resources and being unable to express their curiosity and need for freedom. It's not a big jump from a defence of the frontier, as the only place where authentic humanity can be found, to a defence of the free market. This is a familiar translation, with freedom having both a spatial and an economic character. So, within the space libertarian community, there is much talk of deals with various companies – the media, venture capitalists speculating on future income, sponsors who want publicity and so on. In 2002, the libertarian Cato Institute of Washington DC published an edited collection entitled *Space: The Free Market Frontier*, which included a contribution from Dennis Tito (Hudgins, 2002). According to these authors, NASA is now the problem, and needs to be moved out of the way or convinced that commercialisation is the only way, and not relying on tax payers' dollars. NASA must become an organization that doesn't administer or regulate space, but assists in opening it up for private markets.

> This is a dramatic turnaround from a government-funded organization renowned for its arrogance and intellectual superiority. Even the Russians have shown the sort of entrepreneurial zeal more akin to American capitalism' (Kemp, 2007: 50)

The rhetoric of the pioneer, and of the frontier, suggests that ordinary honest citizens will be able to stake their claims. However, as Dickens and Ormrod argue, these self-described space pioneers are not ordinary people, but members of a kind of 'cosmic elite' (2007: 4). Reading Kemp's description of the sort of people who are investing in these companies, it is easy to see what they mean (2007: 5). Added to Richard Branson are the founders of Amazon.com, Microsoft, Pay Pal, Compusearch and a smattering of games designers and hotel magnates. The entry level costs are huge, and the risks are gigantic. Even the people who might be travelling as space tourists will have to be very wealthy indeed. Virgin Galactic are currently asking $200,000 per flight, which is an expensive five minutes. Dickens and Ormrod's materialist analysis of the space industries concludes that off-earth capitalism is pretty much like capitalism on earth, in the sense that it runs into periodic crises that need to be fixed by the development and exploitation of new markets. These 'fixes' are necessarily temporary, but the promise of the 'outer spatial fix' is that it (potentially) opens a variety of ways in which capitalism might be extended beyond the boundaries of the earth. Adopting some ideas from the geographer David Harvey, they argue that the commodification of space allows for various circuits of capital to be re-imagined and a hegemonic model of neo-liberalism to spread skywards.

The relation between the military industrial complex and the war state is crucial in this regard, with space technologies including surveillance satellites, missile guidance, and the 'weaponization' of space being obvious gains. This much is clear from NASA onwards. However, the link between (for example) military satellites and communications and monitoring devices is clearly a very close one. Hence, access to the military high ground also means access to sur-veillance and media power over the entire planet, and this goes for both states and 'defence' companies. A further circuit is that of space tourism, clearly a domain only accessible to the hyper-rich, but further markets include the exploi-tation of materials from the moon, asteroids or planets; solar energy; off-earth manufacturing; colonies and terraforming projects. All of these would come with their attendant spin-off industries, such as clearing up space junk, provi-sioning off-planet habitats, accounting and legal services, security and so on.

For Dickens and Ormrod, this is a problem, but for the space libertarians, it is an opportunity to make money and assert freedoms.

> It is incumbent on NASA – and upon those who have an influence on its work – to create a space market, not control it. (. . .) this market remains dominated by a handful of heavyweights who work hand in glove with NASA to block competition. (. . .) NASA has convinced lawmakers and most of the private sector that it alone has the ability to safely send humans into space (Klerkx, 2004: 212).

Throughout his book *Lost in Space*, Greg Klerkx describes NASA as a bloated bureaucracy rife with overspending, accounting errors and inflated payments to a select list of contractors. He quotes a commentator on the close relationship between NASA and Boeing saying 'If they fuck up, they get more money.' (Klerkx, 2004: 214). Even the contracts that look as if they are commercial – such as the 'United Space Alliance' and Lockheed's 'Consolidated Space Operations' contract – are actually no different in practice from the practices that preceded them. In 2000, NASA spent $12.5 billion, 83 per cent of its budget, on outsourcing to companies, universities, agencies and so on. 74 per cent went to private industry, of which 53 per cent of that (nearly $5 billion) went to Boeing and Lockheed (*op. cit.*: 254). To make matters worse, the demand that NASA be a vast jobs-generation machine for all US states, com-bined with the practice of 'earmarking' funding for a politician's favourite project in return for a vote in Congress, means that much of the money isn't even spent on space anyway.

'Founded as a trailblazer and innovator, NASA has become a barrier' (Klerkx, 2004: 338). The organization that once stood for national pride, high technology and family values, is preventing access to the frontier through its regulatory relations with the state, and its complicity with big business. The solution is that it needs to be broken up, or privatized, or have its budget slashed even further. Only when the final frontier becomes a commercial frontier will pioneers once again be able to make money by expressing their freedoms.

Bureaucracy and value

If we go back to Weber's distinction between technique and value, we can see that it is rather an useful way of understanding these space libertarians. If one were to write 'The Protestant Ethic and the Spirit of Space Exploration', then value and the technique coincide in the ideology of the frontier. It is the very spirit of the American that is at stake here, and hence constructing the organizational and financial structures that might enable the calling to be met is a task of considerable seriousness. This is not merely about making money, but a reflection of the character of the pioneer, and the freedoms that they require. Such a position also allows NASA to be described as an organization within which such a fusion happened once, perhaps from 1962 to 1972, but that is now merely a zombie bureaucracy that has forgotten why it exists. Its task is to continue existing, a 'mechanized petrification, embellished with a sort of convulsive self-importance' populated by 'Specialists without spirit, sensualists without heart' (Weber, 1930: 182). The libertarians are suggesting NASA is all means and no ends, all red tape and no red touch paper. But does that mean that we have to concede that space is the new frontier for business, and the state had better get out of the way?

In response to the 1957 Sputnik furore and the idea that the Soviets were suddenly near to occupying the military and technological high ground, MIT President James R Killian was appointed to the position of Science Advisor to President Eisenhower. The Killian committee's report in March 1958 concerned arguments for a space programme, and it gave several reasons as to why the USA should invest in such a project. First was 'the compelling urge of man to explore and discover, the thrust of curiosity that leads men to go where no one has gone before'. Second, 'the defense objective'. Third, 'national prestige'. Fourth, 'scientific observation and experiment which will add to our knowledge and understanding of the earth, the solar system, and the universe' (in Smith, 1983: 193–4). The subsequent formation of House and Senate committees, which listened to evidence from a variety of respondents with a vested interest in a state funded programme, did not prevent expansive declarations about frontiers, pioneers and exploration, yet discussion of commercial issues and inventions was vague (Smith, 1983: 196–7).

It seems to me that this was rather an important moment in defining the terms on which the commercialization of space could be imagined. It was primarily the state which was setting the agenda here, and primarily in ways that articulated either common human values – science, exploration – or specifically 'traditional' US values that were worth protecting.

> In many respects the Apollo space capsule was also a time capsule, allowing the nation's Space van Winkle's to carry a vision of the fifties intact through My Lai and Watts, assassinations and campus riots, and the Tet offensive. For many commentators, both friend and foe, the social function of Apollo was to sustain a pre-Vietnam dream of conquest (Smith, 1983: 205).

While it is easy enough to question the content of these values, they are values which are not explicitly concerned with commercial interests. Indeed, as DeGroot argues, many members of the Eisenhower administration were well aware of the dangers of a co-optation by Big Aerospace, and attempted to minimize talk of the Sputnik threat precisely because:

in the councils of government, we must guard against the acquisition of unwarranted influence, whether sought or unsought, by the military-industrial complex. The potential for the disastrous rise of misplaced power exists and will persist (Eisenhower's farewell address, in 1961, quoted in DeGroot, 2007: 124).

That term, 'military-industrial complex', has rung down the intervening half century, and its condensation of state and capitalist power might lead us to assume that the state is inevitably co-opted in such ways. But perhaps a different sort of diagnosis is possible, one that does not leave space as a battleground between free market libertarians and the Lockheed-NASA-Boeing space alliance.

Leaving space for others

I began with Doritos advertising in 2008, and it seems appropriate that I should end with it, just as spaceflight was beginning. Imagine Neil Armstrong's parents, watching him go to the moon, in July 1969.

> Because Neil's parents still had only a black-and white television, the TV networks gave them a large color set on which to watch the mission. On a daily basis, a local restaurant sent down half a dozen pies. A fruit company from nearby Lima delivered a large stock of bananas. A dairy from Delphos sent ice cream. Frito-Lay sent large cartons of corn chips. A local dairy, the Fisher Cheese Co., Wapakoneta's largest employer, proffered its special 'Moon Cheeze'. Consolidated Bottling Company delivered crates of 'Capped Moon Sauce', a 'secret-formula' vanilla cream soda pop (Hansen, 2005: 7).

Uninvited or not, business interests will continue to find their way into space. A year before the Armstrongs were watching TV, Stanley Kubrick had placed a rotating Hilton hotel and a Pam Am shuttle plane in *2001: A Space Odyssey*. The brands may change, and the future will not happen as quickly as we think, but unless we imagine massive state interventionism on a Soviet scale, capitalism will go into space.

Dickens and Ormrod claim that it already has, at least in terms of near earth orbit, and that the key issue is to engineer 'a relationship with the universe that does not further empower the already powerful' (2007: 190). In other words, a Marxist political economy of space would suggest that the military-industrial complex has already empowered the powerful, but would presumably be equally sceptical about the space libertarians' claims to be representing the ordinary citizen. Of course we might conclude from this that the answer is simply to turn away from space. The whole programme has not been without its critics, whether of capitalism, imperialism, patriarchy, techno-fetishism, bad science, bad policy making or even new world order conspiracy (Etzioni, 1964; DeGroot, 2007). Even at the height of space euphoria, in the summer of 1969, we find dissenting voices. 'The moon is an escape from our earthy responsibilities, and like other escapes, it leaves a troubled conscience' said Anthony Lewis in the *New York Times*. An *Ebony* opinion leader, asking what we will say to extra-terrestrials, suggested 'We have millions of people starving to death back home so we thought we'd drop by to see how you're faring'. Kurt Vonnegut, in the New York Times Magazine, put it with characteristic élan.

> Earth is such a pretty blue and pink and white pearl in the pictures NASA sent me. It looks so *clean*. You can't see all the hungry, angry earthlings down there – and the smoke and the sewage and the trash and sophisticated weaponry.' (all cited in Smith, 1983: 207)

In summary, the money could be better spent, and we would be better off tending our own gardens.

But even the best, and only, Marxist sociology of space has its authors making claims that go beyond the economic materialism they deploy. They claim that the desire to go into space is 'cosmic narcissism', a sort of projection of capitalist individualism onto the universe (Dickens and Ormrod, 2007; Dickens this volume). This is, in Weberian terms, a value, even if it is a value that Dickens and Ormrod dislike. Presumably they would prefer more communitarian or collectivist understandings of human values, in which we look more carefully at others, and not merely our own reflections. I might well agree with their politics, but I think that we should not dispose of a radical imagination so rapidly. In other words, there are ways in which we can think about the future that escape the clutches of Virgin Galactic, and that can still leave us misty-eyed about Armstrong.

Dickens and Ormrod are not keen on science fiction, seeing its utopianism as usually a distraction from hard thinking about the world. But a great deal of SF has been very engaged with the politics of its times, and persistently opened the possibility that the future (often, off earth and in the future) might be different. As a form of speculation suspended somewhere between utopias, fantasy and sociology, one definition of SF is that it involves systematically altering technological, social or biological conditions and then attempting to understand the possible consequences. Though much of SF has involved re-locating cowboy plots into spaceships, or constructing fantasies which re-tell ancient myths, much has also involved political thought experiments. It is hardly surprising that many radicals (whether counter-cultural or political) have found in SF a mirror for their own longings (see Jameson, 2005; Shukaitis, this volume). As Mannheim put it –

> Wishful thinking has always figured in human affairs. When the imagination finds no satisfaction in existing reality, it seeks refuge in wishfully constructed places and periods. Myths, fairy tales, other-worldly promises of religion, humanistic fantasies, travel romances, have been continually changing expressions of that which was lacking in actual life (1960: 184).

But, for Mannheim, utopianism was also at the heart of political demands for change

> A state of mind is utopian when it is incongruous with the state of reality in which it occurs (1960: 173).

As I suggested at the beginning, the idea that the world could be other than it is must be at the beginning for a demand that it can be different. Constance Penley suggests that the blended cultural text she calls 'NASA/Trek' is radical in just this way (1997). The dreams of Apollo, the nostalgia for a space age that never arrived (Benjamin, 2004; Parker, 2007, 2008), the sheer enormity of seeing the earth from space, are all examples of a science fiction that actually happened. To assume that we know, in advance, that the future must be either Big Business, or Big State, is to close down the possibilities that make the future worth spending time thinking about.

For me, there is something nauseating (or saddening) about imagining that the inhabitants of 47 Ursae Majoris would want Doritos, but I don't think that this means that space must be left for the capitalists. I don't share Kemp's craven enthusiasm for 'Gaia capitalism' (2007: 249), but I do find the pictures of Armstrong on the moon to be inspiring in ways that make me want the future, rather than being frightened of it. Mailer suggested that Apollo 11's paradox was that:

> American capitalism finally put together a cooperative effort against all the glut, waste, scandal, corruption, inefficiency, dishonesty, woe, dread, oversecurity and simple sense of boredom which hounded the lives of its corporate workers (Mailer, 1971: 175).

Apollo promised something else. Not a solution, or a blueprint, though it generated enough of those, but literally 'something else'. Perhaps even something sublime (Nye, 1994: 237 *passim*). The idea that our world might be different, both larger and smaller than we normally imagine, and that human beings can do extraordinary things. An idea that makes me nostalgic for the future.

Notes

1 Thanks to David Bell for his comments.
2 No astronauts were allowed to appear in advertising whilst they were working for NASA, but after the final Apollo flight in 1972, several ex-astronauts did lend their names to various transportation based industries.
3 Not developed for NASA, but first produced in 1957.
4 Developed in 1938, the 1940s, the 1950s and 1958 respectively.
5 It is not the topic of this paper, but Golden Age space continues to be part of the economy. The 1995 film *Apollo 13* made £355 million at the box office; space artefacts, autographs, stamps, models, soundtracks, licence plates available in many online shops; and conventions make a living for ex-astronauts who are prepared to sign photos for a day.
6 There were, of course, wider diplomatic ramifications to these arrangements too. It was being paralleled by the Soviet 'Intercosmos' arrangement, in which astronauts were selected from Warsaw Pact and sympathetic states.
7 All heavily subsidized by NASA.
8 The Soviet programme was also influenced by Nikolai Federov's mystical vision of humankind populating the galaxy, and being able to use science to resurrect everyone who had ever lived (see Klerkx, 2004: 181, Groys, 2006).
9 An idea nicely echoed in the film *The Astronaut Farmer* (2006) in which dogged individualism and family values outsmart the smarmy regulators and lawmakers from the state.

References

Associated Content (2007), 'Congressman Wants NASA to Sell Ad Space in Outer Space', www. associatedcontent.com/article/233147/congressman_wants_nasa_to_sell_ad_space.html5, [accessed 12 April 08].

Benjamin, M., (2004), *Rocket Dreams*, London: Vintage.

Commercial Alert (2003), 'Business on Board', www.commercialalert.org/news/featured-in/2003/03/business-on-board-nasa-shifts-strategy-for-selling-outer-space, [accessed 12 April 08].

DeGroot, G., (2007), *Dark Side of the Moon. The Magnificent Madness of the American Lunar Quest*, Jonathan Cape: London.

Dickens, P. and Ormrod, J., (2007), *Cosmic Society: Towards a Sociology of the Universe*, London: Routledge.

Etzioni, A., (1964), *The Moondoggle*, New York: Doubleday.

Groys, B., (2006), *Ilya Kabakov. The Man Who Flew into Space from his Apartment*, London: Afterall Books/University of the Arts.

Hansen, J., (2005), *First Man: The Life of Neil Armstrong*, London: Simon and Schuster.

Hudgins, E., (ed.) (2002), *Space: The Free Market Frontier*, Washington DC: Cato Institute.

Jameson, F., (2005), *Archaeologies of the Future*, London: Verso.

Jones, T. and Benson, M., (2002), *The Complete Idiots Guide to NASA*, Indianapolis, IN: Alpha Books.

Kemp, K., (2007), *Destination Space*, London: Virgin Books.

Klerkx, G., (2004), *Lost in Space*, London: Secker and Warburg.

Mailer, N., (1971), *A Fire on the Moon*, London: Pan Books.

Mannheim, K., (1960/1936), *Ideology and Utopia*, London: Routledge and Kegan Paul.

Morton, O., (2002), *Mapping Mars*, London: Fourth Estate.

Nye, D., (1994), *American Technological Sublime*, Cambridge, MA: MIT Press.

O'Neill, G., (1989), *The High Frontier*, Burlington, Ontario: Collector's Guide Publishing.

Parker, M., (2007), 'After the Space Age: Science, Fiction and Possibility', in Grebowicz, M. (ed.), *SciFi in the Mind's Eye: Reading Science Through Science Fiction*, Chicago: Open Court: 275–288.

Parker, M., (2008), 'Remembering the Space Age: From Apollo to Cyberspace', *Information, Communication and Society* 11/6: 846–860.

Penley, C., (1997), *Nasa/Trek*, London: Verso.

Press Release (2008), 'One small step for man, one giant leap for advertising', University of Leicester, www2le.ac.uk/ebulletin/news/press-releases/2000-2009/2008/03/nparticle.2008-03-07.396974412, [accessed 11 Mar 2008].

Pyle, R., (2005), *Destination Moon*, London: Carlton Books.

Scott, D. and Leonov, A. with Toomey, C., (2004), *Two Sides of the Moon*, London: Simon and Schuster.

Sharman, H. with Priest, C., (1993), *Seize the Moment*, London: Gollancz.

Spencer, J. with Rugg, K., (2004), *Space Tourism*, Burlington, Ontario: Apogee Books.

Smith, M., (1983), 'Selling the Moon', in Wightman Fox, R. and Jackson Lears, T. (eds), *The Culture of Consumption*, New York: Pantheon: 177–236.

Wachhorst, W., (2000), *The Dream of Spaceflight*, New York: Basic Books.

Weber, M., (1930), *The Protestant Ethic and the Spirit of Capitalism*, London: George Allen and Unwin Limited.

Space is the (non)place: Martians, Marxists, and the outer space of the radical imagination

Stevphen Shukaitis

I'm looking for my first trip up into space. Whatever training needs doing count me in. Wages can be negotiated. Any job considered. Oh and one more thing I don't have the uniform and am a little scared of heights, hope this isn't a problem. (Anonymous, 'freelance Astronaut' advertisement on Gumtree.com, London, 24 April 2008)

Joe Hill, the famous labour activist and songwriter, in a letter he wrote the day before his execution, said that the following day he expected to take a trip to Mars during which, upon his arrival, he would begin to organize Martian canal workers into the Industrial Workers of World. Why did he do this? After all, it might seem a bit odd that Hill, famous in his songwriting and reworking for consistently mocking the promises and deceits of religious reformers offering 'pie in the sky' (and that's a lie) to oppressed and exploited migrant workers more concerned about getting some bread in the belly (and maybe some roses, ie dignity, too). Hill continues to say that with the canal worker he'll sing Wobbly songs 'so loud the learned star gazers on Earth will for once and all get positive proof that the planet Mars is really inhabited' (Smith, 1984: 164). So why the reference to some form of other worldly-ness, one in which, rather than promising salvation or escape from the trials and tribulations of this world, Hill rather imagines himself as extending and continuing the very same social antagonism that brought him to the day before his execution in the first place? Aside from the personal characteristics of Hill's immense wit and humor (Rosemont, 2002), this chapter will argue that there is something more than that, something about the particular role outer space and extraterrestrial voyage play within the radical imagination. It will explore the idea of voyages out of the world as an imaginal machine for thinking and organizing to get out of this world that we want to leave behind. In other words, how themes and imagery of space take part in the construction and animation of socially and historically embedded forms of collective imagination and creativity; how they operate as nodal points in ever-fluctuating networks of collective intelligence animated through the shaping of social reality. For if utopia has 'no place' in this world, no spatiality on our maps, the dream to leave this earth can hold quite a seductive sway for those who desire to found a new earth upon escape from this one.

Within the imaginal space created through the imagery of space travel one can find an outer space of social movement, a smooth space and exteriority made inhabitable through a labour of collective imagination. The image and idea of space, through its circulation and elaboration within stories, myths, and artistic forms, composes a terrain of possibility that operates as an outside to the world as is. For even if it is not possible literally to step outside the world or existing reality, the capacity to imagine other possible worlds creates a terrain where it becomes possible to work towards the creation of another world. Perhaps the best example of this is 'Visit Port Watson', an unsigned fake travel pamphlet written by Hakim Bey/Peter Lamborn Wilson and included in the Semiotext(e) SF Collection (Rucker *et al.*, 1991). When Wilson received mail and questions about actually visiting the utopian destination of Port Watson described in the pamphlet, he responded by saying that Port Watson is that place where one is in the moment where one actually is when you believe that Port Watson could exist: a mobile territory of possibility rather than a fixed location. Port Watson is the location of realizing possible utopias that begins from the space of possibility opened in the imagination. At its best outer space operates in the same way, opening a space of possibility within the present through which other realities become possible.

It is this labour of collective imagination that draws together into collective imaginaries such diverse phenomena as the Misfits' suburban New Jersey punk anthems ('Teenagers from Mars', 'I Turned into a Martian', etc) with Sun Ra's cosmic madness and mythopoetic self-institution, that ties together the Association of Autonomous Astronauts' call for a worldwide network of community based spaceship construction with Red Pilot/Noordung Cosmokinetic Theater's usage of retrofuturist Soviet space design as fodder for their collective imaginings (Dubravka and Suvakovic, 2003; Monroe, 2005). In these spaces of collective creativity, outer space operates as an effective meme because it creates a space for engagement with weighty issues (exodus, escape, racial politics, otherness, militarization, global catastrophe, etc) while allowing an enticing playfulness to be employed. Indeed, one could argue that through much of leftist politics runs the notion of an apocalyptic moment, of some magical event (usually revolution), followed by the creation of a new and better world. The event, or the visitation, can both act as a pole of imaginal recomposition, or a projected hope that provides an excuse for acting in the world as it is, even if to find ways to escape from it. It is the process of negotiating these ambivalences in social movements, making contact with the other to come, where it becomes possible to build, in Bifo Berardi's words, 'spaceships capable of navigating upon the ocean of chaos: rafts for all the refugees that depart from the bellicose and arid lands of late-modern capitalism' (2008: 140).

To infinity and beyond!

> Mannoch drivels on with mindfucking stupidity about 'visiting agitators from Hand-sworth', what a load of fucking bullshit! No, as EVERYONE knows, the riots were started by Communist Alien Stormtroopers from the red planet Bolleaux who landed on the roof of the fucking Ritzy. – Peter from the Class War Federation explaining the true cause of the 1981 Brixton Riots (Quoted in Bone, 2006: 270)

Perhaps an interesting question, or one of them, is not so much a question of whether there is a presence of outer space imagery and extraterrestrial travel residing within the workings of the social imaginary, but of their function. Their presence is felt both when the poet and songwriter Gil Scott-Heron complains that he can't pay his doctor's bills or rent and wonders what could be done with all the resources that would be available if they weren't being spent on getting 'Whitey on the Moon' (1971), and when Stevie Wonder contrasts the utopian conditions of 'Saturn' (1976), which are peaceful and free from capitalist exchange, with conditions and problems of the urban ghettos. The persistence of space imagery in the social imaginary seems relatively straightforward and easy to demonstrate (and could easily turn this chapter into an extended list of examples, which would be a condition better avoided), perhaps because to some degree the unknown and the mysterious are almost by definition of particular fascination to those crafting mythopoetic narratives and imagery. There's simply not enough mystery in the familiar, banal and well known. One can try to evoke a mythos from a faceless man in a grey flannel suit, or any other kind of every-day-everyman type figure, but tend to lead in a completely different imaginal direction. The curious question is why there was an increase in forms of space imagery and narratives during the period of time roughly from the end of the second world war to the early 1970s; since then they have gone through peaks and spurts in their usage within various political milieus.

One way to approach this question, which might seem odd at first, although hopefully will ultimately become clear, can be found within a recent collection on the history of artistic collectivism and practices of social imagination since 1945 edited by Blake Stimson and Greg Sholette (2007). In their introduction they argue that there was a transformation in artistic collectivism in the post-war era, which they identify as a change in the composition of avant-garde artistic practice. The main reason for this is a movement away from communism as an ideological backdrop (although admittedly the relation between the avant-garde artistic practice and communism had been fraught with tension for some time), with existing connections and relations of affinity almost as strong if not stronger with various currents of anarchist thought and politics (Lewis, 1990; Weir, 1997; Antliff, 2001/2007). Putting aside the particular details, this argu-ment is made of part of a broader observation of the forced removal of forms of collectivism from political, economic, and social life of various forms. This can be seen in the blatant attacks on all forms of collectivism through political witch hunts, the purging of more radical organizers from unions, and the general rise of McCarthyism in the US. Paradoxically the destruction of forms of working class collectivism and forms from political life is directly connected to the rise of ingenious forms of capitalist collectivism, such as mortgages, stock options, retirement plans, and so forth, which are then employed in dual capacities as means of discipline and social support for populations enmeshed in them.

What is of interest here is the relation between the disappearance and destruction of certain forms of collectivism, and their reappearance in others. As Stimson and Sholette observe, the disappearance of collectivism from the political realm lead to these forms returning in a 'mutated and often contradictory form within the cultural realm' (2007: 8). It means that the rise of science fiction films in the 1950s with their imagery of bizarre alien races functioning by some sort of incomprehensible totalitarian collectivism, in many ways reflect the recoded and redirected imagery of communism (Smith *et al.*, 2001). The spectre of communism reappears as a UFO. This is perhaps not a new argument in itself, for the imagery used in genre science fiction has been interpreted as coded for communism before, with *Invasion of the Body Snatchers* (1956) as the most commonly used example (Brosnan, 1978; McCarthy and Gorman, 1999; Von Gunden and Stock, 1982). But what is interesting about the Stimson and Sholette spin is their argument for a displacement of energies from the economic and political sphere, embodied in working-class resistance, into mutated forms in the cultural sphere. This can be read as a form of recuperation or co-option in some senses; but it is not so straightforward. As I have previously argued (2007), the Plan 9 from the capitalist workplace is not a clear-cut case of the integration of energies of social resistance into the workings of capitalism, not one that is irreversible. The mutated and contradictory forms of collectivism that appear might start with imagery of an alleged collectivist communist-totalitarianism, but their ambivalence is also a space of possibility, one that can be turned to other uses. The despised other is often also the secretly desired other, a dynamic that can be viewed as imaginal forms, held out as examples of an Other to be rejected, start to be drawn back into other forms of politics, other forms of usage, and the pleasure of these usages. This is a dynamic that emerges more clearly in the 1960s and 1970s, as the utopian traces of a repressed communism, congealed within the imaginal form of outer space imagery, are slowly reclaimed and brought to other uses.

This is not to say that outer space memes and images of technological development have always played a totally progressive role. Indeed, aside from space exploration and technology, there is a longer history of the relation between scientific innovation and discovery and their connection with right wing and conservative politics (Federici and Caffentzis, 1982). Richard Barbrook (2007) has shown quite convincingly that the imaginary futures formed around space and technology animated collective imaginaries across the entire political spectrum, with both the diffuse spectacle of Western capitalism clamoring towards supremacy through technology, and the concentrated spectacle of bureaucratic collectivism capitalism in the East trying to do much the same, albeit framing it in different terms. While early efforts toward cybernetic communism were initially developed within the Soviet Union (until they were crushed by the party who feared, rightly, that they could not control it), Barbrook notes ironically that the first working model of communism as social co-operation through technology was developed by the US military in the form of DARPA Net, which would later become the internet. Despite apparent vast differences across a communist-capitalist divide, there existed a more profound underlying agreement on technological development as a road to the liberation of human potential, one that was shared by autonomist currents who argued that movement toward increased automation of the labour process would reduce necessary labour to almost zero, thus freeing up great amounts of time for activities other than repetitive labour.

Outer space, far from being a pure space that is always available for recomposing imaginal machines, also connects areas of political thought that veer off in strange and bizarre directions, showing that, as Deleuze and Guattari would concur in their more sober moments, absolute deterritorialization can easily end in death, insanity, or absurdity. The mere mention of alien invasion, coupled with anxiety about the worsening conditions of world affairs, famously led to outbursts of panic during the 1938 Mercury Theatre Halloween broadcast of a radio version of *War of the Worlds* that Orson Welles directed. And why is it that alien visitations seem to always happen in small, rural towns where the residents seem more likely to greet the visitors with shotguns rather than curiosity? Among the classic examples of space related judgment-impairment one can find the Heaven's Gate cult led by Marshall Applewhite and Bonnie Nettles. In 1997, 39 members of the cult committed suicide to coincide with the Hale-Bopp comet passing the Earth, an act they believe would allow themselves to be transported to a spaceship following the comet, thus averting the impending wiping clean and recycling of the planet (Theroux, 2005).

Further back in the history of the diffuse wonders of the wingnut international, one can find the baffling case of Juan Posadas and the Fourth International. Posadas was an Argentinean Trotskyist and, at one point, a relatively well known football player. During the 1940s and 1950s he came to the leadership of Fourth International affiliates in Latin America, known later for their role in the Cuban revolution. Beginning in the late 1960s Posadas also become quite renowned, or rather infamous, for his views on UFOs. Posadas' logic flows in quite a simple way: as Marx tells us, more technologically advanced societies are more socially advanced. Because of this, the existence of space aliens demonstrates the existence of intergalactic socialism, as the level of technology and social cooperation necessary to advance interstellar travel could only be produced by a communist society. The goal of the party, therefore, should be to establish contact with the communist space aliens, who would take part in furthering revolution on this planet. While Trotsky argued against the possibility of communism in one country, Posadas took the technological fetish to its logical conclusion, that there could not be communism on one planet (Salusbury, 2003). While this was greeted with derision by much of the left, as China Miéville explored in a recent article (2007), the derision was for entirely the wrong reasons. Putting aside the existence or non-existence of aliens, the problem was rather the conclusions that Posadas drew from their existence. If the long-standing problem of authoritarian communist and socialist political organizing is the contradiction of their implementation from above, Posadas transfers this problem to another level, literally. Posadas' politics necessitate socialism from above, *way* above, an outer space that can only be hoped to intervene in the earthly realm and obeyed. The imaginal machine animated by outer space in Posadas' politics therefore contributes almost nothing to the further develop-ment of collective composition in social movement, and through its vanguardist nature, if anything, tends to act against the development of autonomy and self-organization. It is, however, rather amusing.

Although Posadas died in 1981, Posadaist sections of the Fourth Interna-tional have been able to continue to produce apparently new material from him for some time since then, due to what seems to be a very large reservoir of taped materials he left behind. Among the more interesting rumoured aspects about the Posadaists of the Fourth International, although very difficult to verify (except by some members of the Marxist Ufologist Group), Posadaists have been known to appear at CND rallies passing out flyers demanding that China launch a pre-emptive nuclear strike against the US as a first step toward creating socialism. While one of the main subtexts of this chapter, following the excellent work of Jack Bratich on conspiracy panics, is the idea that even the most bizarre-sounding ideas often contain some sort of merit or can be learned from as a form of subjugated knowledge (2008), this, along with Posadas' fondness for dolphins based on the belief that they were a highly sentient alien race, cannot but lead to some chuckling, at least, if not a belly laugh or two.

Due to this, as well as other reasons, outer space travel and imagery has not always figured positively in the workings of the radical imagination, which is not so surprising given the ways that the dystopian future narrative often plays just as prominent a role (although often it is technological development enmeshed in an authoritarian social arrangement that is the problem rather than the tech-nology itself). A notable exception to this is found within anarcho-primitivism, which does not find much considered redeemable within space travel and imagery. This is not surprising given that many primitivist thinkers find nothing redeemable in any technological development, including agriculture itself, which is sometimes argued to contain implicitly all forms of subsequent technological development, and therefore the forms of domination based upon them. This gives an almost mystical, autonomous power of self-development and organiza-tion to the forms of technology themselves, one that does more to reify and mystify technological development then actually to explain its workings in any way constructive to a radical politics. Asking a primitivist about technological development is like asking a neoliberal economist about the economy: they both weave tales of mystification. In this case the imaginal exteriority of space travel has been internalized as a dystopian feature and attributed to forms of technol-ogy themselves, rather than the imaginal processes flowing through and animat-ing the particular assemblages in question.

Mythopoetics and imaginal space

> Do you find earth boring? Just the same old same thing? Come and sign up with Outer Spaceways Incorporated. (Sun Ra, 'Outer Spaceways Incorporated', 1968).

> Oh we were brought up on the space race, now they expect you to clean toilets. When you have seen how big the world is how can you make do with this? (Pulp, 'Glory Days', 1998).

All the efforts expended on technological development and innovation, alas, largely failed to deliver on many of the promises on offer, including unlimited energy, artificial intelligence, robots that cleaned the home and eliminated the need for most manual labour, and so forth. To put it crudely, one could say that while most of the forms of technological achievement anticipated by people living in the early 20th century (cars, radio, rockets, television) were largely achieved by midway through the century, for the second half of the century this was not the case. In the second half of the century much more was promised than actually delivered. People thought that soon they would be engaging in outer space travel, driving flying cars, and other such wonderful things that never appeared. If anything, it seems that the main technologies developed during the second half of the century were mainly premised on their ability to simulate things rather than actually do them. Perhaps Baudrillard was waiting with great anticipation for anti-gravity boots and upon their non-arrival decided his only recourse was to conclude that only simulation was possible now? This does not mean that the imaginary future held out by the seductive sway of the promised future did not continue to have powerful effects. If anything that served to diminish the fascination of outer space and the techno-fetish, it is perhaps, as Barbrook (2007) points out, when people actually began to acquire personally ownable forms of these wonder technologies (personal computers, allegedly programmable VCRs), only to discover that they were far less intelligent and sensible than the mythology surrounding them would like to suggest. The actual technology delivered was somewhat less impressive than a menacing HAL 9000, now reprogrammed for beneficent purposes, for every household.

But more than just the disappointment of not receiving those anti-gravity boots for Christmas, techno-utopian space dreams often came with less desired attributes. It was often a case of desiring a transformative war machine, in Deleuze and Guattari's sense of the potentiality of exteriority and its transformation, and instead getting an actual war. To find oneself caught playing a bait and switch game of dreaming of space travel and getting Star Wars as a missile defence system instead. After all, this trick only worked for Reagan precisely because of his ability to tap into and draw from the utopian trace of space imagery. In order to justify and narrate a nationalist-militarist project, Reagan very well might have been making policy decisions based on movies he remembered seeing (or acted in); but this was as much a source of ridicule as a certain kind of populist appeal derived out of his confusion. To some degree there is a large population out there that wishes it was living in a movie set, and these desires congealed in Reagan's confusion and rhetorical bombast. An analysis of this dynamic can be found in the work of Dean and Massumi (1992), who explore the relation between the role of the Emperor's body in the first Chinese empire and the mass mediated role of Reagan's body in the workings of the US Empire. Dean and Massumi argue that President Bush (the first one) attempted to engage in a similar kind of populist media politics, but failed. Extrapolating from this it seems arguable that the second President Bush attempted much the same, even attempting to revive the Star Wars missile defence system. Likewise this has been of mixed success. Many children, including the author, at one point during the 1980s wished to grow up to be the president like Reagan. It is likely that there are far fewer children making the same wish in regards to President Bush. And yet again, one premised on having to confront the all-menacing threat of the communist other and the evil empire. All this is to say that the imaginal space attached to technological development and dreams of space is highly ambivalent, dragging along with it a post-apocalyptic bad-new future.

This makes the role of outer space as a theme for imaginal recomposition much more complicated than it might be otherwise and also more directly politically relevant, to the degree that the provision of imaginal energies, imagery, and resources are necessary to the continued existence of capital and the state. To put it simply, they function a lot better when people have some reason and justification for their actions. Often it is the dreams of escape from the drudgery of wage labour and the banality of the everyday that creates spaces for fermenting these 'new spirits of capitalism', to borrow Boltanski and Chiapello's argument (2005). Why then might outer space emerge more prominently as a theme for imaginal recomposition in the period of the 1960s and 1970s? Aside from the previously mentioned point of mutation of collectivist energies from working-class resistance, one could also say that there was a shift in the nature of imagined exodus. While previously it might have seemed possible that exodus could take an immediately physical form (go westward young man, or take to the high seas, or finding a promised land), this no longer seems possible as the borders of the global frontiers seem to disappear. The world seemed to have most of its territories mapped and at least somewhat known, even if not totally. Outer space provided other avenue of possible exit for those desiring an exodus from the world as we know it, or at least a route to be imagined for this purpose.

In a way, while the map is not the territory, an imaginal landscape is a precondition for actually finding a northwest passage in the physical world. A shift to imaginal recomposition around outer space themes is part of the shift from a conception of exodus in physical terms to one in terms of intensive coordinates. In other words a shift towards an exodus that does not leave while attempting to subtract itself from forms of state domination and capitalist valorization. This is perhaps seen most clearly in the development of late 1960s so-called 'drop out culture', even more so the case of places like Italy where it is organized in terms of the collective and the development of other forms of sociality and collectivity, rather than a sort of individualized notion of withdrawal (which became much more the case in places like the US). This is part of an overall transformation of political antagonism towards forms that inhabit a mythic territory and space of composition and are involved in forms of semiotic warfare and conflict.

A shift toward a mythic terrain of conflict and image generation can be seen in Afrofuturism, which as a literary and cultural movement is based on exploring the black experience through the relation between technology, science fiction, and racialization (Eshun, 2003; Nelson, 2000; Williams, 2001; Weiner, 2008; Yaszek, 2005). While Afrofuturism is a wide-ranging area of cultural production, what is of most interest for the purposes of this chapter is the way it provided a space for going 'black to the future', to borrow Mark Dery's phrasing (1995): in other words, to fuse together an engagement with historical themes and experiences and the ways that they play out within a contemporary racialized experience. In Paul Miller's Afrofuturist manifesto he framed it as a 'a place where the issues that have come to be defined as core aspects of African-American ethnicity and its unfolding . . . [are] replaced by a zone of electromagnetic interactions' (1999). In other words, as the space of publicness for the exploration of these dynamics that had faded or withered, or has become transformed into a paradoxical form of publicity without publicness through hypervisibility, Afrofuturism exists as an imaginal machine for this exploration, coded within forms that are perhaps not instantly recognizable as dealing with the political content they actually work through.

Afrofuturism was first elaborated by Sun Ra in the 1950s (Szwed, 1998; Cutler, 1992; Elms *et al.*, 2007). The Sun Ra Arkestra continues to play to the present day, fusing together hard bop, experimental jazz and electronic music with outer space imagery and Egyptian themes. The Sun Ra Arkestra was one of the first ensembles to make extensive use of electronic musical equipment, synthesizers, and instruments in their performances. They directly combined a continued engagement with new forms of technology and experimentation at a time when most jazz performers who were trying to be taken seriously avoided them (but then again they also avoided appearing on stage in Egyptian garb, claiming that they were from another planet). Perhaps more importantly for the discussion here, Sun Ra elaborates a sort of mythological performance and cosmogony based around fusing together ancient Egyptian imagery and scientific themes. This is clearly expressed a scene from the 1974 film *Space is the Place* (in which Sun Ra engages in a cosmic duel over the fate of the black race, who Sun Ra hopes to transport to another planet in a form of space-age Marcus Garvey-esque exodus). In a discussion with some youth in a community, Sun Ra, when asked if he is real, responds

> How do you know I'm real? I'm not real. I'm just like you. You don't exist in this society. If you did your people wouldn't be struggling for equal rights. If you were, you would have some status among the nations of the world. So we're both myths. I do not come to you as the reality, I come to you as the myth, because that's what black people are, myths. I came from a dream that the black man dreamed long ago. I am a present sent to you by your ancestors (1974).

As we can see from this quote, Sun Ra used this as a means to formulate and develop a politics based around this mythological self-institution. Over five decades the Arkestra released almost seventy albums and gave countless performances while living communally and elaborating forms of mythic narrative and imagery as part of the process of creating a philosophical system, or equation, as Sun Ra referred to it (Wolf and Geerken, 2006). The potentiality in the creation of such imagery does not depend on whether or not Sun Ra is really from Saturn, but rather on the social energies and desires that flow through the creation of these images. The Sun Ra Arkestra were also among the first ensembles to experiment in a serious way with collective improvisation, which can be understood in as an emergent model for a self-organized communist mode of production and social organization.

These themes have been picked up and elaborated since then by artists such Parliament-Funkadelic and George Clinton in the 1970s, whose work contained frequent references to the mother ship and other-worldly exodus, fusing together space themes with cultural black nationalism. This can also be seen more recently in the work of the hip hop project Deltron 3030, with its descriptions of intergalactic rap battles and strategizing industrial collapse through computer viruses (2002). Similar themes can be found in the work of artists including Octavia Butler, Samuel Delany, Colson Whitehead, and in films such as *The Brother from Another Planet*, and most famously in *The Matrix*. Across the many particularities within the work of these various artists one can find what Fred Moten describes as the ontology of black performance, a performance primarily animated through a 'blackness that exceeds itself; it bears the groundedness of an uncontainable outside' (2003: 26). At first this might sounds rather strange, but it makes precisely my core point: that it is not necessarily the feasibility of space travel or literal other-worldly exodus, but it may even be the case that the imaginal machine based around space imagery is made possible by its literal impossibility. In the sense that this possibility cannot be contained or limited, it becomes an assemblage for the grounding of a political reality that is not contained but opens up to other possible futures that are not foreclosed through their pre-given definition.

It is in this sense that outer space plays its most powerful role in the building of imaginal machines, despite and through the ambivalent roles that it has and continues to play in some regards. This is the very point made by Eduardo Rothe in an article he wrote in 1969 for the journal of the Situationists in which he argued that science, scientific exploration and discovery had come to play the role formerly played by religion in maintaining spectacular class domination. The heavens, formerly the province of priests, were now to be seized by uniformed astronauts, for those in power have never forgiven the celestial regions for being territories left open to the imagination. Space then becomes the possibility of escaping the contradictions of an earthly existence, which Roth frames in ways that makes him sound much closer to the priestly caste he claims to despise so much:

> Humanity will enter into space to make the universe the playground of the last revolt: that which will go against the limitations imposed by nature. Once the walls have been smashed that now separate people from science, the conquest of space will no longer be an economic or military 'promotional' gimmick, but the blossoming of human freedoms and fulfillments, attained by a race of gods. We will not enter into space as employees of an astronautic administration or as 'volunteers' of a state project, but as masters without slaves reviewing their domains: the entire universe pillaged for the workers councils (1969).

The messianism bubbles palpably within his rhetoric, seductively so. For many within autonomous movements of the 1960s and 1970s (as well as for many before and after that), what was previously conceived of as the inevitable march of dialectical progress towards a communist future, propelled along by the laws and motion of historical progress, seemed at best something of antique or a myth. But it was that imaginal machine that provided a great deal in terms of nourishing the resistant imaginary. It was this narrative that provided an outside from which critical thought and interventions were possible. In the same way that the narrative of progress towards a communist future was based around a forward projection of an outside to capitalism enabling a space of possibility in the present, here one can see outer space functioning in much the same way: a moment where a unity is reclaimed within the wealth of social knowledge and production (in this case in terms of the alienation of science and technology through state usage) which then enables a communist future in the present, one that overcomes the master-slave dialectic and an outburst of creativity in the organized form of workers councils. A mythopoetic creation indeed, but that is exactly the point, for the capacity to structure an imaginal machine is not necessarily based on the feasibility of enacting the ideas contained within it, but rather in acting as a compositional point for collective social desires. And if today we live, as Stephen Duncombe argues (2007), in an age of fantasy, our developing ability to understand, intervene, and work within the flows of imaginal desires and flows is precisely the ability to think through a collective radical politics despite and because of the ambivalence that the desires of the multitude contains.

A more recent example of space as a pole of imaginal recomposition comes in the form of the Association of Autonomous Astronauts (AAA), which formed in 1995 as a response to the continued militarization of space through programmes such as Star Wars. The AAA operated as an umbrella organization, or as a collective name for the autonomous activities of many different groups operating across numerous cities. While the AAA initially emerged very much out of the mail art and pscyhogeography scene, their efforts were intended to take the practice of the collective name and extend it from being an artistic practice to a wider form of organizing and political action (Home, 1997). For the AAA the collective name opened the possibility of creating a collective phantom (Holmes, 2007), one that 'operates within the wider context of popular culture, and is used as a tool for class war' (Anonymous 2004). Thus they, in a diffuse sense, proceeded to formulate a five year plan to boldly establish a planetary network to end the monopoly of corporations, governments and the military over travel in space. Although in a certain sense one might say that the AAA 'failed' in that they did not actually establish any sort of autonomous network of space exploration, that would be to mistake their stated goals for actual goals rather than as points of imaginal recomposition, a sense in which they were much more successful. Or, as Neil Starman frames it, the AAA was an attempt to turn nostalgia for the future into an avenue for political action, to 'make good some of the unkept promises of our childhoods' (2005). People dreamed that they would be able to explore space but, as the Pulp song intones, they only found themselves in dead-end, precarious jobs cleaning toilets or something equally uninteresting.

Among the AAA's most noted actions was a protest outside the London headquarters of Lockheed Martin against the militarization of space held in 1999 as part of the J18 'Carnival Against Capitalism'. It featured the strange sight of police blocking men in space suits from entering the building. This also marked the beginning of the 'Space 1999 – Ten Days that Shook the Universe' festival. Given the then waxing expansion of the anti-globalization movement one might think that this would be an opportune moment for the expansion and proliferation of the AAA. Rather, it became the moment when the AAA decided that it was time, according to their own previously charted five-year plan, to move towards self-dissolution. This might seem a bit odd, but as explained by Neil Disconaut:

> So why stop now? Well even the wildest of adventures can become routine, startling ideas clichés and the most radical gestures a source of light entertainment. Space imagery has become increasingly banal and retro, featuring in numerous adverts and pop videos. We don't want to be the space industry's court jesters when capitalism itself is being openly contested, as seen in Seattle and the City of London in the last year (2000: 13)

The point made here by Disconaut is quite clear. While the AAA was intended to, and did, act as a pole of imaginal recomposition, it was not intended to be an end in itself. One can find something of a parallel to the AAA in the Men in Red radical Ufology group, which grew out of the student movement in Italy in the early 1990s. For Men in Red, radical Ufology starts from a politics founded in disputing the proposition that the universe is made in man's image, and proceeds to think of ways to engage in autonomous contact with extraterrestrial life forms. In a parallel to the AAA as collective phantom, Men in Red state that they themselves wish to remain at a level that is the same as what they study, namely unidentified. To act as an end in itself would all too easily slip into a form of aesthetic escapism that might be said to characterize many forms of science fiction not particularly concerned with its politics. But the AAA did not want to fall into such a trap, did not want to end up generating more imaginal fodder for the capitalist image machine, and thus chose to dissolve in 2000. ET sold out to a capitalist communication company, but the AAA had no intention of doing so. In other words, the members of AAA sensed the potentiality of space imagery as a point of recomposition at one point, and also realized that it was not permanent and that would it would be strategically better to move to something else.

Outer space and the communist other to come

> We really don't think it's worth going through all the effort of getting into space just to live by the same rules as on earth. What attracts us to space exploration is the possibility of doing things differently. We are not interested in finding out what's its like to work in space, to find new ways of killing. We want to find out what dancing or sex feels like in zero gravity. (Association of Autonomous Astronauts flyer for J18 Anticapitalist Carnival, 1999)

Lastly, let us turn to the lovely example of the recently created Martian Museum of Terrestrial Art, which existed at the Barbican in London from 6 March to 18 May, 2008. The museum was coordinated by Martian anthropologists visiting Earth for reconnaissance purposes, sent on a mission to reconsider whether the previous classification of Earthlings as an unsophisticated and backwards population amongst the cosmos is as accurate as previously thought. This particular section of the Martian Museum took on multiple functions, including both playfully engaging with the commonly felt near incomprehensibility of contemporary art as well as the othering and alienating effects contained within unreconstructed uses of traditional anthropological methods (ethnography, fieldwork, living amongst the primitives). To put it bluntly, it was clear from the arrangement that the Martian ethnographers were quite baffled, although they tried with great valour to understand the function and purpose of contemporary art. Agent 083TOM33McC5THY, one of the more astute among their team, made the following comment in a red paper that accompanied the creation of the museum:

> The fact that art occupies a symbolic stratum – and, moreover, does so with a rationale whose key or legend seems to elude both Martian *and* Terrestrial observers – has led to a suspicion that it forms an encryption that among Terrestrial codes has hitherto eluded deciphering. That it serves both as repository and index of the population's desires, fantasies, and so on suggests it as potential field for mind control activities – yet one that must be mastered, or alternatively, neutralized by Martians lest it be directed against us. (2008)

This is quite an astute observation. Here we find an observation of the large degree of incomprehensibility of the artistic world mingled with some vague premonitions that there could be something dangerous happening. Art could lead to mind control, which could be potentially used against the Martian forces. Quickly, let us do away with the incomprehensible other for there could be something dangerous here. This is not far from the attitude of many secret service organizations or colonial regimes, although it is one that would tend to dispute the previously argued for, inherently progressive, politics required for cooperative space exploration.

But, again, there is an ambivalence that is also a possibility. When you think about it, the emergence of a radical future, communist, anarchist, or otherwise, is almost always necessarily defined by its very otherness from the world as is (see Parker, this volume). It is the other future that emerges through struggle and to some degree necessarily seems alien from the world as is, because otherwise it would not be (an)other world at all, but merely a rearrangement of the present. While Juan Posadas and the Fourth International may have argued that space aliens would inherently be communist, maintaining an open relation to encountering the other means having to confront the realization that despite all our wishes, space aliens might in fact not be communists at all! The becoming-other of the communist future can be found in the becoming-other and abjection of the present as well as the past, an abjection which brings together the twin dynamics of rejection and desire in an otherness already in the process of becoming. This is perhaps why the Zapatistas, when they call for an encuentro, often frame it as being an intergalactic encuentro. Not that they actually believe a delegation from another universe will arrive, but in the sense of maintaining an open relation to the actually existing other, the other of the future. It is in these spaces where, among many others, one finds cracks in the imagery of a present that is often not nearly as hegemonic as thought, imaginal breaks and tesseract through which other voyages and transformations become possible. A communist future is not an uncritical celebration of this otherness but rather an ethics of engagement with an Other that is truly other, and a politics founded through that. The question is not really whether there are little green men or communist partisans on the red planet bolleaux, but what can be gained through the imaginal gymnastics of imagining our relation to them. As the Association of Autonomous Astronauts always say, 'Above the paving stones, the stars.' What to be found beyond the stars is an open question, an unidentified future, and that is precisely the reason why it is the only one worth living. Out there, somewhere, Joe Hill is still singing.

Acknowledgement

Thanks to all my friends and comrades from whose collective intelligence I have learned very much, especially Richard Barbrook, Enns Chung, Stepano Harney, Ben Meyers, Martin Parker, Falian Tompsett and Alberto Toscaro. Special thanks to Agart Schreven for the provision of intergalactic documents.

References

Agent 083TOM33McC5THY, (2008), 'Letting It Be: A Red Paper on Terrestrial Art', *Martian Encyclopedia of Terrestial Life, Volume VIII: Art.* London: Martian Museum of Terrestrial Art.
Anonymous, (2004), 'Multiple Names', *Mail-Art Encyclopedia*, available at www.sztuka-fabryka. be/encyclopaedia/items/multiple_name.htm. [accessed 7 Nov 2008]

Antliff, A., (2001), *Anarchist Modernism: Art, Politics, and the First American Avant-Garde*, Chicago: University of Chicago Press.

Antliff, A., (2007), *Anarchy and Art: From the Paris Commune to the Fall of the Berlin Wall*, Vancouver: Arsenal Pulp Press.

Barbrook, R., (2007), *Imaginary Futures: From Thinking Machine to Global Village*, London: Pluto Press.

Berardi, F. 'Bifo' (2008), *Félix Guattari: Thought, Friendship, and Visionary Cartography*, translated by Giuseppina Mecchia,. New York: Palgrave.

Boltanski, L. and Chiapello, E., (2005), *The New Spirit of Capitalism*, translated by Gregory Elliot, London: Verso.

Bone, I., (2006), *Bash the Rich: True-Life Confessions of an Anarchist in the UK*, Bath: Tangent Books.

Bratich, J. Z., (2008), *Conspiracy Panics: Political Rationality and Popular Culture*, Binghamton: SUNY Press.

Brosnan, J., (1978), *Future Tense: The Cinema of Science Fiction*, New York: St. Martin's Press.

Camatte, J., (1995), *The World We Must Leave and Other Essays*, Brooklyn: Autonomedia.

Cutler, C., (1992), *File Under Popular: Theoretical and Critical Writing on Music*, Brooklyn: Autonomedia.

Dean, Kenneth and Brian Massumi, (1992), *First & Last Emperors: The Absolute State and the Body of the Despot*, Brooklyn, NY: Autonomedia.

Deltron 3030, (2000), *Deltron 3030*, San Francisco: 75 Ark.

Dery, M., (1995), 'Black to the Future: Afro-Futurism 1.0', available at www.levity.com/markdery/black.html.

Disconaut, N., (2000), 'Mission accomplished but the beat goes on: the Fantastic Voyage of the Association of Autonomous Astronauts', *See you in Space: the Fifth Annual Report of the Association of Autonomous Astronaut*, London: Association of Autonomous Astronauts.

Dubravka, D. and Suvakovic, M., (eds), (2003), *Impossible Histories: Historical Avant-gardes, Neo-avant-gardes, and Post-avant-gardes in Yugoslavia, 1918–1991*, Cambridge: MIT University Press.

Duncombe, S., (2007), *Dream: Re-Imagining Progressive Politics in an Age of Fantasy*, New York: New Press.

Elms, A., John Corbett and Jerri Kapalsis, (eds) (2007), *Pathways to Unknown Worlds: Sun Ra, El Saturn and Chicago's Afro-Futurist Underground, 1954–68*, Chicago: WhiteWalls.

Eshun, K., (2003), 'Further Considerations on Afrofuturism', *CR: The New Centennial Review* Volume 3, Number 2: 287–302.

Federici, S. and Caffentzis, G., (1982), 'Mormons in Space', *Midnight Notes*: 3–12.

Holmes, B., (2007), *Unleashing the Collective Phantoms: Essays in Reverse Imagineering*, Brooklyn: Autonomedia.

Home, S., (1997), *Mind Invaders: A Reader in Psychic Warfare, Cultural Sabotage and Semiotic Terrorism*, London: Serpent's Tail.

Lewis, H., (1990), *Dada Turns Red: Politics of Surrealism*, Edinburgh: Edinburgh University Press.

McCarthy, K. and Gorman, E., (1999), *'They're Here . . .' Invasion of the Body Snatchers: A Tribute*, Berkeley: Berkeley Boulevard Books.

Miéville, C., (2007), 'The Struggle for Intergalactic Socialism', *Socialist Review*. January 2007, available at www.socialistreview.org.uk.

Miller, P., (1999), 'Afro-Futurism: A Statement of Intentions – Outside In, Inside Out', available at www.afrofuturism.net/text/Manifestos/Miller01.html.

Monroe, A., (2005), *Interrogation Machine: Laibach and the NSK*, Cambridge, MA: MIT Press.

Moten, F., (2003), *In The Break: The Aesthetics of the Black Radical Tradition*, Minneapolis: University of Minnesota Press.

Nelson, A., (2000), 'Afrofuturism: Past Future Visions', *Colorlines* (Spring), available at www.arc.org.

Ra, S., (1968), *Outer Spaceways Incorporated*, El Saturn Records.

Ra, S., (1974), *Space is the Place*, directed John Coney, El Saturn Records.

Rosemont, F., (2002), *Joe Hill: The IWW and the Making of a Revolutionary Working Class Counterculture*, Chicago: Charles H. Kerr Publishing.

Rothe, E., (1969), 'The Conquest of Space in Time and Power', *Internationale Situationniste* No. 12, translated by Ken Knabb, available at www.bopsecrets.org/SI/12.space.htm.

Rucker, R., Robert Anton Wilson, Peter Lamborn Wilson and Bart Plantenga (eds), (1991), *Semiotext(e) SF*, New York: Semiotext(e).

Salusbury, M., (2003), 'Posadism for Beginners', *Fortean Times*, available at www.forteantimes.com.

Scott-Heron, G., (1971), 'Whitey on the Moon', *Pieces of a Man*, New York: Flying Dutchman Records.

Shukaitis, S., (2007), 'Plan 9 from the Capitalist Workplace: Insurgency, Originary Accumulation, Rupture', *Situations: A Project of the Radical Imagination*, Volume 2 Number 2: 95–116.

Smith, G. M., (1984), *Joe Hill*, New York: Gibbs Smith.

Smith, W., Higgins, M., Parker, M. and Lightfoot, G., (2001), *Science Fiction and Organisation*, London: Routledge.

Starman, N., (2005), 'Nostalgia for the Future: The Darker the Night, the Brighter the Stars'. Talk given at the 'Art is not Terrorism' event on April 23rd, 2005, Paris, available at www.geocities.com/redgiantsite/paris.html.

Stimson, B. and Sholette, G., (eds), (2007), *Collectivism After Modernism: The Art of Social Imagination After 1945*, Minneapolis: University of Minnesota Press.

Szwed, J., (1998), *Space Is the Place: The Lives and Times of Sun Ra*, Cambridge: De Capo Press.

Theroux, Louis, (2005), *The Call of the Weird*, New York: Pan Macmillan.

Von Gunden, K. and Stock, S. H., (1982), *Twenty All-Time Great Science Fiction Films*, Arlington: Arlington House.

Weiner, J., (2008), 'Lil Wayne and the Afronaut Invasion', *Slate* June 2008, available at www.slate.com.

Weir, David, (1997), *Anarchy & Culture: The Aesthetic Politics of Modernism*, Amherst, MA: University of Massachusetts Press.

Williams, B., (2001), 'Black Secret Technology: Detroit Techno and the Information Age', *Technicolor: Race, Technology, and Everyday Life*, (eds), Alondra Nelson and Thuy Linh Tu, New York: New York University Press: 154–176.

Wolf, J. and Geerken, H., (2006), *Sun Ra: The Immeasurable Equation: The Collected Poetry and Prose*, Herrsching: Waitawhile.

Wonder, S., (1976), 'Saturn', *Songs in the Key of Life*, Detroit: Motown Records.

Yaszek, L., (2005), 'Afrofuturism: Science Fiction and the History of the Future', *Socialism and Democracy*, Volume 2 Number 3.

The space race and Soviet utopian thinking[1]

Iina Kohonen

Introduction

'Once the Sky lay near the Earth. But when people started wiping their dirty hands on it, it escaped to the heavens, out of our reach' (Vail and Genis, 1988: 3–12).

Countdown: the International Geophysical Year

The programmes that resulted in the launching of the first artificial earth satellites were run by the Soviet Union and the United States within the overall framework of the International Geophysical Year. (henceforth IGY). The IGY was an ambitious international undertaking, comprising a network of planetwide geophysical studies that was initiated in 1952 and implemented in 1957–1958. It united scientists globally: sixty-seven national scientific teams with diverse cultural, political and economic backgrounds participated in different ways. The IGY agreements guaranteed the free exchange of information acquired through scientific observation, including that obtained by artificial satellites. Almost all the members of the two rival alliances contributed to the year's events, in spite of the fact that many of the scientific subjects of study had a considerable military and scientific significance. And, indeed, in the depth of the Cold War there actually *was* some degree of useful scientific interaction and exchange. This was remarkable, bearing in mind the generally hostile relations between the countries of NATO and the Warsaw Pact (signed only two years before the opening of the IGY) (Bulkeley, 2000: 125–152; Wilson, 1961: 72).

On July 1955 President Eisenhower announced that the United States Navy had been assigned the task of launching *Vanguard* satellites as part of the programme of the IGY. Soon afterwards the Soviet Union declared that it would do the same. The race into space had begun.

At the climax of the space race both superpowers, the USA and the Soviet Union, suspected, at least in theory, that the other had the technology to launch the first artificial space satellite. When the Soviet Union won the race the message was clear: the first satellite, *Sputnik 1*, became a symbol of the success of the socialist system. Space became a symbol of modern life. In the United

States this caused a crisis of confidence in the effectiveness of American technology (Peoples, 2008: 55–75).

The Soviet space industry was born within the military industrial complex; but the space programme was never merely a military programme. It was an unusual fusion combining military aspirations, state propaganda and utopian thinking (Barry, 2000: 95–115; Harford, 2000: 108). In this chapter I shall try to consider all of these interconnected aspects of the Soviet space programme. First, I will consider how the utopian elements were connected historically to the idea of space exploration; secondly, by taking the beginning of the 1960s as an example, I intend to consider how these elements were transformed into visual propaganda after the first manned space flight; and, finally, I shall consider how disillusionment took over soon after that.

Cosmic utopia and the space race

I have chosen the beginning of the 1960s, and in particular the year 1961, for my 'close reading' of the visual propaganda for two reasons. First, the year 1961 was the year when the space race culminated with the Soviet Union achieving the greatest victory of all: it triumphed over the United States by sending the first human into space. Secondly, the year 1961 was the year when cosmic utopianism reached its zenith in the Soviet Union. The new programme of the Communist Party of the Soviet Union, which had evolved during 1958–1961, laid the foundation for the official Khrushchevian utopia. It heralded the construction of communism, and the central argument of the programme was that communism would be achieved by the year 1980, so that 'this generation will live under it' (*Programma KPSS*, 1961: 142 and passim. See also Genis and Vail, 1988: 3–12; Renkama, 2006: 284–332). This utopianism surrounded people through visual representations, and everyday problems did not appear to exist in such a world. The contradiction between these illustrations and people's everyday lives was obvious: it was as if two parallel worlds existed simultaneously. The utopian world was the world of the future. Beautiful, smiling people such as Yuri Gagarin were the children of the new era, the age of Space.

The creation of a material-technical basis of communism became the guideline for Khrushchevian policies. The cosmos became a powerful symbol of modernization and the future. Technological utopianism and the worship of science were built into the revolutionary ideology, and space was closely associated with modernization and technological progress. At its height, this ideology was beautified via visual representations. Fantasy crept into the scientific discourse through these utopian visions. The utopia called communism was soon to come into being.

Visual representations of space – propaganda and dreams

The enthusiasm with regard to cosmic space was promoted and skilfully taken advantage of by the propaganda machine of the party state. The role of photography in this process was prominent. Visual propaganda had been a significant determinant of Soviet utopian thinking and the country's concepts of the future ever since the birth of the nation. Over the years, posters, paintings and photography had played a major role in Soviet propaganda, and the 1920s in particular is often regarded as the golden age of Soviet political art and photography. In the early 1960s then, the cult of scientific and technological progress and modernization – elements so evident in the Khrushchevian era – created a favourable climate for a rebirth of photography. It was promoted as a modern technological medium and was widely used to propagandize the successes of Soviet science, notably the space programme. Photography was seen above all as a means of proving that the Soviet utopian project was being put into practice (Reid, 1994: 33–39).

In this chapter, I will concentrate on photographic expressions of the Soviet utopia. The empirical material is divided into two spheres. The first area of interest is material which was published in the Soviet Union during the years 1957–1969. For this chapter I have collected all the space-related photographs from the popular, widely distributed periodical *Ogonyok* (Flame), a weekly illustrated magazine from the first years of the 1960s. The other part of my study consists of archival material from the Russian State Archive of Scientific and Technical Documents, located in Moscow. This archive holds substantial numbers of documents related to the Soviet space programme, and includes not only technical documentation, but also films, photographs and audio recordings of historic achievements in rocket design and space travel.

The fact that these photographs were used for propaganda purposes is taken as axiomatic, and there is no intention of revealing the real, objective truth behind them. So rather than *objective* truth, this study will seek the discursive construction of *narrative* truth, in which coherence serves as a decisive factor for the production of intelligible and appealing narratives (Sumiala-Seppänen and Stocchetti, 2007: 336–343). The central idea is to search for new critical ways of understanding photographs as historical documents by investigating how images communicate: the means by which they convey their message, the devices employed, the appeals they make, the conventions they reinforce; and to treat them not as pictures alone or as documents but as cultural texts. The greatest historical interest might be found less in what the photograph literally depicts than in the way it relates to and makes visible the culture of which it once was a part (Trachtenberg, 1989: xiii–xvii; Brothers, 1997: 22).

The dreamers

Origins of the Soviet cosmic utopia

The beginning of the Space Age was not the first time that the triumph of the cosmos was treated as a victory over time and place and as transcendence of all earthly hardship. The dream of space flight had enjoyed a long tradition in the Soviet Union. At least one seed of this thought can be found in the writings of a truly original thinker, Nicolay Fyodorovich Fedorov (1829–1903). For

Fedorov, a voyage to the cosmos was connected with the idea of the brother-hood of all mankind and of universal happiness. For him, the most important task for humans was to unite humankind, to conquer the universe, to create a cosmos from chaos, and even to conquer death: resurrecting the dead by future advances in science and technology was not beyond his imagination. There is magic and pure fantasy in Fedorov's thought. He profoundly opposed passivity, believing that one should actively participate in changing what is into what ought to be (Fedorov, 1906, 1913; Zenkovsky, 1953: 588–604; Yegorov, 2007).

'Mankind will not be bound to Earth forever', wrote Konstantin Tsiolkovsky (1857–1935), a unique self-taught rocket designer, space philosopher, writer and teacher from the small provincial town of Kaluga. He was the first to connect the theory of a cosmic utopia to more practical considerations of rocket technology, and many of his inventions were later proved to work. Apart from his technological studies, he was also a sincere theorist of cosmic philosophy, an enthusiastic reader of Jules Verne and an adherent of Fedorov, who at the time of Tsiolkovsky's student years in Moscow was working as a librarian at the Rumiantsev Museum (now the Russian State Library) in Moscow (Kozhenikov, 1906; Boym and Bartos, 2001).

Tsiolkovsky did his work in isolation, unconnected to the scientific community; but a growing popularity of the idea of space travel was in the air. In the Soviet Union, as well as in Western Europe, the idea of interplanetary exploration caused a phenomenon in the 1920s that can rightfully be called a Space Boom (Geppert, 2008: 262–285). Science fiction literature flourished and the idea of space flight was taken seriously – in an era when even electric lighting was a luxury. Flying machines real and imagined were, as Susan Buck-Morss puts it, 'invested with transformative social meaning' and utopian impulses were tolerated and even supported by the ruling power. Interplanetary travel was a preferred form of social utopian expression. (Buck-Morss, 2000: 45) Several space clubs were organized. In them serious-minded scientists undertook practical research and organized public courses and launches of rocket models. Officially these clubs were public but in fact they were controlled by the government and financed mostly by the military (Gorin, 2000: 23).

At the very end of his life Tsiolkovsky finally received public recognition within the Soviet Union: the Soviet government used him as a living example of 'an ordinary person who had become a great scientist when freed from the oppression of the bourgeoisie'. At this point he also made contact with the West through German space pioneer Hermann Oberth (1894–1989), and he was published outside the Soviet Union (Gorin, 2000: 17–22; Tsiolkovsky (n.d.)).

'Dreaming is a serious mental disease' (Zamyatin)

Within the Soviet Union, the idea of space flight came to an abrupt end in the 1930s. Because the idea of space flight challenged the notion of Stalin's unique ability to foresee the future, it was officially crushed in 1934, condemned as useless daydreaming. Nearly all the leading space scientists and engineers were either killed or imprisoned during the Great Purges of 1937. Science fiction literature was declared forbidden.[2]

The idea of rocketry was reinvented during World War II – there was not much room for cosmic dreaming or utopia at this point though. During the final days of the war both Americans and Soviets had captured German scientists who had been employed in the Nazi missile programme, the so-called V2 programme at the Peenemunde Research Centre. Both superpowers started their missile programme (and consequently their space programme) on the basis of this German know-how (Maddrell, 2006: 25–26; Winter, 1990: 55–58).

Re-birth of cosmic enthusiasm

After Stalin's death, ideological suppression substantially eased and science fiction literature experienced a renaissance. Writing about the possibility of space flight began to flourish in the press after 1953. Even the *Bolshaya Sovetskaya Entsiklopedya* (The Great Soviet Encyclopaedia) contributed to this discussion in the 1954 edition, which included an article entitled 'Interplanetary Communications', a topic which had been an official taboo under Stalin. (*Bolshaja Sovetskaja Entsiklopedya*, 1954: 51–53). This 'Second Space Boom' clearly prepared public consciousness for the possibility of a space flight and these early publications were a major contributing factor to the public's perception of space flight as potential reality (Gorin, 2000: 11–42).

By the year 1961, the Soviet Union had launched fourteen artificial satellites and rockets. There had been one stunning success after another. The list of 'firsts' is admirable: the first satellite, Sputnik 1, in October 1957; the first living being in orbit, Layka in Sputnik 2 in November 1957; the first human-made object to escape Earth's gravity and be placed in orbit around the Sun, Luna 1 in January 1959;[3] the first pictures of the far side of the Moon, Luna 3 in October 1959; the first return of living creatures from orbital flight, Sputnik 5 in August 1960, carrying the dogs Strelka and Belka.[4] The concept of space flight was visible everywhere; science fiction novels and films were extremely popular, while pictures of sputniks and space dogs could be found on every possible product from cigarette boxes to tea cups – the Soviets clearly knew how to merchandize these early achievements in space travel. Visually the Soviet Union was a society living in the Space Age.

On April 12, 1961, Major Yuri Gagarin flew into space, the first person in the world to do so. This was something that had been anticipated, yet no one could have even dreamed of the impact and propaganda value his face would have. The flight also aroused enormous attention in the West. This is how the leading Finnish newspaper *Helsingin Sanomat* described him immediately after the flight: 'His smile is good and honest. There is no need to add that this man, who was the first to have the courage to fly into outer space, to greet the stars, a man who has been the first to look down on our Earth, has a truly dignified character. This is seen in his smile, in his intelligent eyes' (*Helsingin Sanomat* 13.4.1961).

After that date this smile was seen everywhere. There are myriad photographs of Yuri Gagarin. Soon he was accompanied by other heavenly heroes as the list of firsts lengthened: the first day-long space mission in August 1961, by Gherman Titov; the first long-duration space flight in August 1962, when the cosmonaut Andrian Nikolayev spent four days in space; the first woman in space, Valentina Tereshkova in June 1963; the first multi-person mission in October 1964, carrying cosmonauts Komarov, Yegorov and Feoktistov; and the first spacewalk, by Alexei Leonov in March 1965 (Launius, 2000, xi–xii).

The year 1961 was also a watershed in political ideology: three months after Gagarin's flight, on 30 July, *Pravda* published the third party programme (Genis and Vail, 1988: 3–12; Renkama, 2006: 284–332). The programme was adopted at the 22nd Party Congress in October 1961. This was not a minor happening – publicly it was celebrated as a major ideological turning point. The programme defined plans for the internal development of the Soviet Union for the next twenty years. In particular, there were detailed plans for the technological and economic development of the Soviet Union. According to the third party programme, there were two stages involved in the building of communism in the Soviet Union. In the first decade (1961–1970) the Soviet Union was supposed to surpass the United States in production. The welfare of the population would be greatly improved: the programme envisaged progress in housing conditions, an increase in the production of consumer goods and a reduction of working hours to the fewest in the world. During the second stage (1971–1980), the material and technical base for communism would be built and Soviet society would approach the communist goal of a distribution of goods according to one's needs (*Programma KPSS*, 1961: 65–66). In this context, photographs from the cosmos can be seen as manifestations of an official but publicly embraced cult of science which viewed technology as the solution to all social and economic problems. The significance of the space flights was not only technological but also social (Josephson, 1990: 169–177). Never before had a utopian dream had such a tight schedule, such a precise point of achievement in the future.

Cosmic utopianism in 1961

The cosmic utopianism of Fedorov and Tsiolkovsky had begun to develop at the same time as Russian Marxism (Yegorov, 2007), and Fedorov can rightly be called the founding father of the Soviet philosophy of cosmism. He was virtually forgotten during the Soviet era however, unlike Tsiolkovsky, who was canonized as a 'Father of the Soviet space program' and was a frequent visitor in the pages of *Ogonyok* (eg *Ogonyok* 28/57; *Ogonyok* 37/60). Whether the philosophical thoughts of Fedorov were acknowledged by Khrushchevian reformists is not known, but there are strikingly Fedorovian thoughts to be found, eg in the '*Onsovy Marxisma-Leninisma*' (Bases of Marxism-Leninism, published in 1959), an ideological handbook of Soviet Marxism-Leninism. The book is a broad introduction to a society that is about to reach utopia (communism, that is). It was edited by Otto-Wille Kuusinen, an eager reformist and an original thinker himself. The Fedorovian fantasy begins to flourish in the very last pages of the book, where Kuusinen is proclaiming the future society. In communism, the book explains, it will be possible 'to extend the lifetime of an individual to approximately 150–200 years, . . . and to resurrect people when premature death occurs' (1960: 731; Vihavainen, 2003: 30).

The theme of death and resurrection is crystallized in Soviet Russia in one place in particular: in the Mausoleum of Lenin in Red Square. It was the symbolic centre, the 'holy shrine' where the ideology was given a concrete form (Lane, 1981: 210–212). The building was designed by architect Aleksey Shchusev but inside the building is work by another architect: Konstantin Melnikov designed the sarcophagus where Lenin's embalmed body is lying. Melnikov was an original figure on the Soviet architectural scene – and, incidentally, a true follower of Nicolay Fedorov.

The decision to display Lenin's body was rich in symbolic significance for an Orthodox Russian population and inevitably stimulated discussion of death and resurrection. That Lenin could die and yet somehow continue to live held out the prospect of a new type of immortality in a post-Christian Russia. If Christianity had derived its strength from the *spiritual* victory over death, the communist state would use science to achieve *physical* immortality (Starr, 1978).

In 1961, this Mausoleum was at the centre of attention. It served as the ritual stage for the homecoming ceremony of cosmonauts after their heroic flights. At the top of this building the cosmonauts were embraced by the ruling elite and presented to the people for the first time. It is tempting to think that it was indeed the metamorphosis of the same cosmic myth, which had originated with Fedorov, that made the cosmonauts climb to the roof of their beloved leader's tomb. At the time, Stalin was also lying beside Lenin, but he would be hastily removed from the Mausoleum in October 1961 (McNeal, 1974: 281–282). Surely it was not desired that *he* be resurrected, as Yevgeny Yevtushenko put it in his poem 'Stalin's Heirs' from that year:

> Mute was the marble.
>   Mutely glimmered the glass.
> Mute stood the sentries,
>   bronzed by the breeze.
> Thin wisps of smoke curled over the coffin.
>   And breath seeped through the chinks
> as they bore him out the mausoleum doors.
> Slowly the coffin floated,
>   grazing the fixed bayonets.
> He also was mute–
>   he also!–
>   mute and dread.
> Grimly clenching

his embalmed fists,
   just pretending to be dead,
      he watched from inside. . . . (Yevtushenko, 1961)[5]

Melnikov had himself hinted at the idea of a sleeping Tsarevna, a Russian version of the tale of Sleeping Beauty. In this tale, as we all know, the Princess appears dead, but is only sleeping in her innocent beauty until the Prince enters the room and, by kissing her, brings her back to life (Starr, 1978). Would the cosmonauts be the princes to kiss Lenin back to life? They were, after all, living proof that utopia had landed on Earth.

Utopia and propaganda

Responses to Sputnik; East and West

As much as it was a cause for euphoria in the Soviet Union, the launching of Sputnik 1 came as a shock to the United States. How was it possible that the backward society of the Soviets could outshine the most powerful technological superpower? The unexpected nature of the Soviet launch gave the US cause to rethink its vulnerability to outside attacks. As Peter Gorin (in a slightly pro-vocative tone, perhaps) shapes it, the shock effect of Sputnik was a by-product and creation of the politically motivated ignorance of Western mass media – there had been many hints of the coming launch in the Soviet press, but these had been ignored in the West (Gorin, 2000: 11–42). The reason for this hysteria was not only the political humiliation caused by the defeat, but something more concrete: the vehicle for putting the little satellite into space was basically an intercontinental ballistic missile. At the tip of the rocket, a nuclear warhead could be substituted for the satellite. The confidence in American superiority in technology, science and education instantly evaporated. Sputnik was an indica-tion that the Russians could build ballistic missiles capable of hitting any chosen target anywhere in the world. Technological optimism in the United States was struck by a new dimension of *technophobia* (Gorin, 2000: 11–42; Peoples, 2008: 55–75).

The Western public was not appropriately informed, since the Western media was generally not profoundly interested in the content of the propaganda that filled the Soviet press (Gorin, 2000: 11–42). In the Soviet Union the situation was very different. The Soviet public was well prepared for the launching of Sputnik. Soviet satellite development combined tight secrecy with controlled 'leaks' of information stemming from the fact that space technology was deeply connected to the development of strategic weapons. These leaks, in addition to the popular space enthusiasm, prepared the public for the launch of Sputnik.

What the Soviet media was *not* ready for was the public response that Sputnik caused in the West. After the launch, *Pravda* published only a small routine-like bulletin from TASS concerning a successful satellite experiment (Soobshchenie Tass 5.10.1957); only after realizing the reaction of the Western media did Khrushchev become conscious of the propaganda value of these flights. He hastily ordered Sergey Korolev, chief designer of the Soviet space programme, to send another satellite into space to coincide with the anniversary of the Great October Revolution. Korolev succeeded and within a month the Soviets astonished the world with yet another Sputnik, this time even with a living creature inside: a small dog called Layka. This same hasty manoeuvre was repeated after Gagarin's flight when Khrushchev again ordered a quick repetition of the flight; yet again this was a success and Gherman Titov became the second person to orbit the Earth in August 1961. The flight conveniently distracted the world's attention from the construction of the Berlin wall, an affair more or less discomforting for Khrushchev (Taubman, 2003).

Whether the cosmonauts in fact would kiss Lenin back to life was a thought left in obscurity, but they gave utopian ideologists concrete evidence that this really was the dawn of a new era: images of outer space gave reality to these otherwise abstract political and intellectual concepts of a fantastic future global utopia. The first really sensational photograph was the first picture from the far side of the Moon, taken by Luna 3 in October 1959. The naming of features of the far side of the Moon by the Soviet Union was highly controversial, so the responsibility for naming features on the surface of the Moon was given to the Paris-based International Astronomical Union, a federation of professional astronomers from around the world. Here we can find Tsiolkovsky again: Among the names submitted by the USSR Academy of Sciences to the International Astronomical Union to be given to the newly found craters on the dark side of the Moon was that of Tsiolkovsky as well as of his inspirational hero, Jules Verne. The two early dreamers about space had finally made it to the Moon (Barabashov *et al.*, 1961).

Visual representations of space in Ogonyok

The weekly illustrated periodical *Ogonyok* was established as a truly national publication. The magazine was produced in Moscow, took ten days to print and up to one month to reach the far eastern regions of the Soviet Union. It was ideologically mild, available at hairdressers, clinics and airports, and, thanks to its crossword puzzles and full-colour reproductions of art works, attracted a general readership (Porter, 1990: 3). One of the main features characterizing *Ogonyok* was its photojournalistic ambition. *Sovetskoe Foto*, a monthly photography journal and mouthpiece for photographers, published pictures from *Ogonyok* in nearly every number (eg *Sovetskoe Foto*, 1963, vol. 1–12 passim). Such prominent photographers as Vsevolod Tarasevich, Dmitrii Baltermants and Isaak Tunkel were included in the photographic branch of *Ogonyok* in the 1960s.

In the beginning of the 1960s, pictures from space were highly visible in this publication. If we compare the political rhetoric of the time and the photographs published, the first thing that strikes us as contradictory is the relationship with technology. Soviet rhetoric representing the conquest of space portrays a society that worshipped science and technology. Marxism was defined as science itself, and revolution was its greatest achievement. By the year 1961 it was obvious that *visually* the theme of technology had fulfilled its purpose. It was the cosmonauts in particular who had the role of new, quintessentially utopian, heroes. Even before Gagarin's flight, technology is strikingly absent from Soviet photographs representing the conquest of space: the utopian future seems to be a pastoral idyll, a never-ending holiday in Sochi. In the photographs, cosmonauts are living happy and trouble-free lives in their beautiful homes, spending quality time with their happy and sophisticated spouses and children (see Sage, this volume).[6]

The second noticeable attribute to be discerned in the photographs is the plain *ordinariness* of the figures in them. The represented Soviet future is not as smooth and glossy as was verbally illustrated in the third party programme. Actually it was quite shabby, ordinary and disordered. This ordinariness is emphasized in different ways: the surprise at one's sudden success is a common theme: a cosmonaut is gazing at his/her photograph on the first page of *Pravda*, discomfited at the new status; or a cosmonaut is spending leisure time fishing or cooking, playing chess or reading (eg *Ogonyok* 26/61; *Ogonyok* 27/61). I believe that this was neither a mistake, nor a minor detail. By showing ordinary Soviet men who had accomplished heroic deeds, the future was drawn into the present. It is as if these photographs were proclaiming that the heavenly creatures were already living among ordinary people. The present and the future became indistinguishable.

This immediate equation of 'is' and 'will be' was built into the inner logic of Socialist Realism, and thus was nothing new to the viewers (Fitzpatrick, 1999: 9–67; Holz 1993: 74; See also Bonnell, 1997). The present had been a permanent progression towards the future since the 1930s, but now the future was something that was comprehensible to all. Perhaps the predictions of the third party programme became more plausible, when the depicted actors bore a resemblance to actual, living people? The photographs hold out the promise that the Soviet utopia was truly coming into being and was right around the corner. This would, however, make the later disillusionment perhaps even more bitter.

Cosmonauts, as it turned out, were not confined to the sky, either: they travelled over the Earth's surface to far-off lands to promote the great Soviet utopia. In many photographs cosmonauts are depicted greeting film stars and political superheroes of the time (eg *Ogonyok* 30/61). To the average Soviet citizen this second journey around the world might have appeared just as miraculous as the actual space flight itself. These were truly citizens of the globe, uniting the whole world in the forthcoming utopia. Photographs from space illustrated the utopia foreseen in the third party programme.

The heroic journey

What, then, goes into the making of this cosmic hero? In the Soviet visual discourse surrounding the cosmonauts there seems to be confusion as to whether the heroism is something that is built into the character itself or something achieved through an extraordinary deed. The reason for this confusion might be in the dialectic of invisibility and conquest that was characteristic of the Soviet space programme in general: the cosmonaut's journey beyond Earth's atmosphere and his return from the frontiers of our existence was a dream that was thoroughly choreographed. The making of the dream had to be kept mysterious. This created an illusion that cosmonauts just flew by themselves – or actually didn't fly at all[7] (Boym and Bartos, 2001, 91). When we examine photographs from *Ogonyok* this is strikingly true: we can see cosmonauts in ritualistic welcoming ceremonies, in their childhood, in their preparation for the flight, in their daily routines and during their leisure pursuits (eg 1–2211, 1–14923, 1–2209; Ogonyok 31/61, Ogonyok 34/62, Ogonyok 43/64). But the *actual heroic deed*, the conquest of earthly bounds, is left in obscurity. The few photographs from beyond the atmosphere are blurred, unclear and faded – as if to increase the mysteriousness of the flight (*Ogonyok* 12/65). Notwithstanding the evident role played by the technical challenges in this new branch of photography, these first cosmic photographs also created politically incorrect associations. After his flight, Yuri Gagarin was constantly asked about the whereabouts of God in Heaven and no denial or reference to scientific atheism helped: he had been closer to God than anyone, and therefore was considered to embody a certain sacredness (*Ogonyok* 52/61).

A contrasting analysis of Ogonyok materials with archival photographs confuses the picture even further. In the archive we can find depictions of heroes and heroines who have arrived from the borders of our reality. One photograph in particular is illuminating: RGANTD 0–878 (Figure 3). In this photograph, Valentina Tereshkova is sitting in a field, in the middle of cosmic debris, like a fallen angel. She has just arrived from space, not quite ready to be embraced

Figure 1: *Cosmonaut Gherman Titov is praciticing his sense of equilibrium in an apparatus that was at the time called "skillet" by the cosmonauts. Courtesy of RGANTD.*

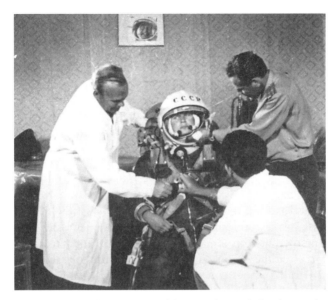

Figure 2: *Cosmonaut Valentina Tereshkova is being helped into the space suit before her flight. Courtesy of RGANTD.*

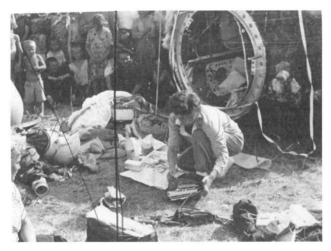

Figure 3: *Cosmonaut Valentina Tereshkova after her landing in the Pavinskiy Collective Farm, Altai region, near Kazakhstan border, in June 19, 1963. Note the censors excision at the left hand side of the photo. Courtesy of RGANTD.*

by the people, by the media. She looks perplexed and disoriented in her flight equipment, while the audience gathered around this *miracle* from the sky stands in clear contrast to those celebrating in the pages of *Ogonyok* (eg *Ogonyok* 26/63): poor, barefooted children with muddy knees; peasants with confused and uncertain facial expressions. You can almost hear their silence, sense the wonder in their eyes. There she is, not a heroine yet, but not quite an ordinary woman anymore. She is in a stage of liminality, between two different existential planes.[8] The metamorphosis from an ordinary human being to a heroine will happen in an official ritual later. That ritual will be repeated in countless media representations. Innumerable duplications of the same motif assured that the significance of the deed got across to the public. It was the repetition of the photographs of ritual homecomings that created the symbolic power of the cosmonauts. The significance of their deed was on the surface of the Earth. The cosmos was left in murkiness.

Disenchantment

The new utopia was soon to disappear. The inability of the Communist Party to fulfil its promises became apparent almost immediately after the adoption of the programme. It failed in almost every respect (Taubman, 2003: 519–523). The world witnessed the USA's victory in the race to the moon in 1969, but the disillusionment in the Soviet Union became obvious years before that. Khrushchev was removed from power three years after Gagarin's flight and all utopian references gradually vanished from the political rhetoric, as the ideology rapidly became something quite different.[9] The bright utopian future gave way to an era of stagnation. The new Soviet society turned to its past achievements, foremost among them the victory in what in Russia is termed the Great Patriotic War. As Svetlana Boym has pointed out, by the end of Brezhnev's era, the Soviet Union had enormous difficulty sustaining its commitment to space travel, not only because it lacked the necessary resources but because the intimate connection between technological development, state ideology and the utopian myth had been broken (Boym and Bartos, 2001: 84). Cosmonauts, those daredevils of space, gradually fossilized into political monuments. The scientific optimism of the early 1960s, describing a utopian vision of a future Earth, stands in poignant contrast to the disillusionment of later decades.

Conclusion

Marshall Berman has commented on modernity in the following words: 'To be modern is to find ourselves in an environment that promises us adventure, power, joy, growth, transformation of ourselves and the world – and at the same time, that threatens to destroy everything we have, everything we know, everything we are' (Berman, 1982: 15).

The Soviet space programme was a complex hybrid. It was shamelessly used by the Khrushchevian propaganda machinery, deeply connected to the military industry and to the arms race. At the same time, it had roots in and connotations for utopian cosmic dreaming that were profoundly apolitical. In this sense it was very much a modern phenomenon, sharing the basic notion that modern life is radically contradictory at its base.

The Soviet achievements in the field of space exploration resonated in numerous areas of Soviet political, mythological and popular culture. This was the first time that the Soviet Union had led the way in a totally new technological sphere – until October 1957 the Soviet Union had been striving to catch up with the West in technological competition. Now it had not only caught up with the West but had overtaken it. The impact on national self-esteem was obvious, and the propaganda value of space flight was enormous. The Soviet propaganda machinery eloquently mixed cosmic utopianism with patriotic sentiments. Space was an influential emblem of modernization, the Promethean victory of Man over nature, freedom from gravity and from past horrors, and the promise of a bright, shimmering future. Widely published photographs showed cosmonauts who had already travelled beyond the horizon, to the bright future. Indeed, space was a symbol of utopia landing on Earth, as Peter Vail and Aleksandr Genis put it (Vail and Genis, 1988: 3–12). But in the midst of the Cold War policies and the technological utopianism so closely attached to the space race, the photographs that I have studied clearly show that visually it was not the *machine* that was celebrated. It was the man who had broken the barriers of Earth's gravity and survived, the cosmonaut, utopian hero and modern man.

This cosmonaut was a radically new kind of hero in Soviet history. There had been heroes who had commented on the future throughout Soviet history but the materials examined here clearly show that the heroic cosmonaut was a more complex figure than meets the eye; and it was specifically through visual representations that this complexity was heralded. Through visual representations of the time we can discover a man possessed of all the virtues, a true hero with all the utopian qualifications needed for the future. To use Reinhart Koselleck's phrase, the images of space were 'pregnant with the future' (Koselleck, 1985: 75, see also Kohonen, 2005). The photographs that I have studied do not offer the satisfaction of a single narrative, but leave open a maze of narrative possibilities and hints of probable histories. Furthermore, these illustrations show the *creative* side of propaganda – power could work in ways that were inventive, and not only repressive.[10]

The beginning of the space age renewed interest in utopianism. This spirit is hard to imagine in our age of scepticism, since utopianism is so unreasonable (see Parker, this volume). How could anyone have seriously believed in a radiant future, totally different from the chaotic past and miserable present? The problem of understanding this dream is all the greater because of the distance between the utopian vision and actual Soviet reality. It is tempting to dismiss the vision as simply deception and camouflage. It cannot finally be dismissed, however. It was part of most people's everyday experience in the 1960s. The Soviet citizen might or might not have believed in this, but could not have been ignorant of the fact that it was promised (See also Bonnell, 1997).

Today we know that in the Soviet Union the anticipated year 1980 resembled the dystopian society depicted in Orwell's book *Nineteen Eighty Four* far more than the brilliant future promised in the third CPSU party programme (Orwell, [1949] 1978). The intercontinental ballistic missile had been created alongside space technology – or, depending on your angle of vision, the space programme had been a mere side effect of military ambition. There may have been an agreement about a free exchange of scientific information as part of the IGY, but there was never any plan to exchange information about the prime requisite for putting the satellites into orbit: powerful and dependable rocket engines (Wilson, 1961: 72). Soon after the first human space missions, as if a logical outcome of this development, technological progress and political tension came to a head in the Cuban missile crisis. This moment is often regarded as the point at which the Cold War came closest to escalating into a nuclear war. Thus ended the cosmic utopia of universal brotherhood, before it even got started.

The photographs that I have studied are pictures from a forgotten future, the remains of a failed utopian project. There is a sense of melancholy in them that comes from this disillusionment. They are photographs of the past, not the way it was, but of a past the way it *could have been*. The study of this kind of material might be useful for an alternative history that includes conjectures and contradictory visions and possibilities. The symbolic use of space exploration was equally as powerful as the scientific one.

Sputnik, the '*fellow traveller*', as the name translates into English, was about the size of a beach ball and took 98 minutes to orbit the Earth. This was not a spectacular phenomenon; still, the satellite was visible to the naked eye, like a steadily moving star, several times a night.[11] This gave people their first real impression of the globe. The length of the flight was the length of a feature film, one and a half hours – a measure of time that was comprehensible to everyone (Anttila, 1989: 90–91). So small is our planet, so easily conquered, covered, encompassed; so fragile and alone in space. Seeing our globe against the immensity and vastness of space, there could have been an opportunity for man to discover the essential unity of all mankind. This, I think, was one of the purposes of the International Geophysical Year.

Archival material

RGANTD: The Russian State Archive of Scientific and Technical Documents, Moscow (Rossiskij gosudarstvenyi arhiv nauchno-tehnicheskoi dokumentatsii)

Sources

Bolshaja Sovetskaja Entsiklopedya, 1954. Moskva: Gosudarstvennoe Nauchnoe Izdatelstvo.
Helsingin Sanomat 13.4.1961. Helsinki: Sanoma Osakeyhtiö
Krokodil 1957–1961. Moskva: Pravda
Ogonyok, 1961–1969. Moskva: Pravda
Programma KPSS 1961, Moskva: Pravda

Notes

1 This article is a part of a larger ongoing research project. For my doctoral dissertation I am studying photographic representations of space in the Soviet Union in the first decade of the so-called space age.

2 According to Richard Stites no genuine science fiction was published between 1931 and 1957. This seems not to be entirely true. For example *Tehnika – Molodezhi* and *Znanie-Sila* published space-related articles regularly in the 1940s. (See eg Kosmicheskij polyot 1941; Pavlov 1935; Pokrovskij 1944; *Polyot na Mars* 1940) There were also books that could be counted as science fiction or popular astronautics all through the 1930s, 1940s and early 1950s (eg Ivan Yefremov's *Zveznye korabli* was firstly published in *Znanie-Sila* 1947. See also Shternfeld 1949). Stites is right, though, in his claim that SF 'as a whole was greatly reduced in output, narrowed in focus, and lowered in quality'. (Stites, 1989, 236)

3 Luna I was actually targeted at the moon, but missed due to an error in navigation. The media turned the failure into a triumph: the Soviet Union, it proclaimed, had succeeded in launching an artificial planet. Luna I still circles the sun in an orbit situated between the Earth and Mars.

4 Strelka and Belka were extremely popular. They had even a minor role in the earthly Cold War aggravations: one of the puppies of the dog Belka was given as a gift to Kennedy's daughter as a token of friendship – a good example of Nikita Khrushchev's sense of humor.

5 Translated by George Reavey, 1963.

6 The cosmonauts themselves were a generation that grew up without fathers, so in this sense these photographs also illustrate hope for a better future without war –a sentiment that was more or less universal in the 1950s and early 1960s. (See eg *Ogonyok* 34/62, *Ogonyok* 43/64; also RGANTD 1–15266, 1–15268, 2–413)

7 For example Sergei Korolev, head engineer of the whole Soviet space program, got the media-attention he deserved posthumously in January 1966. (*Ogonyok* 4/66) Before that he was known to the public only under the mysterious pseudonym 'Chief Designer'.

8 This photograph was not published at the time. It was not politically explosive, but perhaps too human.

9 Even inside the Lenin mausoleum the utopian expectation of Lenin's actual resurrection faded in 1973 as the Fedorovian version of the sarcophagus was superseded by a bulletproof version, designed by sculptor Nikolai Tomsky.

10 This is of course very Foucaultian thought, drawing from the assumption that power is a creative force that determines the relationships between people, institutions, and concepts. (Foucault, 1990: passim.)

11 It was, in fact the rocket of the satellite that was visible to the naked eye. Sputnik itself was too dim to see without binoculars – a fact not known at the time.

References

Anttila, L., (1989), 'In Search of the Earth', in Synnyt – Sources of Contemporary Art, Helsinki: Museum of Contemporary Art: 79–96.

Barabashov, N. P., Mikhailov, A. A., Lipsky, Y. N., (eds) (1961), *Atlas of the Other Side of the Moon*, Oxford: Pergamon Press.

Barry, W. P., (2000), 'Sputnik and the Creation of Soviet Space Industry', in Launius, R. D., (2000), (ed.), Reconsidering Sputnik. Forty Years Since the Soviet Satellite, Amsterdam: Harwood Academic Publishers: 95–116.

Bendavid-Val, L., (1999), Propaganda and Dreams. Photographing the 1930s in the USSR and in the US, New York: Edition Stemmle.

Berman, M., (1982), *All That is Solid Melts into Air: The Experience of Modernity*, New York: Simon and Schuster.

Bonnell, V. E., (1997), Iconography of Power. Soviet Political Posters under Lenin and Stalin, Berkeley: University California Press.

Boym, S. and Bartos, A., (2001), Kosmos: Rembrances of the Future, Princeton: Architectural Press.

Brothers, C., (1997), *War and Photography*, London: Routledge.

Buck-Morss, S., (2000), Dreamworld and Catastrofe. The Passing of Mass Utopia in East and West, Cambridge: The MIT Press.

Bulkeley, R., (2000), 'The Sputniks and the IGY', in Launius, Roger D., 2000. (ed.) Reconsidering Sputnik, Forty Years Since the Soviet Satellite, Amsterdam: Harwood Academic Publishers: 125–160

Fedorov, N. F., (1906), Filosofija Obshchego Dela. Stati, Mysli I Pisma, Tom I. Vernyj: Moskva.

Fedorov, N. F., (1913), Filosofija Obshchego Dela. Stati, Mysli I Pisma, Tom II. Vernyj: Moskva.

Fitzpatrick, S., (1999), Everyday Stalinism. Ordinary Life in Extraordinary Times: Soviet Russia in the 1930s, New York: Oxford University Press.

Foucault, M., (1990), History of Sexuality, New York: Vintage Books.

Geppert, A. C. T., (2008), Space Personae, Cosmopolitan Networks of Peripheral Knowledge, in Journal of Modern European History, Vol 6. 2008/2. München: C. H. Beck: 262–286.

Gorin, P. A., (2000), 'Rising from the Cradle. Soviet Perceptions of Space Flight Before Sputnik', in Launius, R. D., (ed.) (2000), Reconsidering Sputnik. Forty Years Since the Soviet Satellite, Amsterdam: Harwood Academic Publishers: 11–42.

Harford, J. J., (2000), Korolev's Triple Play: Sputniks 1, 2, and 3, in Launius, R. D., (ed.) (2000), Reconsidering Sputnik. Forty Years Since the Soviet Satellite, Amsterdam: Harwood Academic Publishers: 73–94.

Holz, W., (1993), Allegory and Iconography in Socialist Realist Painting, in Bown, M. C., (ed.) (1993), Art of the Soviets. Painting, Sculpture and Architecture in a One-Party State 1917–1992, Manchester: Manchester University Press: 73–85.

Josephson, P. R., (1990), 'Rockets, Reactors, and Soviet Culture', in Graham, L. R. (ed.) Science and Soviet Social Order, London: Harvard University Press: 168–191.

Kenez, P., (1985), The Birth of the Propaganda State. Soviet Methods of Mass Mobilization 1917–1929, Cambridge: Cambridge University Press.

Kohonen, I., (2005), 'Gagarinin kengännauhat ja muita reittejä neuvostotodellisuuteen.' Synteesi 4/05. Helsinki. Suomen Semiotiikan Seura: 38–49.

Koselleck, R., (1985), *Futures Past: On the Semantics of Historical Time*, Cambridge, MA: The MIT Press.

Kosmicheskij polyot, (1941), in *Tehnika – Molodezhi* 6/1941 Moskva: VLKSM Zk Detizdat (np).

Kozhenikov, V. A., (1906), 'Predlislovye', in Fedorov, N. F. (ed.) (1906), Filosofija Obshchego Dela. Stati, Mysli i Pisma, Tom I. Moskva: Vernyj: i–iv.

Kuusinen, O.-V., (1960), Marxismi-leninismin perusteet, Petroskoi: Karjalan ASNT: n valtion kustannusliike.

Lane, C., (1981), The Rites of Rulers. Ritual in Industrial Society – the Soviet Case, Cambridge: Cambridge Univiversity Press.

Launius, R. D., (ed.) (2000), Reconsidering Sputnik. Forty Years Since the Soviet Satellite, Amsterdam: Harwood Academic Publishers.

Maddrell, P., (2006), Spying on Science. Western Intelligence in Divided Germany 1945–1961, New York: Oxford University Press.

McNeal, R. H., (ed.) (1974), Resolutions and Decisions of the Communist Party of the Soviet Union. Vol. 4 The Khrushchev Years 1953–1964, Toronto: University of Toronto Press.

Orwell, G., [1949] (1978), *Vuonna 1984*, Porvoo: WSOY.

Pavlov, A., (1935), Kosmicheskij reijs, in Tehnika – Molodezhi 5/1935. Moskva: VLKSM Zk Detizdat (np)

Peoples, C., (2008), 'Sputnik and 'skill thinking' revisited: technological determinism in American responses to the Soviet missile threat', in Cold War History Vol. 8 No. 1 Feb. 2008: 55–75.

Polyot na M., (1940), in Tehnika – Molodezhi 12/1940 Moskva: VLKSM Zk Detizdat (np)

Pokrovskij, G., (1944), Novyi sputnik zemli, in Tehnika – Molodezhi 2/1944. Moskva: VLKSM Zk Detizdat. (np)

Porter, C., (1990), 'Introduction', in Korotich (ed.), The Best of 'Ogonyok.' The New Journalism of Glasnost, London: Heinenman: 2–6.

Programma KPSS (1961), Moskva: *Pravda.*

Reid, S. E., (1994), 'Photography in the Thaw' in Art Journal, Vol. 53, No. 2, Contemporary Russian Art Photography (Summer, 1994): 33–39

Renkama, J., (2006), Ideology and Challenges of Political Libralisation in the USSR 1957–1961, Helsinki: SKS.

Shternfeld, A., (1949), Polyot v Mirovoe Prostranstvo, Moskva: Gosudarstvennoe Izdatelstvo Tehniko-teoreticheskoij literatury.

Soobshchenie TASS, in: *Pravda: Organ tsentralnogo komiteta KPSS* 4.10.1957, Moskva: Pravda: 1.

Starr, S. F., (1978), Melnikov: Solo Architect in a Mass Society, Princeton: Princeton University.

Stites, R., (1989), Revolutionary Dreams: Utopian Vision and Experimental Life in the Russian Revolution, New York: Oxford University Press.

Sumiala-Seppänen, J. and Stocchetti, M., (2007), Father of the nation or arch-terrorist? Media ritual and images of the death of Yasser Arafat, in *Media, Culture & Society*, Vol 29 (2007): 2. London: Sage: 336–343.

Taubman, W., (2003), Kruschechev. The Man and His Era, London: Simon and Schuster.

Trachtenberg, A., (1989), Reading American Photographs. Images as History. Mathew Brady to Walker Evans, New York: Hill and Wang.

Tsiolkovsky, K., (no date). *The Call of the Cosmos*, Moscow: Foreign Languages Publishing House.

Vail, P. A. G., (1988), 60-ye: Mir sovetskogo Cheloveka, USA: Ardis.

Vihavainen, T., (2003), O. W. Kuusinen ja Neuvostoliiton ideologinen kriisi vuosina 1957–64, Helsinki: Suomalaisen Kirjallisuuden Seura.

Wilson, T. J., (1961), IGY the Year of the New Moons, London: Michael Joseph.

Winter, F. H., (1990), Rockets into Space, Cambridge, MA: Harvard University Press.

Yegorov, B. F., (2007), Rossiskie Utopii. Istoricheskij Putevoditel., St. Petersburg: Isskustvo – SPB.

Yefremov, I., (1947), Zveznye korabli, Moskva: Vsesojusnoe obshchestvo, 'Znanie'.

Yevtushenko, Y., [1961] (1963), *Olen vaiti ja huudan*, Helsinki: Kirjayhtymä.

Zamyatin, Y., [1920] (1959), *Me*, Jyväskylä: Gummerrus.

Zenkovsky, V. V., (1953), A History of Russian Philosophy, vol. two, London: Routledge.

The archaeology of space exploration

Alice Gorman

Introduction

Since the Second World War, the exploration and commercial development of space have created an increasingly complex material record of places and objects. In 1947, four rocket ranges were established in Algeria, Australia, the USSR and the USA, the first generation of Cold War facilities where the production of missiles also created the capability of penetrating outer space. In 1957, the launch of Sputnik 1 heralded the beginning of the orbital age. In 1969, humans first set foot on the surface of another celestial body when the Apollo 11 mission landed on the Moon, leaving behind a flag, bootprints, and a myriad of other material remains. After 50 years of rocket launches, there are now more than 10,000 pieces of human-manufactured material in Earth orbit alone.

These places and objects have been extensively documented and are represented in space museums across the world; but until recently they have not been considered as an archaeological record. To do so raises a number of questions: what can the artefacts of the space age tell us that the documentary record cannot? How has space exploration altered or created landscapes on Earth and in space? How do people interact with the artefacts and landscapes of space exploration? And, perhaps most importantly, what are the heritage values of this archaeological record?

For many, the history of space exploration is also that of the 'Space Race': a narrative that emphasizes the adversarial relationship of the Cold War superpowers and downplays international collaboration and the contributions of 'Third' and 'Fourth' world people. In this chapter I propose to sidestep the 'Space Race' approach and examine the archaeological record of space exploration with particular reference to launch facilities in Australia and Algeria, and early amateur satellites such as Australis Oscar V.

The material culture of the space age

Space travel begins on Earth, where the principle classes of space sites include launch areas, research and development facilities, and ground stations. There are also places on the continents and the bottom of the ocean where human artefacts, such as the Mir space station, have fallen from orbit. Earth orbit itself contains millions of objects from the micromillimetre size to massive satellites weighing thousands of kilogrammes; and spacecraft orbit the Sun and several planets in the solar system. Of the celestial bodies, the Moon, Mars, Venus, Titan and the asteroids carry the traces of crewed and robotic landings.

Two factors have impeded the recognition of this material as amenable to analysis in the same way as other material culture: its relatively recent date, and what had been called 'technological somnambulism' (Winner, 1977: 324): the assumption that technologies are culturally neutral, developing under their own imperatives divorced from social forces (see also Lubar, 1993: 211). This traditional ontological division between technology and society, 'between the moral purposes of human beings and the instrumental work of technology' (Brown, 2007: 331), is a disjunction through which archaeologists can examine the interaction of humans and the matériel of space.

In the absence of written documents and living memories, archaeologists study artefacts, spatial and chronological relationships and landscapes to make hypotheses about past human behaviour, inferring the intangibles of social relations and beliefs from the physical remains of both human bodies and objects. Closer to the present, historical archaeologists use material culture to understand the lives of those excluded from documentary records dominated by literate and political elites, for reasons of race, class, gender and ethnicity, in the period of European colonial expansion, from the 1400s until the 1900s (eg Hall and Silliman, 2006; Orser, 1996).

More recently, archaeologists have also been considering how to approach the 'contemporary past' which coincides with living memory (Buchli and Lucas, 2001), looking at World War I and II, the Cold War, ephemeral processes like protests, and the 'conquest' of outer space (eg Cocroft and Thomas, 2004; Gorman, 2005a; Saunders, 2004, Schofield *et al.*, 2002; Schofield *et al.*, 2003; Spenneman, 2004; O'Leary, 2006). As Schofield has commented, several factors mitigate against comprehensive knowledge of the contemporary past: its very familiarity undermines its perceived value; military and commercial secrecy prevent public access to information, and a rapid rate of change means that 20th century technology may be less understood than life inside an Iron Age hill fort (Schofield, pers. comm.). Given this situation, archaeological methodologies have the potential to illuminate aspects of the culture of space exploration that are unremembered or undocumented.

An archaeological approach to the material culture of the space age employs the same approaches used to investigate the far distant past: chronological and technological trajectories, deep time spans, the influences of climate and landscape, sources of raw material, cultural exchange and cultural contact. By doing this, we can contextualize cultures of space travel against the background of broader human engagements with technology and the environment.

Alternative narratives of spacefaring

Much of the development of space exploration has coincided with and been driven by the Cold War; the Space Race is inextricably intertwined with the Arms Race. The pervasiveness of this trope obscures other motivations and directions in the history of space exploration, such as the scientific exploration of the solar system, the participation of non-spacefaring nations and Indigenous people, international co-operation in space, and amateur space initiatives. Running parallel with the Space Race narrative are others which draw our attention to different kinds of objects and places (Gorman, 2005a).

Two of the early Cold War launch sites, Woomera in Australia and Colomb-Béchar-Hammaguir in Algeria, are no longer in the mainstream of space exploration. They represent the early period of military space development, before telecommunications opened space to civil and commercial enterprises. They were also technological enclaves in colonized territories, where high technology came face-to-face with the Stone Age (Gorman, 2005b). Neither Algeria nor Australia became a spacefaring nation with its own launch capacity; but the resources provided by these colonies were crucial in the development of the European Space Agency, a contribution which is often overlooked. But in addition to their role in developing rocket and satellite technology, these launch sites were places of cultural contact between locals, Indigenous people and the new sciences of space.

Fire across the desert: launch sites in Algeria and Australia

In 1947, two years after the end of WW II hostilities, those nations which had been fortunate enough to secure the physical remnants and personnel of the German V2 program established rocket ranges with the initial purpose of developing nuclear missiles. The US began its launch programme from the White Sands Proving Ground in New Mexico; the USSR built a vast range which crossed the border into Kazakhstan at Kapustin Yar; in Australia, a joint project with the UK saw the creation of the massive Woomera Prohibited Area. France utilized its colonial territories in Algeria.

This first generation of launch sites had a common thread: the influence of German design from Peenemunde and Mittelbau, and a location in desert/steppe regions, far from populated centres. Rocket and missile tests had a high failure rate; and metropolitan populations could not be put at risk from explosions and crashes. Moreover, in order to test a missile designed to reach another continent, a very long firing range was needed. Neither France nor Britain could meet these conditions within their national borders.

Algeria: une rencontre 'lunaire'

In 1903 the French General Lyautey, charged with establishing order in the frontier zone, established a military post just outside the Saharan oasis of

Béchar on the Moroccan border, to control frequent border disputes and subdue local resistance. The oasis was a rich date cultivation area with well-fed aquifers (Moyal, 1959: 331). Two years later, the railroad from Oran reached the settlement, now called Colomb-Béchar (Trout, 1970). The discovery of coal at nearby Kenadza, after World War I, led to further development in the region.

The presence of existing military and civil infrastructure, as well as water, reliable weather, clear and dry conditions, and relative low population, made Colomb-Béchar an attractive base for France's first long range weapons testing range. The Centre Interarmées d'Essais d'Engins Spéciaux (CIEES) was established there in 1947. Soon, hundreds of men were stationed around the oasis, and accommodation, administrative buildings, workshops, test facilities, research offices, power plants, communications and transport networks, hangars, cinetheodolites, tracking antennae, and launch pads sprang up in the formerly featureless desert (Ducarre, 1959; Penot, 2000: 16).

B0 was the first launch area to be constructed, intended for light missiles (Wade, 2008). From 1949, the B1 launch pad for heavier missiles was in operation (Wade, 2008). The Véronique sounding rocket was approved by the French Government in 1949 (Penot, 2000: 9) and required more extensive facilities: these were constructed at Hammaguir (Hamada du Guir), 120 km southwest of Colomb-Béchar. Hammaguir was upgraded in the late 1950s to accommodate ballistic missile launches, with four new launch areas: Blandine and Bacchus were used for sounding rockets, Béatrice was used for surface-to-air missile tests and the Cora rocket, part of the cooperative Europa program in the 1960s, and Brigitte was assigned to the satellite launch series Pierres Précieuses. In 1965, the satellite Astérix 1 was launched on the Diamant rocket from Hammaguir (Figure 1), and three small geodetic satellites were launched in early 1967.

Figure 1: *The Diamant launch pad at Hammaguir. Image courtesy of CNES/L. Laidet.*

The growth of the rocket range reflected international changes in the focus of rocket technology, from missiles to orbital space, as the International Geophysical Year of 1957–58 approached. But there was much more going on in the desert. Colomb-Béchar-Hammaguir was a community of engineers and scientists who imprinted the infrastructure of space on the desert environment. Redfield (1996: 252) has commented that space technology is often represented as universal, modern and placeless: but in every location, the new space migrants had to adapt to local conditions and carry out the activities of everyday life.

Diversions on the range included open-air film screenings, at which spectators could look above them to see the passing of satellites (Marcel Lebaron, quoted in Penot, 2000: 19). For recreation, people roamed the dunes, marvelling at the tenuous life of the desert and collecting flaked stone points from the Late Stone Age (Lebaron in Penot, 2000: 20). To Marcel Lebaron, who joined the sounding rocket program at Hammaguir in 1965, the Sahara seemed as alien as a lunar landscape (Lebaron in Penot, 2000: 19).

Conflict with France had been almost continuous since the annexation of Algeria in 1843. Having served with the French military during the Algerian War of Independence (1954–1962), Lebaron regarded Algerian Arabs as the enemy. His perceptions altered entirely as he made friends with those at Hammaguir. There were other surprises too. One day, while exploring the desert, he encountered a Tuareg camp, where he was offered desert truffles, and photographed the camels. He conceptualized it as culture contact: 'Une rencontre 'lunaire' avec quelqu'un d'un autre monde' (A lunar encounter with someone from another world; Lebaron in Penot, 2000: 20).

The Tuareg were a loose confederation of Berber-speaking tribes who had controlled the trans-Saharan trade routes for two millennia prior to French invasion, which they resisted vigorously (Rodd, 1926). The arrival of French roads and rail radically disrupted this trade monopoly, and Tuareg lives were further impacted by a policy of forced sedentism, aimed at controlling Tuareg movements and preventing uprisings. High security military establishments required political stability, which was far from the case in Algeria. In 1958 and 1959, the Doui-Menia group who lived in the Colomb-Béchar region were confined to a 'tent village' surrounded by barbed-wire fences. Air traffic from the bases at Colomb-Béchar and Hammaguir ensured that they were under constant surveillance (Belaid, 2008). Despite this, Lebaron's encounter demonstrates that Tuareg people continued to resist French control and move freely around the launch polygons.

In 1967, the CIEES facilities were handed to the Algerian government as part of the Evian Accords. Equipment was dismantled or destroyed (Azoulay, 2006). By this time France had established Kourou in French Guiana, and presumably much that was usable found its way to the new launch site, soon to become the base for the Ariane rocket. There was no question of equipping Algeria to establish its own space programme; and after only twenty years of launch activity, Colomb-Béchar-Hammaguir was abandoned.

The red sands of Woomera

By contrast, the Woomera rocket range in Australia resembled a Martian landscape with its red sands (there is even a mock-up of a Martian surface in South Australia; Clarke *et al.*, 2004). Many saw it as 'one of the greatest stretches of uninhabited wasteland on earth, created by God specifically for rockets. . . .' (Southall, 1962: 3). In 1946, the UK government approached Australia to set up the Anglo-Australian Joint Defence Program (Morton, 1989). The headquarters for the resultant Weapons Research Establishment (WRE) was a former munitions factory at Salisbury, on the outskirts of Adelaide. The actual rocket range extended from the rangehead area, 450 km northwest of Adelaide, into Western Australia, enclosing an area larger than the UK and containing the Woomera Village, nine launch areas, workshops, instrumentation buildings, hangars, tracking and meteorological stations, and roads where none had existed before.

Launches from Woomera included a wide range of missiles from the anti-aircraft Sea Dart to the Blue Streak ICBM, sounding rockets like Long Tom and Skylark, and Europa, a joint European vehicle aimed at launching a satellite. The Europa did not succeed in its mission, but in 1967, WRESAT 1, an Australian-designed scientific satellite, was launched on a Redstone rocket donated by the USA.

Although the desert was supposedly empty, the evidence of Aboriginal occupation was everywhere. An early reconnaissance mission in 1947 found that:

Lying on the ground, here, there and everywhere, were tens of thousands of artefacts, discarded knives and spear-points of flaked and chipped stone, dropped by unencumbered generations of black men, and one had to accept the artefacts at their face value. Where one found artefacts, one found water (Southall, 1962: 41).

Woomera village was like 'an oasis in the wilderness' (Chambers, 2000: 20), but the rocket range itself was far from deserted. The area around Woomera was the traditional country of the Kokatha, and the entire Woomera Prohibited Area crossed the country of many Aboriginal groups.

Since the 1800s, Aboriginal people had been alienated from their country by the usual array of colonial processes; they were considered to be a 'dying race' (Gorman, 2005a; Bates, 1938). Residents of Woomera, like the colonial administrators of the preceding century, were fascinated by the culture they saw themselves as superseding. In the 1960s, a Natural History Society was established at Woomera. They organized guest speakers such as Norman Tindale, one of the founders of archaeology in Australia, and undertook expeditions to the gibber desert to collect geological, biological and cultural objects, such as stone tools and artefacts like the woomera or spear-thrower after which the range was named. Souvenirs of Aboriginal inspiration were also purchased by visitors, often making their way back to the UK and other countries (eg Chambers, 2000: 6). While Aboriginal people were regarded as having passed on, leaving the way open for the Space Age, 'half-caste' girls were employed as domestic staff at Woomera, and Native Patrol Officers kept in touch with all those still living in the desert in order to warn them of impending launches (Morton, 1989). At the Giles Meteorological station far in the desert, a fringe camp sprang up: both whites and blacks were sharing the same water resources (Morton, 1989, Gorman, 2009). The 'Space Age' had not replaced the 'Stone Age'; the avatars of both were shaping a new kind of landscape where the wreckage of a rocket might lie undisturbed amidst a stone tool scatter, while the children or grandchildren of those who knapped the tools camped nearby.

Woomera is still used today for various launches; but Australia is no longer a spacefaring state. When the demise of the Apollo missions ended Australia's involvement in the US space programme, and the Europa rocket was moved to Kourou in 1970, Woomera went into decline. Much of the Europa material was sent to French Guiana, and bitterness at the end of Australian space dreams resulted in infrastructure being unnecessarily destroyed (Morton, 1989; Figure 2). As security diminished on the range, Kokatha people were able to re-assert their ties to country through Native Title claims and the resumption of ceremonial activities in places formerly closed to them (Andrew Starkey, pers. comm.).

Cultural exchange on the range

Despite their different imperial origins, the Algerian launch sites and Woomera have much in common. Both had camels (the Bactrian camel having been introduced to Australia in the 1880s; Finlayson, 1943: 107); and 'nomads' in the Tuareg and Aboriginal people who remained on their country. The launch sites were oases of high technology in hostile environments, but the high security boundaries were permeable: space scientists interacted with the environment and the locals. One aspect of cultural exchange was the traditional colonial activity of collecting the artefacts of the vanquished race. In the other direction, we know little about how the presence of this new technology affected the existing technologies of Aboriginal and Tuareg people.

Within the same landscape, we can interrogate spatial relationships between the location of space infrastructure and the places and artefacts left by the non-European inhabitants as they adapted to the imposed barriers of high security

Figure 2: *Europa launch pad, Woomera. Author's photo.*

military facilities. Material culture was used to survive and adapt in different ways for both Aboriginal and Tuareg groups in the desert, and the Cold War migrants. Domination and resistance, themes of archaeological enquiry at sites such as plantations, penal settlements and internment camps, can be explored through the archaeological record (eg Miller *et al.*, 1989). Principally, the artefacts of everyday life and their distribution on these rocket ranges can tell us not just what people said they did, but what they actually did.

The basis of the technology and design derived from the common heritage of the V2 in both places, and both bequeathed material and technology to the Kourou launch site in French Guiana, established in 1964. Following this journey enables us to examine the adoption of national, international and transnational technology in a context of global capitalist economies dating from the industrial revolution. The Algerian and Australian rocket ranges, however, can also tell the story of Indigenous interactions with space in common landscapes, enabling a far more complex understanding of the social significance of space material culture than a focus on technology alone would allow.

Just as Indigenous people rarely figure in the popular and scholarly presentation of space history, the contribution of amateurs and enthusiasts to high technology in the Cold War is frequently relegated to the sidelines. Nevertheless, before the development of the V2 rocket, with its obvious military applications, in the late 1930s, rocket science was dominated by amateur groups and isolated researchers like Robert Goddard in the US and Konstantin Tsiolkovsky in the USSR. The adoption of rocket technology by the Allied powers following World War II did nothing to deter amateur organizations from pursuing their dreams of space travel with any means at their disposal. The materials and approaches they used provide another avenue for exploring the archaeology of space.

Kitchen satellites and space hitchhikers: amateur space programmes

Space technology has not only been pursued at the level of national space agencies or governments. From the time Sputnik 1 started sending its distinctive signal towards Earth, the amateur radio community was keen to participate in the action. Despite the nationalist and ideological motivations for satellite launch, the reality was that anyone with the right optical or receiving equipment could track satellites and intercept their telemetry. Space was also being conquered by passionate individuals who wanted simply to communicate with each other.

Radio hams in space: Project OSCAR

In 1958, a group of radio hams on the west coast of the USA formed Project OSCAR (Orbiting Satellites Carrying Amateur Radio), initiating a tradition of volunteer, international space participation that continues to this day (Baker

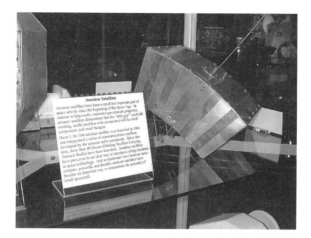

Figure 3: *OSCAR 1. SETI League Photo, used by permission.*

and Jansson, 1994). In 1961, only four years after Sputnik 1, the tiny 4.5 kg OSCAR 1 satellite left Earth on an Agena rocket from Vandenberg Air Force Base in the US, re-entering the Earth's atmosphere approximately 6 weeks later (Figure 3). It was the first secondary payload to be ejected into a separate orbit. Oscar II followed in 1962, and OSCAR III and IV in 1965. The scientific missions of these satellites were facilitated by the return of data from volunteers across the world: for OSCAR I, more than 570 people from 28 countries participated.

OSCAR III was an active telecommunications satellite, carrying a transponder designed to receive uplink signals and re-transmit them to enable radio hams to communicate. Until this time, telecommunications satellites had been passive, mere reflectors of radio signals. OSCAR III was in progress at the time that Telstar 1, the first commercial active telecommunications satellite, was being planned, and according to one story, the Telstar team were not best pleased at the prospect of being beaten into space by an amateur satellite (Baker and Jansson, 1994). In the end, they had nothing to worry about: Telstar 1 was launched in 1962, three years before OSCAR III achieved orbit.

Australis Oscar V

In 1965, the Melbourne University Astronautical Society were already tracking Project Oscar satellites, as well as US and Soviet lunar probes (Hammer and Mace, 1970: 2) when they decided to make their own contribution. The team was led by physics student Richard Tonkin, with Les Jenkins, a senior electronics technician with the CSIRO, Peter Hammer, who was studying the physics of the ionopshere, Owen Mace, studying infrared astronomy, and Paul Dunn, a computer expert (Goode, 1970; Atkinson, 1970). Other collaborators included the Wireless Institute of Australia and the Melbourne University Union, who provided funding; local electrical companies who donated equipment (Goode, 1970); and various Melbourne University clubs and societies (Jones, 1970: 45).

By 1967 they had designed and constructed a satellite aimed at testing the suitability of the 10 m amateur radio band as a downlink frequency for satellite transponders, and a passive magnetic attitude stabilization scheme (Baker and Jansson, 1994). A high frequency transmitter would provide data about the ionosphere. The satellite was a tiny aluminium box weighing 17.7 kg, with dimensions 30.4 × 43.1 × 15.2 cm, powered by a battery and thermally insulated. The antennae were made from spring steel carpenters' tape so they could be wrapped around the satellite to extend on ejection (Jones, 1970). Australis Oscar V was the first amateur satellite to be remote-controlled and to have a complete telemetry system (Hammer and Mace, 1970: 2).

Once again, an amateur satellite threatened the professionals: Australis Oscar V looked as if it might become the first Australian-designed satellite to reach orbit, ahead of WRESAT 1. It was shipped to California in June 1967 but the launch was repeatedly delayed (Atkinson, 1970). By 1969 the Project Australis team despaired of achieving a launch. The foundation of AMSAT (the Radio Amateur Satellite Corporation) from the original Project OSCAR group and an east coast group in 1969 provided impetus for the project: the newly formed corporation made the launch of Australis Oscar V its priority (Hammer and Mace, 1970: 2).

Finally, Australis Oscar V was launched in 1970 on a Thor-Delta rocket from the Vandenburg Air Force Base, piggy-backed onto a TIROS-M weather satellite. It was the first OSCAR satellite to be launched by NASA. To enable tracking, orbital predictions and reporting information were disseminated by radio announcements and newsletters (OSCAR News, 1967). Twenty-seven countries sent in data from tracking Australis Oscar V to contribute to its scientific mission.

According to USSPACECOM data, Australis Oscar V is still in orbit, although its telemetry ceased after 46 days as the batteries ran out. An engineering prototype of Australis Oscar V is in the Scienceworks Museum in Melbourne (James, 1992: 319).

Suburban space: Australis Oscar V ground segments

Like all orbital objects, Australis Oscar V is associated with a range of terrestrial places. They include 'a particular refrigerator and a famous Carlton oven' (Jones, 1970: 45), and a shack in the garden of a house in the Melbourne suburb of Highett, where the team listened to the launch via a radio link (Goode, 1970).

Subsequent tracking of Australis Oscar V took place from a station on the roof of the physics building at Melbourne University (Hammer and Mace, 1970: 2). According to an unattributable newstory in the Museum of Victoria's archives, the tracking station consisted of old car parts, second-hand electric motors, and pieces of an air conditioning plant.

In the Canberra suburb of Torrens, Dr C. Rann, a chemist from the National Biological Standards Laboratory, built a tracking station specifically for Australis Oscar V, with the help of Mr E. Penikis and Mr G. Hover from the Australian National University (Bickel, 1970). They worked for six months to construct an automatically controlled antenna with 50 ft high aerials. Much of it was also made from scavenged junk, including the rear axle of a 10-ton truck, and aircraft propeller pitch motors. NASA lent them two signal converters (Bickel, 1970).

This pattern was by no means unusual. The success of OSCAR I's 'bargain basement' approach to procurement and management provided the philosophy for all following OSCARS. The satellites were frequently constructed in the basements and garages of people's homes (Baker and Jansson, 1994). For example, the fibreglass mounting rails for OSCAR 13 were cured in the kitchen oven of one of the AMSAT Vice Presidents (Baker and Jansson, 1994). The satellites were often built with donated leftovers from aerospace industry, and components from hardware and electronic stores (Baker and Jansson, 1994): a domestic, small-scale space technology.

In later years, AMSAT has become truly international, arranging launches for satellites built by amateurs, students, universities and even governments from countries such as Malaysia, Saudi Arabia, Mexico, Korea, Denmark, and Argentina. Most spacefaring nations have provided launch vehicles for AMSAT satellites, including the US, USSR, Japan and France. Of 98 OSCAR and other AMSAT satellites launched since 1961, 89 appear to be still in orbit according to AMSAT's data (AMSAT, 2004–2006).

Despite being outside aerospace industry, AMSAT satellites proved that innovation was not the sole province of the well-funded. AMSAT satellites were among the first to use voice transponders. They also pioneered microsatellite technology – of necessity – at a time when commercial and military satellites were becoming larger and larger (Baker and Jansson, 1994). Today, the trend is towards micro- and nano-satellites.

The amateur satellites demonstrate the diversity of space artefacts and the capacity of the public to participate in high technology. These satellites *look* vastly different from 'professional' satellites. Their design and construction reflect the resources available on low budgets and the ingenuity of scarcity. When it is possible to study orbital hardware from space, these little satellites will stand out from the thousands of commercial, military and scientific satellites by their appearance. In the cultural landscape of orbital space (Gorman, 2005c), their heritage significance is enhanced by their relative rarity; and their very presence in orbit undermines the dominance of the spacefaring states.

Conclusions

These space places exist in vastly different environments: 'remote' terrestrial deserts and the largely invisible umbrella of Earth orbit. A consideration of their social contexts allows us to see a range of different types of places, not usually considered as space sites, that can tell us something about the values of emerging spacefaring societies in the 20th century.

The installations and artefacts demonstrate the use of resources to adapt to new environments. The Australian and Algerian launch sites were positioned to take advantage of a colonial asset, 'empty' lands where nuclear missiles could be tested without impacting on urban populations. On the rocket ranges, ephemeral Tuareg and Aboriginal camps are juxtaposed with the monuments of space infrastructure. Two cultures were simultaneously using the same land-scapes, shaped by the expansion of one and the constraint of the other. To see them as part of the same process enables the heritage significance of Woomera and Colomb-Béchar-Hammaguir to be assessed in a way that takes into account not only the achievements of space exploration, but also the impacts on those ostensibly left behind in the Space Race.

The OSCAR satellites and their infrastructure were improvizations, creating high technology out of the everyday. Suburban places in Melbourne and Canberra are linked to a small and silent black box still orbiting the Earth among the surveillance, earth observation and meteorological satellites of large corporations and national governments. These satellites may not be grand technological breakthroughs, but their social significance to those involved in the international community of amateur space, and to the local communities who supported them, renders them worthy of preservation when proposed orbital debris removals take place (Gorman, 2005c).

Human material culture associated with space travel has created an archaeological record that reflects technology and society as a globalized space-based culture emerges (Gorman in press). From the desert spacescapes to the kitchen-sink mechanics of the OSCARs, we can discern the diverse ideologies of space exploration. But space exploration has not yet led us to the ultimate encounter, ending our loneliness in the universe. Instead, on the lunar and Martian surfaces of the desert launch sites, imperial scientists encountered those who adapted to life on Earth long ago.

References

AMSAT, (2004–2006), A brief chronology of amateur satellites, http://www.amsat.org/amsat-new/satellites/history.php. [accessed 30 Aug 2008].

Atkinson, T., (1970), A satellite that is all-Australian, *Newsday*, 21 January.

Azoulay, G., (2006), Diversité et périmètres du patrimoine spatial, *La Revue pour l'Histoire du CNRS* 14 (Mai), http://histoirecnrs.revues.org/document1750.html [accessed 30 Aug 2008].

Baker, K. and Jansson, D., (1994), *Space satellites from the world's garage – the story of AMSAT*, paper presented to the National Aerospace and Electronics Conference, Ohio: Dayton.

Bates, D., (1938), *The Passing of the Aborigines: A Lifetime Spent Among the Natives of Australia*, London: John Murray.

Belaid, T., (2008), *Abadla*, http://adadla.afrikablog.com/archives/2008/08/20/index.html. [accessed 16 November 2008].

Bickel, L., (1970), The backyard spacemen are ready. . . . And now it's up to OSCAR, *The Australian*, 20 January.

Brown, M.R., (2007), Can technologies represent their publics? *Technology in Society* 29: 327–338.

Buchli, V. and Lucas, G., (eds) (2001), *Archaeologies of the Contemporary Past*, London: Routledge.

Chambers, E.W., (2000), *Woomera. Its Human Face*, Henley Beach, South Australia: Seaview Press.

Clarke, J.D.A., Thomas, M. and Norman, M., (2004), The Arkaroola Mars Analogue Region, South Australia, *Lunar and Planetary Science* XXXV.

Cocroft, W.D. and Thomas, R.J.C., (2004), *Cold War: Building for Nuclear Confrontation 1946–1986*, London: English Heritage.

Ducarre, C., (1959), Sahara test centre, *Flight*, 13 February: 213.

Finlayson, H.H., (1943), *The Red Centre: Man and Beast in the Heart of Australia*, fifth edition, Sydney and London: Angus and Robertson.

Goode, J., (1970), Blast-off time and stony broke, *Newsday*, Tatts Edition, 8 January.

Gorman, A.C., (2009), Beyond the space race: the significance of space sites in a new global context, in Piccini, A. and Holthorf, C. (eds), *Contemporary Archaeologies: Excavating Now*, Bern: Peter Lang. pp 161–180.

Gorman, A.C., (2005a), The cultural landscape of interplanetary space. *Journal of Social Archaeology* 5(1): 85–107.

Gorman, A.C., (2005b), *From the stone age to the space age: interpreting the significance of space exploration at Woomera*, unpublished paper presented at the symposium Home on the Range: The Cold War, Space Exploration and Heritage at Woomera, South Australia: Flinders University, November 2005.

Gorman, A.C., (2005c), The archaeology of orbital space, in *Australian Space Science Conference 2005*, Melbourne: RMIT University: 338–357.

Gorman, A.C. and O'Leary, B.L., (2007), An ideological vacuum: the cold war in space, in John Schofield and Wayne Cocroft (eds) *A Fearsome Heritage: Diverse Legacies of the Cold War*, California: Left Coast Press, Walnut Creek: 73–92.

Hall, M. and Silliman, S., (2006), *Historical Archaeology*, Blackwell Studies in Global Archaeology, Malden MA: Blackwell Publishing.

Hammer, P. and Mace, O., (1970), Student satellite in orbit, University of Melbourne Gazette 26(2): 1–3

Jones, D.W., (1970), Oscar Five, *Newtrino* 3(2): 44–45.

Lubar, S., (1993), Machine politics: the political construction of technological artefacts, in W. Steven Lubar and David Kingery (eds), *Essays on Material Culture*, Washington DC: Smithsonian Institution Press: 197–214.

Miller, D., Rowlands, M. and Tilley, C., (eds) (1989), *Domination and Resistance*, London: Routledge.

Morton, P., (1989), *'Fire across the desert': Woomera and the Anglo-Australian Joint Programme, 1946–80*, Canberra: Australian Government Publishing Service.

Moyal, M., (1959), The need for cooperation in the Sahara, *African Affairs* 58(233): 329–333.

O'Leary, B.L., (2006), The cultural heritage of space, the Moon and other celestial bodies, *Antiquity* 80(307).

Orser, C.E., (1996). *A Historical Archaeology of the Modern World*, New York: Plenum Press.

OSCAR News (1967), Project OSCAR inc, Los Altos Hills, California: Foothill College: July.

Penot, J-P., (2000), *L'aventure des fusées-sondes Françaises (1949–1979)*, Paris: CNES/PEMF.

Redfield, P., (1996), Beneath a Modern Sky: Space Technology and its Place on the Ground, *Science, Technology and Human Values* 21(3): 251–274.

Rodd, F., (1926), The origin of the Tuareg, *The Geographical Journal* 67(1): 27–47.

Saunders, N., (ed.) (2004), *Matters of Conflict. Material Culture, Memory and the First World War*, Abingdon: Routlege.

Schofield, J., Johnson, W.G. and Beck, C.M., (eds) (2002), *Matériel Culture: The Archaeology of 20th Century Conflict*, London: Routledge.

Schofield, J., Beck, C. and Drollinger, H., (2003), The archaeology of opposition: Greenham Common and Peace Camp, Nevada, *Conservation Bulletin* 44: 47–49.

Southall, I., (1962), *Woomera*, Sydney: Angus and Robertson.

Spenneman, D.H.R., (2004), The ethics of treading on Neil Armstrong's footsteps, *Space Policy* 20(4): 279–290.

Trout, F.E., (1970), Morocco's boundary in the Guir-Zousfana river basin, *African Historical Studies* 3(1): 37–56.

Wade, M., (2008), Hammaguira, http://www.astronautix.com/sites/hamguira.htm [accessed 13 Sept 2008].

Winner, L., (1977), *Autonomous technology: technics-out-of-control as a theme in political thought*, Cambridge, Mass.: MIT Press.

Giant leaps and forgotten steps: NASA and the performance of gender

Daniel Sage

Popular portrayals of American spaceflight regularly propose that the history of the National Aeronautics and Space Administration epitomizes the masculinist organization of American post-WWII modernity. Films such as Philip Kaufman's *The Right Stuff* (and earlier book), or Ron Howard's *Apollo 13* (see Llinares, this volume), seemingly correlate the success of NASA, and by extension America and/or humanity, around the fortunes of strong, stoical, active and resourceful men. Meanwhile, women, such as the astronauts' wives, seemingly feature as rather passive, marginalized and abjected. Manly bodies are shown here capable of 'risk taking', 'frontier exploration', 'technical decision making', 'competition' and 'attention to detail', all qualities which Connell (1995) suggested typified 'hegemonic' masculinities and legitimated patriarchies.[1] Popular examples of NASA's articulation of masculinist social power are complemented by various scholarly accounts explaining how NASA has historically subjugated women (Ackmann, 2004; Kevles, 2003; Moule and Shayler, 2003; Penley, 1997; Weitekamp, 2004). This chapter takes the underlying claim found within such studies – NASA articulated a gendered binary – as its starting point. Rather than foregrounding the stories of women in NASA as a revisionist counterpoint, as many of these studies have, I will go further and critically assess the dis/organization of underlying binary oppositions which often frames explanations of the relationship between NASA and gender.

Focusing on the activities of NASA, particularly during the Apollo era, I draw upon Butler's (1990, 2004) work on the performed aspects of gender and identity, to question whether and how NASA as an organization is complicit with the rehearsal of gendered identities through polarized binaries that align 'masculine'/'feminine' with 'male'/'female'? Butler's work provides a particularly apposite starting point to address this question, as will now be elaborated prior to the empirical discussion.

Gender as performance

In contrast to a diverse group of feminist theorists, including Simone de Beauvoir, Kate Millett, Marilyn Frye or Barbara Duden, Butler rejects the idea that feminist epistemology and politics should or can differentiate *a priori* between identities, experiences, values or behaviours based on sexual difference (see Butler, 2004: 210–213).[2] Her critique of the universalism associated with feminist theory echoes some other scholars, including Julia Kristeva, Helene Cixous and Luce Irigaray. Butler (1990), however, goes further than multiplying the category 'Woman', and questions how gender/sexual differences are performed thorough a 'heterosexual matrix': 'The heterosexualization of desire requires and institutes the production of discrete and asymmetrical oppositions between "feminine" and "masculine" where these are understood as excessive attributes of "male" and "female".' (p. 24). She continues: '. . . one is one's gender to the extent that one is not the other gender, a formulation that presupposes and enforces the restriction of gender within the binary pair' (p.30). Consequently, if gender is produced through binary oppositions then, for Butler, the 'us'/'them' of 'masculine'/'feminine' becomes unintelligible outside of these discursive practices and desires. As Butler (1990) puts it, 'There is no gender identity behind the expression of gender, that identity is performatively constituted by the very "expressions" that are said to be its results' (p. 41).

Importantly, Butler explains we should not abandon interest in the normative expressions of male/female binaries per se, rather we must be careful to view such 'choices' as repeated stylized acts regulated by regimes of truth (or discourses) and operationalized within institutions from the welfare state, modern medicine and perhaps also spaceflight, not part of any natural order of things (compare with Holmes, 2007; Parker, 2002). 'To conflate the definition of gender with its normative expression is inadvertently to reconsolidate the power of the norm to constrain the definition of gender' (Butler, 2004: 42). And so, while 'Gender is the mechanism by which notions of masculine and feminine are produced and naturalized . . . gender may very well be the apparatus by which such terms are deconstructed and denaturalized' (Butler, 2004: 42). Crucially for Butler, the contingency and transformability of gendering binaries becomes most evident in those situations when we feel unsure of the authenticity of a gender act, hence 'Gender Trouble' (Butler, 1990). Butler's work has been of particular relevance to studies of transgender and homosexual cultures that accentuate the phantasmic *construction* of gender, by separating gender and biological sex, and thus challenging dominant regimes of truth around gender (see Parker, 2002: 152). Yet Butler (2004) argues that all gendered identities can be witnessed as phantasmic, because these 'abstract norms' always 'exceed the lives they make – and break' (p. 56). Butler's passion for the mutability of authentic/fictional gender acts bleeds into her broader political strategy (Parker, 2002) as she seeks to concurrently describe and challenge the disciplining of modern *beings* through powerful regimes of truth and afford us more creativity to *become* (Butler, 2004: 175).

Her celebration of transgression is, however, more than simply a multiplication of gendered identities; indeed as she explains, via Foucault's understanding of power, transgression from a norm can equally help refine the disciplinary techniques by which any norm is produced (Butler, 2004: 52). There are resonances here with Law's (2002) concept of fractional coherence that illustrates how postmodern reverence for multiplicity to resist modernist singularity – the modus operandi of much work on gender – often unhelpfully simplifies the nuanced practices through which gendered subjects are de/constructed.

Arguably, the American space programme, especially during and before the Apollo-era, perhaps presents a rather strange association with Butler's thesis – ostensibly it is permeated with repetitive gender acts where 'authentically' masculine men are opposed to feminine women, and has become somewhat of a leitmotif for the gendering of American modernity (Penley, 1997; Weitekamp, 2004). In many respects, however, such labelling only fuels the intellectual and political exigency for a more nuanced interrogation of some of the historical gendering practices surrounding space flight. Butler's approach provides a useful frame in which a historical, largely text-based, analysis of gender can mitigate a tendency to assume *a priori* the coherence of essentialist gender roles. My decision to focus here primarily upon encounters between women and NASA develops Butler's (1990) position that the category 'woman' articulates a conceptual fracturing of subjectivity – a fluid becoming not a fixed being (Grosz, 1994): women, as Butler (2004: 204–229) describes, are historically both inside and outside a politics based on group-recognition and representation.[3] Encounters between women and NASA can simultaneously expose and transform normative gender practices, disclosing the phantasmagoric de/construction of femininities and masculinities. Having introduced this performative approach, I will now turn towards three genderings within and surrounding NASA: (i) astronauts' wives, (ii) women working within NASA and (iii) female astronauts.

Engendering others? Astronauts' wives

Astronaut identities have ostensibly long been constructed alongside their 'Other': the seemingly supportive yet demure, passive, domestically bound and rather abject astronauts' wife. For example, in 1959 *Life* magazine ran two covers back-to-back, depicting the original Mercury Seven astronauts and their wives (see Figures 1 and 2).[4]

Here the physical contrasts between the astronauts and their wives (clothing, hair-length, jewelry and make-up) are aligned with discursive binaries between men and women as public/personal actors. For example, the men are described as part of an 'epochal mission', seemingly conjuring up images of extensive heroism, while the focus on the wives' 'inner thoughts and worries' returns us to ostensibly more 'feminine' interests.[5]

Similar gendered contrasts are articulated in the *The Right Stuff* film adaptation of Tom Wolfe's same-titled novel. In one scene, for example, the wives of prospective astronaut test-pilots sit indoors describing their anxieties about their husbands' work, while their husbands exemplify stoicism – appearing relaxed as they recall their missions around the BBQ outside. Later in the film,

Figure 1: Life *magazine cover 14 September 1959.* Ralph Morse / Time Life Pictures / Getty Images

the Mercury 7 astronauts are unveiled to the press and asked how their wives feel about their work. John Glen declares: 'My wife's attitude towards this has been the same as it has been all along my flying career, if it's what I what to do, she's behind it'. Meanwhile their wives, including some who had earlier expressed doubts, clap along with the gathered press crowd. Throughout the film we are presented with scenes of the wives supporting their husbands in public, despite expressing some private fears or concerns. At no point, however, do the wives appear to desire more active involvement in the space programme themselves; appearing instead content with their role as domestic supporters. Notably all the NASA employees in the film, with the exception of nurses, are portrayed by men.

As Llinares argues (this volume) Ron Howards' Oscar-winning film *Apollo 13* presents equivalent genderings. Here, seemingly uncontested expressions of masculinity/femininity are essentialized in exactly the terms Butler seeks to problematize. Men appear as active agents who are strong, heroic and creative, while women – the astronauts' wives – appear as nurturing, demure and domestically bound, seeing space exploration, as a threat to this identity. In one scene,

149

Figure 2: Life *magazine cover 21 September 1959.* Ralph Morse / Time Life Pictures / Getty Images

for example, Marilyn Lovell tells her husband she cannot attend his launch because their kids are busy at school. Penley (1997) captures the masculine-heroic aura of the rest of the film: 'Using only duct tape and gumption NASA teamwork turned into deliverance . . . [Ron Howard's Apollo 13] recreates an era when NASA appeared faultless and heroic' (pp. 12–13).

Despite the seeming ubiquity of gendered binaries – between public/private, active/passive, mind/body, reason/emotion, production/reproduction *etcetera* – these images are often presented as performances rather than uncontested essentialisms. Indeed, in one scene in *The Right Stuff*, one of the astronauts' wives reveals her lie to the astronaut selectors about the normative appearance of her family – at this point in the film she had decided to live away from her husband after feeling isolated. Moreover, the actual astronauts' wives themselves readily acknowledge the managed nature of their identities, as Susan Borman (wife of Apollo 8 commander Frank Borman) recalls:

> They had people looking into the background of the men, [and] they also had people looking into the background of the wives because they didn't want an oddball . . . it

wasn't discussed, it wasn't written, but . . . you had better be in every sense of the word, the All American Family in everything you say and do! . . . (quoted in PBS, 2005)

Nasa wanted perfect wives, perfect children, perfect homes. There was certainly some pressure there. (quoted in Cuddon, 2007)

Tom Wolfe similarly describes his perceptions of the astronauts' wives: 'As far as the wives were concerned, their outlook was the same as that of officers' wives generally, only more so. The main thing was not to say or do anything that reflected badly upon your husband' (Wolfe, 1979: 132). As Butler (1990, 2004) suggests, normative genderings require mental and physical effort, and self-discipline to be maintained.

The Right Stuff also highlights the performativity of masculinities within NASA. In one scene, for example, the Apollo astronauts' challenge the rocket scientists' desire to perfect a fully automated space capsule and call instead for a piloted spacecraft. This scene speculates on the way contrasting hegemonic masculinities (Connell, 1995) – rational control versus heroic agency – are shifting and ambiguous. However, it is important not to over-celebrate the presence of multiple shifting masculinities, or indeed their performativity. Following Law's (2002) concept of fractional coherence, we might argue that while these manly identities are multiple, and even contrasting, they still added up to a non-coherent masculine discourse that was precisely able to exclude women because it could employ multiple dominating narratives and defer its essence (compare with Connell, 2007). Or, as Law (2002) puts it: 'the singularities of the 'modern project' arise from the interferences between multiplicities produced in that characteristic oscillation between one and many' (p. 143). As will be shown later in this chapter, struggle with masculine narratives that legitimate patriarchy can be rendered all the more difficult, not easier, if that masculinity is fluid or reflectively performative, rather than singular. A deconstructive reading of masculinity is not, as Connell (2007) illustrates, enough on its own to eviscerate patriarchies.

The astronaut's wives frequently identify the media gaze surrounding the astronauts' houses as implicit confirmation of Butler's (1990) claim that the disciplinary techniques buttressing normative genderings are performative. Similarly, Borman recalls, 'Some of them [the press] actually moved into the home so they could photograph us watching the launches on television. We used to call it the death watch' (see Cuddon, 2007). A comparable binarized masculinist abjection of female emotion occurred after Elliot See (prospective Gemini 9 Commander) died in a plane crash. John Young called Marilyn Lovell (wife of astronaut John Lovell) and asked her to visit See's wife. She was disbelieving: 'You want me to tell her that Elliot was killed?' Young replied, 'No. I want you to do something much harder – not tell her. Somebody should be there with her right now, but she can't be told anything until I can come over and notify her officially. We don't want some overeager newspaperman knocking on her door' (quoted in PBS, 2005).

Gendered binaries were further legitimated through a discourse of rampant workaholism, as Valerida Anders, wife of Apollo astronaut Bill Anders, recalls:

> You were, in effect, a single parent for the week. And when the men came home on the week-end in their T-38s [airplanes] they flew in and their first obligation was to go to the office at the Manned Spacecraft Center [Houston] and catch up on their mail, do their business at the office and then come back and spend time with the family in the time that was left of the weekend, which was generally late Saturday afternoon and all day Sunday (quoted in PBS, 2005).

Such sacrifices maintained a spatial division of labour (McDowell, 1999), that preserved a public/private (or production/reproduction) binary of masculine/ feminine work. Faye Stafford (former wife of Apollo 10 astronaut Thomas Stafford), for example, describes how 'Most of us were still homemakers. I would have liked to have had a career. Especially once the children left home. It was isolating' (quoted in Cuddon, 2007). The accounts of Dotty Duke (wife of Apollo 16 astronaut Charlie Duke) are particularly poignant. Duke describes how: 'Charlie was a complete workaholic. The space programme was all he thought about. I knew he would never be able to show me the love I needed or make me a priority and I became suicidal' (quoted in Cuddon, 2007).

The presence of suicidal thoughts, resistance towards the press and NASA's mission, and perhaps above all the acknowledgement of the performed, quixotic and specious 'feminine' identity in the 'all-American family', immediately throws into doubt not just the *content* but the *concept* of essentialized gender binaries, and indeed singular identities. Indeed, often the routines of the space programme meant that wives, and indeed astronauts, ended up by necessity cultivating social roles outside of heterosexual desire. For example, the wives would frequently support each other through friendships that functioned as extended families while their husbands were away. Gracia Lousma (wife of astronaut Jack Lousma) remembers how, 'We kind of filled in for each other when the men were away. We'd have dinner together and look after each other's children' (quoted in Cuddon, 2007). Equally many of the wives were compelled to undertake domestic duties that would perhaps more normally be the responsibility of men in suburban American. Dotty Duke recalls her experiences:

> . . . to make sure that my husband was taken care of in such a way that he could do the best job possible. I tried not to bother him with mundane burdens at home. Most [astronaut] wives cut the grass, took out the garbage, and kept the house and kids in order. That was our contribution to the US effort in space. (quoted in Shayler and Moule, 2003: 110)

Similarly the astronauts themselves cultivated multiple identities, such as close friendships, beyond heterosexual desire, that have endured over the decades since the Apollo program, often longer than their marriages, as illustrated in various biographies and autobiographies (Cernan and Davis, 1999; Scott and

Leonov, 2004). While, as Connell (2007: 146), argues such homo-social cultural practices prefigure the exclusion of women, they also promote a disarticulation of the heterosexual identities that may have initially rendered such practices legitimate.

The self-disciplining experiences of the astronauts' wives, and their representation in popular culture, initially confirms Butler's (1990) thesis that essentialized gendered binaries revolve around the performed repetition of a 'heterosexual matrix' (p. 6) of desire. Similarly, the possible presence of multiple, performed masculinities within NASA, as exampled above in *The Right Stuff*, may also only serve to police rather than to alter such normative genderings, nevertheless, the lives of these women, and indeed of their husbands, reveals how they often experienced difficulty internalizing and repeating such singular identities, causing stress, anxiety and frequently embodied transformations of such prescriptive identities (Butler, 1990: 192). The next section will continue to engage with normative gendered binaries, looking at some of the experiences of women working for NASA, illustrating femininities organized through desires for creativity, technical skill and activity, not a heterosexual matrix, experiences that are notably absent from both *The Right Stuff* and *Apollo 13*.

Working with the 'other' – women inside NASA

During the Apollo programme, many NASA employees were, as McCurdy (1993: 56–60) describes, young people, overwhelmingly men, living in hotels and motels, working long hours well into the evening and seeing their friends and family perhaps only one day a week. NASA Apollo-era management analyst Charles Bingham echoes this image as he describes how his staff at Johnson Space Center:

> . . . had the opportunity to select very high-quality people to come work on the staff, which means that most of them were very highly self-motivated. It was not a question of people in dull, sluggish jobs, and you have to try to pump them up in order to get them to get away from the water cooler. It was not like that at all. Almost without exception, the people who came to work there were just charged with this emotion (Bingham, 2000).

This intensive work ethic operated as a gendering process, as it presupposed that NASA required people who would dedicate themselves solely to the space programme, exceptional people whose lives could be eulogized as beacons of the bodily regime required to organize America's exceptional destiny (McCurdy, 1993, 1997). While concluding his 1961 'Moon Landing' speech President Kennedy emphasized the character of NASA's work ethic in these terms:

> It [the lunar landing] means a degree of dedication, organization and discipline which have not always characterized our research and development efforts. It means we cannot afford undue work stoppages . . . [he then asks that] every scientist, every

engineer, every serviceman, every technician, contractor, and civil servant gives his personal pledge that this nation will move forward, with the full speed of freedom, in the exciting adventure of space (Kennedy, 1961).

Such sentiments were frequently reiterated by NASA's senior management. For example, deputy administrator Hugh Dryden was quoted in NASA's *Future Program Task Force Document* stating: 'We must not delude ourselves or the nation with any thought that leadership in this fast-moving age can be maintained with anything less than determined, whole-hearted sustained effort' (quoted in NASA 1965: 19). By conflating utopian exceptionalism with highly contingent bodily practices and work regimes, both Kennedy and Dryden presented the values which an image of a 'better' humanity would not just desire but inevitably require.

In this manner, NASA's demarcation of the 'expert body' within the recruitment policy of 'exceptional people' tacitly constructed different bodily practices, knowledges, spacings and technologies including those in the home or even the mall as somehow perhaps more 'passive', 'banal' or 'marginal' to this exciting epicentre of American modernity. Feminist scholars of technology and science provide some important insights into the dichotomous constructions of gender/technology across different spaces and times (compare with Lerman *et al.*, 2004). For example, Judith McGraw (2004) explains how in post-WWII America woman and domestic technology were mutually rendered feminine and invisible, as both were viewed as serving the basic biological functions of food, clothing or shelter, rather than as a part of a broader project of 'human creativity' or 'progress' (p. 32). This distinction can be readily positioned within the interlinked dualisms of public/private – active/passive – productive/reproductive and masculine/feminine spaces (see Cowan, 1976 and Pacey, 1999). Bettyann Kevles (2003) characterizes this division as an extension of the mapping of Cold War geopolitics into the American home, wherein 'The Soviets promised women equal opportunities in careers like medicine and engineering; capitalists offered women consumer goods and the luxury of remaining at home to use them' (p. 3). Presumably, for these 'capitalist women', freedom was to be equated not with equal opportunities to work but with freedom from the exhaustion of domestic work, a freedom nevertheless bound up with domestic space. And yet, as Kevles (2003) acknowledges, post-WWII labour shortages and less time-consuming domestic responsibilities as a result of household technologies, together with broader economic changes (Massey, 1994), increasingly meant that women desired, and were sought after in, a variety of conventionally 'masculine' careers, including NASA.

Unquestionably NASA was never solely a male employer. By the mid 1960s it employed thousands of women, as had its predecessor organizations such as the NACA (National Advisory Committee for Aeronautics), from seamstresses working on space suits to aerodynamics engineers and in-flight physiologists (see Moule and Shayler, 2003: 92–107). Moreover, women were often placed in key positions of responsibility, such as computing the flight trajectory for the first manned Apollo (Apollo 8) mission to orbit the Moon and return to Earth (p. 97). Tellingly however, in the latter case, it was a male flight controller whom was officially praised, until revisionist accounts (as in Moule and Shayler, 2003).

In a December 1961 advertisement in *American Girl* magazine, President Kennedy sought to encourage women to work for NASA:

> In our many endeavors for a lasting peace, America's space program has a new and critical importance. The skills and imagination of our young men and women are not only welcome but urgently sought in this vital area. I know they will meet this challenge to them and to the nation with vigor and resourcefulness. (quoted at p. 92)

While NASA recruited women, this does not automatically prohibit the organized persistence of normative gendering practices. Indeed, by the 1960s women had long been contributing to American aeronautical science and engineering, especially during WWII, while binary assumptions persisted about the alignment of 'masculine'/'feminine' and 'male'/'female' work under the rubric of American progress (Kevles, 2003). Many women working for NASA during the 1960s and 1970s testify to pervasive disciplinary and self-disciplinary techniques that articulate normative gender binaries.

Donna Shirley recalls her experiences working as a mission engineer in NASA's Jet Propulsion laboratory during the 1960s and 70s:

> Well, things are a lot better than they used to be. There's an episode in the book where my horny old boss at McDonnell Aircraft was chasing me around, a married guy, and how I finally got rid of him by subterfuge and trickery. But I don't think that the overt sexual harassment of professional women – I don't think it's quite as bad. I mean, you hear a lot more about it, but it used to be there wasn't any sense in reporting it because nobody would do anything about it so it didn't make any difference. My impression is that the really bad stuff, for the most part, is a lot better than it used to be (Shirley, 2001).

Shirley goes on remembering her accomplishments, though largely in terms of her ability to negotiate active discrimination and gender norms:

> I think just being able to accomplish as much as I was able to accomplish with a lot of strikes against me, mainly being female – the aerospace industry is a cold warrior kind of industry, and it's not easy for a woman to do well in it. There are no female center directors. There's only been one, Carolyn Huntoon, and she didn't last long. Carolyn Griner was the deputy of Marshall for a long time, never became center director. Plenty of opportunities to promote her but she wasn't. There are no women AAs [Associate Administrators] in NASA except things like public relations and policy and things like that. And the same is true across the centers, there's not very many females in power positions at all, and it's very true across the whole industry. If you go to the aerospace industry, you will not see any female faces except maybe human resources.

Tellingly perhaps, Carloyn Huntoon repeats uncontested gender oppositions to articulate her experiences of gender discrimination:

There were individuals in the program that did discriminate, did make life hard for me and other women. Luckily, they moved on. I outlasted most of them. So I think the idea of women not being just like men, some people can't get over that. They would [hire] women [to] do jobs, and the fact that they didn't behave just like another guy would do meant they couldn't do the job. [Some managers] weren't willing to give them a chance to develop their own way of doing things. I ran into that several times. Other women have, too. It's not unique to me (Huntoon, 2002).

She continues:

But I decided that what I was accomplishing and what I was able to get done in spite of all that was worth it to me to stay there and do it, and that's why I did. A lot of women did not, would not do that. A lot of women have left, not just NASA, but other places at mid or high-level careers because they just didn't want to put up with what you had to put up with. To me, it was worth it, and, as I said, in general I was treated very well by most people. There was a few that did not, but that's life. It's not always good (Huntoon, 2002).

Feminist scholars have observed (Lerman *et al.*, 2004) that the presence of women in such stereotypically 'masculine' careers did eventually provide a repertoire of case studies that would help feminist writers and activists later challenge the straightforward alignment of 'masculine'/'feminine' with 'male'/'female'.

Given such experiences within NASA, it is perhaps not surprising to find how Charles Bingham, who once worked for NASA human resource development at Houston, expressed the pessimism felt by women (and ethnic minorities) towards employment in NASA during the Apollo era:

If you know NASA at all, you know this is not where women and minorities would normally turn as a first opportunity for a job. At that time [during Apollo] particularly even with the best women in the world, there were not that many women taking advanced engineering programs. That's not to say that they were not out there, but it is to say that you had to work harder to go find them or to make the fact known that Houston was a good place for women and minorities to work. A lot of them didn't believe it. A lot of them didn't believe that you could go into an old-fashioned engineering shop and ever be given any responsibility or become a real partner in the organization (Bingham, 2000).

It is important to note that while normative gendered binaries continue to be performed within NASA into the 21st century (even in the accounts of women previously suffering from such narrow identity prescriptions), the enduring passion and skill with which many women invested themselves in spaceflight subverts many gender essentialisms, not least the premise that womanly and manly desires can only be understood through a neat heterosexual matrix of oppositions (Butler, 1990). Indeed, as Butler (2004) suggests, it is inaccurate to equate any measure of institutional identity with either strictly masculine or feminine identities, values or behaviours. Rather we should describe the on-going dis/organization of normative gender practices and foreground those moments – as Carolyn Huntoon's account might example – when the easy mapping of concepts of gender and sexual difference onto organizational and technical efficacy becomes problematic. The next section develops this line of thinking about transgressive desires and bodily competences by attending to a set of bodies that offered potentialities to throw into relief perhaps one of the most popularly understood 'masculine' technical environments: the spacecraft.

Risky bodies? The lovelace women in space project

The masculine self-identity of pilots has often been understood through an eroticized desire for risk and suffering, or what Law (2002) terms 'Thrills and spills' (p. 32). Similarly, McCurdy (1993), quotes one Apollo astronaut as saying, 'Recognition of risk is what made us as good as we were' (p. 62), while another states 'But if it [risk of death] was like, one in one hundred, you would do it, you take it . . . There were so many ways it could happen' (p. 63). Across such statements astronauts' fetishized tolerance of risk as a part of the performance of manliness; risk became part of the astronauts' identity, contributing to what Tom Wolfe's novel (1979) famously referred to as 'The Right Stuff'. Yet this attitude towards physical and mental subjugation was not mere blind masochism; it was, also predicated upon a set of techniques concerned with the control of bodies wherein the astronauts were rigorously tested to confirm a high degree of corporeal control and calculation over their own bodies and perform tasks in this hostile environment – to maintain control in a situation despite the discomfort and vulnerability and get the job done.

Within all these images of the astronaut there exist mutually shaping essentializing associations between masculinity, corporeality, outer space, risk and high-technology that prefigure the identity construction of 'The Right Stuff'; becoming increasingly evident when challenged with transgressive Other(s), namely female bodies.[6] Such an instance occurred in 1962, when a small group of women successfully passed the some of same physical and psychological tests as the *Mercury* astronauts, in a privately funded women astronaut study organized by a physiologist called Dr. William Lovelace (see Shayler and Moule, 2003; Weitekamp, 2004). The women now sought NASA's support to become astronauts. 'Lovelace's Women in Space Project' (Weitekamp, 2004) or 'The Mercury 13' (Ackmann, 2004) de-stabilized many of the iterative bodily performances enacted through NASA that prescribed binary gendered assumptions.[7] The desire of these women to become astronauts and their embodied suitability, transgressed the tacitly masculinist spatio-temporal categorization of different bodies under modernity (Massey, 2005: 93).

These bodies offered, in Judith Butler's (1990) terms, a sense of hope 'in the possibility of a failure to repeat, a de-formity, or a parodic repetition that exposes the phantasmatic effect of abiding identity as a politically tenuous construction' (p. 192). Just as some homosexual bodily performances may present a particular body in an opposing gender role (see Butler, 1990: 167–170), thus exposing the de-stabilized 'ground' of both gendered identities, these astronauts tacitly desired to place a female body in a hegemonically masculine guise. Yet equally, as Butler (1990) makes clear, such transgressions, while sometimes transformative, are frequently accompanied by 'punishments that attend not agreeing to believe in them' (p. 190). For example, in 1962 Dr. Lovelace sought the Navy's permission to expand his use of their facilities to provide further evidence of the women's suitability. The official reply to the Navy was that 'NASA does not at this time have a requirement for such a program' (Weitekamp, 2004: 128). This reply was then made known to Dr. Lovelace and the women involved; it effectively cancelled the nascent woman into space project. Here, the twin spectres of technological determinism and instrumentalism (Feenberg, 1999) are used to conjure up a belief in value-neutral, automatic and unilateral technical decision-making. In turn, this meant that the space programme could be constructed as if it were an inevitable temporal sequence, expressing natural gender roles and bodily practices, and devoid of ethno-political import (Shayler and Moule, 2003).

The decision was re-examined in a heated Congressional hearing in July 1962, in which the Lovelace Women, led by Geraldine 'Jerrie' Cobb, were cross-examined by Congressmen partly in an attempt to illustrate their technical worth objectively, above and beyond their male peers (Shayler and Moule, 2003, p. 149). The women demonstrated the capacity of their bodies to pass the same flight-tests as men, as well as possessing some important advantages, not least their requirements for less food and oxygen – on account of their smaller size (Penley, 1997: 55). Ultimately, however, the women's transgressive bodily desires were blocked through quasi-judicial significations of risk. Namely, a belief asserted by NASA that astronauts had to be jet test pilots, a profession women were already barred from, because only jet test pilots possessed the necessary experience to undertake high-risk flight experiments. This point appeared already undermined by NASA's own demonstration that spacecraft could fly automatically in outer space (Penley, 1997), combined with the rejection of many skilled test pilots by the astronaut selectors, such as Chuck Yeager. NASA's Chief of Manned Space Flight, George Low, then explained to Congress how NASA support for the women-in-space project would set his work back, despite the fact that Lovelace had requested the very limited use of Navy not NASA facilities (Ackmann, 2004: 166). More implicitly, it appears the decision revolved around a belief that women were excluded from becoming jet test pilots (or astronauts) because it was deemed too risky (Weitekamp, 2004: 149). In this case, a masculinized relationship between technology and risk within American modernity proved intractable; accordingly men were able to dictate thresholds of female risk. As Weitekamp (2004) explains, the male construction of female risk prevalent in NASA was two-fold: on the one hand, NASA seemed reluctant to subject women to degrees of risk because 'the prospect of subjecting a woman to mortal danger betrayed the rigidly defined gendered roles asserted in post-war America' (p. 3). On the other hand, this paternalist designation of women as needing protecting might itself lead the public to conclude that if women flew in spacecraft then the craft themselves might be deemed too straightforward and safe. Thus as Weitekamp (2004) puts it, if 'a woman could perform those tasks [it] would diminish their prestige' (p. 3).

The appropriation within NASA of risk as the legitimate means by which to exclude women from outer space appears only strengthened through its seemingly contradictory blending of different masculine identities. In this case, risk is alternately, and seemingly paradoxically, constructed as both a cipher for the rational management of hazards and the manly celebration of danger. Here the capacity to render masculinity fractionally coherent (Law, 2002) renders it more, not less, persistent in justifying patriarchal norms.

The Mercury astronaut John Glenn, who had just returned back to Earth to a ticker-tape parade after being the first American to orbit the Earth, summarized his verdict in a final statement within the hearing:

> I think this gets back to the way our social order is organized really. It is just a fact. The men go off and fight the wars and fly airplanes and come back and help design and build and test them. The fact that women are not in this field is a fact of our social order. It may be undesirable (quoted in Weitekamp, 2004: 151).

While Glenn's reference to 'undesirable' may be telling of shifting attitudes towards women, he nevertheless asserts that there is something inherently masculine about these interactions between bodies, risk and technology, so that only particular bodies were deemed not just more desirable but almost factually suitable. After the hearing, female astronauts were frequently the subject of further derision, often evoking the 'heterosexual matrix' of submissive female sexuality, as Wernher von Braun demonstrated in a speech given at Mississippi State College (19 Nov. 1962):

> Well, all I can say is that the male astronauts are all for it. And as my best friend Bob Gilruth [director of Johnston Space Center of manned spaceflight] says, we're reserving 110 pounds of payload for recreational equipment (from *Parade Magazine* Sunday Supplement, December 1962 – quoted in Kevles, 2003: 4).

Harry Hess, a Princeton Professor and Chair of the Space Studies Board at the National Academy of Sciences, adopted a similar approach to explain away female astronauts by stating unequivocally that 'leaving the kids behind was not part of womanhood's idealized image' (quoted in Kevles, 2003: 47).

Ultimately, as Weitekamp (2004) surmised of the Apollo era: 'NASA had no room in its mission objectivities for acting as an agent of social change' (p. 157). Indeed it was not until 1978, and the development of the shuttle programme, that NASA would select women as astronauts.[8] By this point frontier analogies were being drawn upon retrospectively to excuse the omission of women from past astronaut selections; NASA's media rhetoric talked of the shift from explorers to pioneers, or from surveyors to homesteaders (Kevles, 2003: 56). Making a similar nod to spatialized gender roles, Carolyn Huntoon, describes what she saw as the reasons behind the new policy for astronaut selections to the space shuttle: 'It was going to have more space in it for the crews. It was going to have some of the conveniences of home that previous space capsules had not had. And the laws were changing in our country that women could no longer be discriminated against. The decision was made that we would select qualified women to fly in space' (2002). Again the domestication of space missions appears to go hand-in-hand with the presence of women in outer space. In both cases, stereotypical gender roles, frequently made through a gendered (mis)reading of American frontier expansion in the 19th century, provided an ill-fitting though seemingly seductive temporal analogy to explain away almost thirty years of institutionally prejudicial accounts of bodily difference and space exploration. This re-telling of a spatial division of labour, as a teleological sequence, where male explorers precede female pioneers, reveals the way prescriptive bodily performances were retrospectively legitimated within a heterosexual matrix, even by women themselves.

Eventually in 1983, over thirty years after the Lovelace women's plight, Sally Ride would become the first American female astronaut to fly into space (Penley, 1997: 55); though not until Eileen Collins in 1999, over 40 years since its founding that NASA would give a woman the opportunity of commanding a spacecraft (p. 13).[9] As Kevles (2003) optimistically puts it, 'women can now decide risks for themselves' (p. 56). Today many more women are entering science and engineering disciplines and training to be pilots. Even so, only 10 per cent of astronauts being selected are women, as Carolyn Huntoon reports. Perhaps the institutionalized desire to uphold this assemblage of American modernity as a male domain is changing, albeit slowly.

Concluding comments

Across these varied sources, from films to oral histories, I have sought to render visible some of the performances surrounding the dis/organization of gendered identities within NASA. Just as Butler (1990) proposes, my methodological choices are manifestly also my political strategy. I have focused on those moments within and surrounding NASA where gender roles became disengaged from a straightforward alignment with biological sex. My intention here has been to reveal the lived circumstances and embodied practices through which totalizing gender discourses are enacted. Following Butler (1990), I have focused on the way embodied performances, from grass-cutting to astronaut testing, inscribe and transform normative binaries. My reading of NASA is, of course, partial, developed from a particular theoretical stance towards gender, combined with three extended, though unavoidably limited, slices of NASA history. I have sought to foreground how a diverse set of statements concerning gender implicitly perform the gendered subjects they were explicitly trying to represent. The elision of the performativity of gender, which is perhaps best exampled by John Glenn's reference to the social factuality of gender roles, both obscures and reinforces its normative power-effects. My focus upon women and NASA, while in keeping with Butler's (2004) own understanding of women as a necessary aspect of treating gender as a 'becoming', has ostensibly downplayed some of the multiple masculinities within NASA. However, as the tensions between the Mercury 7 astronauts and rocket scientists near the start of this chapter reveal, as well as NASA's use of a non-coherent concept of risk in the 'Lovelace' hearing, I suggest that multiplying gendered identities, whether male or female, does not necessarily help expose and challenge their normative power-effects. Put more formally, perhaps it is problematic to valorize 'Self' multiplicity and then risk overlooking the way multiplicity can sometimes subjugate that which appears 'Other'.

This reading of the experiences of women within NASA illustrates the sacrifice and cost for women who failed to repeat a recognizable gendered identity, yet perhaps equally it provides a great deal of potentiality to rethink the prevalent reading of NASA, particularly during the Apollo era, as an uncontested masculinist realm. As Judith Butler (1990) maintains, gendered identities must be constantly performed, hence are capable of being otherwise. While the accounts of Carolyn Huntoon testify how NASA, and in particular the human spaceflight programme, continues to remain a male-dominated institution it is perhaps encouraging to note here the many embodied examples – from Dotty Duke's lawn-mowing to female rocket trajectory programmers and Geraldine Cobb's 'expert' body – where binary categorization, prejudice and discrimination only fuelled, and indeed frequently necessitated, transgression of prescriptive and oppressive gendered identities.

Notes

1 The phrase 'hegemonic masculinity' was first coined by R.W.Connell in the book *Masculinities* (see Connell, 1995). Connell's thesis is that masculinities are intentionally constructed from a repertoire of choices, never given *a priori*, and are therefore capable of being multiple. Connell identifies a series of normative traits associated with men, such as risk-taking, physical prowess, competitiveness, domination, logic and control, which have all been historically used to justify the subordination of women.

2 The assumption of a natural opposition between universalized male and female experience can also be found in some writing on masculinity (see for example Connell, 1995).

3 The concept of becoming is developed by Butler (2004) through her reading of Deleuze and Guattari's concept of 'becoming-women'. Deleuze and Guattari (1987) explain, 'It is perhaps the special situation of women in relation to the man-standard that accounts for the fact that becomings, being minoritian, always pass through a becoming-women' (p. 291). While the man-standard reifies dualisms, a becoming 'has neither beginning nor end, departure nor arrival, origin nor destination . . . A becoming is neither one nor two, nor the relation of the two; it is the in-between' (p. 293). Hence if a man escapes such dualisms and identification, he must also pass through a becoming-women on the way to 'becoming-imperceptible'.

4 Notably, part of the contract with *Life* magazine meant that the astronauts would be protected by a life assurance policy and that the family would receive a stipend from the magazine. Hence despite the growing funding for the early space programme, NASA perhaps reflected a patriarchal bias that disconnects public and private spheres: work and home. See: http://www.pbs.org/wgbh/amex/moon/peopleevents/p_wives.html [accessed 2 April 2008]

5 Heroism is frequently associated with masculinities. Perhaps the best way to think about this is in terms of a sense of subjective autonomy – an exaggerated sovereign agency – capable of think-

ing and acting independently of external relations. Here heroism suggests the apotheosis of a mind/body dualism – the marginalization of the mind-body and a God-like aggrandization of a dispassionate mind (compare with Haraway, 1991).

6 The bodies of animals, in particular chimpanzees, similarly illustrate masculinist assumptions surrounding NASA. Indeed, chimpanzees were used in the early days of the space programme to test the effects of weightlessness for later human astronauts. While the presence and competence of such passive explorers might seem to challenge masculine identities based on heroic action, as Haraway (2004: 93–95) explains, their role is actually more complicit with masculine identities than might be suspected. They were, as she puts it, 'neonates, born of the interface of the dreams about a technisist automaton and masculinist autonomy' (p. 94). Or, in other words, they were repressed subjects whose symbiotic relations with telemetric technology made them appear fully controllable, predictable and ordered, all under the watchful gaze of man (for further discussion on NASA and animals, see Gray, 1998).

7 As Weitekamp explains (2004: 192), it is perhaps inappropriate to refer to the women as the 'Mercury 13', because they had no formal connection with NASA or the 'Mercury 7'. Moreover, the women never met each other, or knew each other, as a single group.

8 During the period before 1978, steps towards eradicating essentialist gender roles in NASA's selection process had been slow. For instance, two 'Lovelace' scientists in the mid 1960s recanted on their early work and testified to NASA that female astronauts were prone to be more 'emotionally unstable', supported by 'unspecified studies of menstrual women' (Kevles, 2003: 13). This study is lamented by Kevles (2003: 13), principally because of its tautological logic – that because there were no female astronauts in NASA then why would further research be required to disprove such prejudicial accounts of bodily difference?

9 In a rather explicit act of NASA criticism, on her first launch into space Eileen Collins invited all the surviving 'Lovelace' women and even carried mementos into orbit from these women (see Penley, 1997: 89).

References

Ackmann, M., (2004), *The Mercury 13: The True Story of Thirteen Women and the Dream of Space Flight*, New York: Random House.

Bingham, C., (2000), interview with Butler. C., Johnston Space Center Oral History Project, 9 April, available at: http://www.jsc.nasa.gov/history/oral_histories/a-b. [accessed 25 March 08]

Butler, J., (1990), *Gender Trouble*, London: Routledge.

Butler, J., (2004), *Undoing Gender*, London: Routledge.

Cernan, E. and Davis, D., (1999), *The Last Man on The Moon*, New York: St Martin's Griffin.

Connell, R. W., (1995), *Masculinities*, Berkley, CA: University of California Press.

Connell, R. W., (2007), 'Masculinities, Power and Alliance Politics', in Ashe F. (ed), *The New Politics of Masculinity: Men, Power and Resistance*, London: Routledge.

Cowan, R. S., (1976), 'Two Washes in the Morning and a Bridge Party at Night: The American Housewife Between the Wars', *Women's Studies*, 3(2): 147–172.

Cuddon, S., (2007), *The Astronaut Wives' Club*, BBC News, [internet], 8 November, available at: http://news.bbc.co.uk/1/hi/magazine/7085003.stm, [accessed 12 July 08]

Deleuze, G. and Guattari, F., (1987), *A Thousand Plateaus: Capitalism and Schizophrenia*, London: Continuum.

Duke, C., (1990), *Moonwalker*, Nashville, TN: Thomas Nelson Inc.

Feenberg, A., (1999), *Questioning Technology*, London: Routledge.

Fiftiesweb (2008), *Index Fiftiesweb*, [online] http://www.fiftiesweb.com/ [accessed 12 August 08]

Gray, T., (1998), *A Brief History of Animals in Space,* [internet] Washington D.C.: NASA History Office. available at: http://history.nasa.gov/animals.html [accessed 15 June 08]

Grosz, E., (1994), *Volatile Bodies: Toward a Corporeal Feminism*, Indiana: University Press.

Haraway, D. J., (1991), *Simians, Cyborgs, and Women: The Reinvention of Nature,* London: Free Association Books.

Haraway, D. J., (2004), *The Haraway Reader*, London: Routledge.

Holmes, M., (2007), *What is Gender?* London: Sage.

Huntoon, C., (2002), Interview with Butler, C., Johnston Space Center Oral History Project, 5 June, available at: http://www.jsc.nasa.gov/history/oral_histories/herstory.htm [accessed 3 April 08]

Kennedy, J. F., (1961), Special Message to the Congress on Urgent National Needs, in Joint Session of Congress, Washington D.C. May 25th, 1961, available at: http://www.jfklibrary.org/Historical+Resources/Archives/Reference+Desk/Speeches/JFK/003POF03National Needs05251961.htm. [accessed 12 June 08]

Kevles, B. H., (2003), *Almost Heaven the Story of Women in Space*, Jackson TN: Basic Books.

Law, J., (2002), Aircraft Stories: Decentering the Object in Technoscience, Durham, NC: Duke University Press.

Lerman, N. E., Oldenziel, R. and Mohun, A. P., (eds), (2004), *Gender and Technology: A Reader*, Baltimore: John Hopkins University Press.

Massey, D., (1994), *Space, Place and Gender*, Oxford: Blackwell.

Massey, D., (2005), *For Space,* London: Sage.

McCurdy, H. E., (1993), *Inside NASA: High Technology and Organizational Chance in the U.S. Space Program,* Baltimore, MD: John Hopkins University Press.

McCurdy, H. E., (1997), *Space and the American Imagination*, Washington D.C.: Smithsonian Institution Press.

McDowell, L., (1999), *Gender, Identity and Place: Understanding Feminist Geographies*, Cambridge: Polity Press.

McDougall, W. A., (1985), *A Political History of the Space Age*, Baltimore, MD: John Hopkins University Press.

McGraw, J. A., (2004), Why Feminine Technologies Matter, in N. E. Lernan, R. Oldenziel and A. P. Mohun, (eds), *Gender and Technology: A Reader*, John Hopkins University Press: Baltimore.

NASA, (1965), Summary Report: Future Program Task Group, in Logsdon J. *et al.* (eds), (1995), *NASA and the Exploration of Space*, Volume 1. Washington D.C.: NASA History Office.

Pacey, A., (1999), *Meaning in Technology*, Cambridge, Mass: MIT Press.

Parker, M., (2002), 'Queering Management and Organization', Gender, Work and Organization, 6(2): 146–166.

PBS (2005), *NASA Wives and Families*, Public Broadcasting Service [online] available at: http://www.pbs.org/wgbh/amex/moon/peopleevents/p_wives.html [accessed 12 April 08]

Penley, C., (1997), *NASA/Trek: Popular Science and Sex in America*, London: Verso.

Scott, D., and Leonov, A., (2004), Two Sides of the Moon: Our Story of the Cold War Space Race, London: Simon Schuster.

Shayler, D. J. and Moule, I. A., (2003), Women in Space – Following Valentina, New York: Springer.

Shirley, D., (2001), Interview with C. Butler, Johnston Space Center Oral History Project, 17 July, available at: http://www.jsc.nasa.gov/history/oral_histories/herstory.htm [accessed 12 March 08]

Weitekamp, M. A., (2004), Right Stuff, Wrong Sex: America's First Women, Baltimore, MD: Johns Hopkins University Press.

Whitehead, S. and Barret, F., (2001), *Masculinities Reader*, Cambridge: Polity Press.

Wolfe, T., (1979), *The Right Stuff*, London: Bantam Press.

Idealized heroes of 'retrotopia': history, identity and the postmodern in *Apollo 13*

Dario Llinares

The astronaut's revered position as an icon of the 20th century is inculcated culturally as much as historically. Innumerable media representations have contributed to an intertextual mythology which constructs the astronaut as an ideal embodiment of American identity. Elements such as competitiveness, individualism, patriotism, family values and even religious morality inform characterizations of the astronaut in both the photojournalism of magazine and literary accounts of the space race such as *The Right Stuff* (Wolfe, 1979) and *A Fire on the Moon* (Mailer, 1970). Television characters like Buck Rogers and Capt. Terry Nelson in *I Dream of Jeannie* further shape a distinctive symbolic repertoire affirming the coherence of astronaut identity. Underpinning this cultural mythology is an intrinsic conceptualization of masculinity which, drawing from Barthes (1957), becomes 'naturalized', outside historical context, as an efficacious notification of some eternal truth. The embedding of a specifically masculine ideal can be understood as a discursive process, sanctioning boundaries concerning the perception of gender. In these terms the representative idealization of the astronaut posits him as an exemplar of 'hegemonic' masculinity (Connell, 1995, Sage, this volume).

Cinema has invariably drawn upon and perpetuated narratives that reinforce the idealized (hegemonic) masculinity of the astronaut. This is underpinned by a correlation between paradigms of the astronaut myth and what Kellner and Ryan (1990) describe as the 'Hollywood worldview'. Like the cowboy and the war hero, the astronaut has become an archetypal protagonist in film, reflective of a specific social and political context, yet indicative of assumptions about the intrinsic nature of masculinity. Ron Howard's 1995 blockbuster *Apollo 13* is a quintessential example of this discourse at work. The film intertextually draws upon familiar markers producing a meticulously crafted embodiment of the astronaut as a masculine ideal. The film's attention to visual and historic accuracy, I suggest, imbues the text with an aura of symbolic 'authenticity'. This can be defined by what Tim Prokop (1995) describes as the film's 'absolute verisimilitude'.

The power of such 'authenticity' perpetuates a cultural perception in which the film itself becomes a historical document, structuring knowledge and memory. For Jameson, however, such cinematic re-creations imbue a, 'pseudo-historical depth, in which the history of aesthetic styles displaces 'real' history' (1984: 67). This 'historicizing' derives from the film's visual techniques and extends to the production of social context. A flawless illusion of 1970s America is created which masks inherent ideological underpinnings and presents a nostalgic, romanticized view of the past. I define this in terms of a postmodern 'retrotopia' in which 'stylistic innovation is impossible, because everything has already been tried, and all that remains is to recombine or evoke past styles and methods in an ironic, playful, reflexive manner' (Brown *et al.*, 2000). I argue however, that *Apollo 13* forgoes such playful reflexivity, instead invoking an 'authenticity' predicated on idealized representations of history in which cultural ambiguity and social contradictions are filtered out.

The ideological effect of this 'retrotopian' historicizing I relate specifically to the film's construction of masculinity. *Apollo 13's* 'absolute verisimilitude' authenticates the traditional symbolic repertoire of the heroic American astronaut while simultaneously negating his hegemonic potential. This occurs through a series of re-articulations that define a masculinity of progressive, empathetic homosociality. The highly fluid vicissitudes characterized, however tenuously, by 'the postmodern', provide a framework for the depiction of masculinity here that has to amalgamate disparate and oppositional paradigms to retain its idealized understanding. My reading derives from a poststructuralist, feminist perspective that seeks to highlight the discursive hierarchies of power in the construction of gender identity. In this context I deploy 'the postmodern' as a theoretical tool in two distinct yet interrelated ways.

The *postmodernism* of *Apollo 13* implies 'authenticity' derived from the fusion of embedded cultural markers of the past, combined with contemporary filmmaking technologies which form a seductive and nostalgic 'reality'. This very process however annihilates any organic sense of history and defines discursive boundaries of knowledge. Within this framework of producing meaning I foreground how traditional tenets of masculine heroism are rearticulated through the fractious nature of identity within *postmodernity*. The exact social conditions and temporal specificity of postmodernity are open to argument. The notion of unstable and fluid identity formulations, however indicative of the postmodern condition, informs my critical reading of masculinity as a consistent, coherent and unchanging form. I suggest that *Apollo 13* constructs the astronaut as a transcendent masculinity formed within a representational nexus between the modern and the postmodern, the past and the present, the traditional and the progressive which facilitates the maintainence of an idealized and, in turn, dominant status.

Total verisimilitude and historicizing myth

Apollo 13 recreates what would have been the third mission to land on the moon. When an oxygen tank explodes on the command module, a lunar landing becomes impossible and the crew must overcome a series of emergencies to get back to Earth. The narrative focus is threefold: how the astronauts deal with the disaster in space; NASA's teamwork in providing the procedures for them to return home safely; and the reactions of the astronauts' families. The cinematic effectiveness of *Apollo 13* however, stems from its ability to induce a notion of the 'authentic'. In engendering what might be described as 'total verisimilitude', the film creates a 'documentary-like' accuracy which, paradoxically derives from processes of cinematic construction. For Prokop:

> What makes its skilful recreation of the event even more extraordinary is the fact that, unlike previous films recounting America's space program, not one shot of NASA stock footage was used in its making. From the awe-inspiring launch sequence to the suspenseful splashdown, every significant moment of the Apollo 13 mission was created through a combination of live action photography on sets and full-scale mock-ups, practical effects, motion control model work and computer generated artifice (1995: 61).

An inherent contradiction emerges in this assessment. It posits the notion that the use of visual technologies in the film-making process produces a level of artifice which prescribes a greater authenticity. Prokop defines the film as compelling through its ability to recreate, copy or simulate the 'real'.

On one level *Apollo 13* depicts a perspective of history; a rendering which offers a way of viewing the past. Yet its tools of production effectively go beyond mere representation. Its absolute precision visually shapes a past which *becomes the authentic reality of the event*. For Baudrillard, cinema, 'in its current efforts is getting closer and closer, and with greater and greater perfection, to the absolute real', and in turn produces an 'implacable fidelity to the materiality of the past' (1981, trans. 1994: 46–47). The postmodern cinematic spectacle is the epitome of Baudrillard's 'hyperreality' which, when depicting historical events, defines the boundaries of what is perceived and therefore what is known. What is interesting is how this authentic past is a simulation constructed from a range of already recognizable visual signifiers. History thus becomes a re-processing of symbolic markers which are used as the foundation of 'authenticity'.

The visually impressive launch scene in *Apollo 13* is an example of such historicizing. The entire sequence derives its authenticity from its precise simulation of recognizable cultural reference points. The ritualistic 'suiting-up' of the astronauts, the nervous wives taking their seats in the public gallery, the astronauts walking out to board the rocket carrying their life support systems by their side, are all familiar iconographies. Mission control, with its rows of computer terminals in front of a large screen, appears simultaneously futuristic and 'out-of-date'. The familiarity (and authenticity) of the milieu however, is indisputable. This is underpinned by the sublime seduction of the film's visual effects.

The camera pans up and down the side of the Saturn V rocket almost in reverence to the perfection of the simulation. Minute details such as the sun casting shadows across the rocket add aesthetic depth to a text that collapses boundaries between documentary, period drama and science-fiction. Science-fiction is, in fact, a generic inaccuracy. *Apollo 13* should be viewed as science-non-fiction or science 'reality'. The moment of lift-off itself is an event so distant, yet so familiar, that it dissolves the boundary between direct experience and mediated knowledge. What a rocket launch looks, sounds and feels like, is defined by this spectacle. The raw visceral power is so overwhelming that acceptance of its authenticity is not asked of the viewer, but demanded. Captured through a series of vertical camera angles and top-to-bottom pans, the explosiveness of the ascension is underscored by the sound of roaring jet engines and shaking cameras. The dramatic score builds to a crescendo climaxing when the immortal phrase 'we have lift off' is uttered.

'Authenticity' here does not derive from an arbitrary collection of visual and thematic tropes. The precision in the deployment of recognizable reference points cultivates historical 'reality'. Two shots during the launch sequence, each lasting less than five seconds, epitomize this discourse. Firstly, as the Saturn rocket ascends into the sky the camera remains static, as large red letters spell out 'UNITED STATES', passing upwards through the frame one at a time. The second shot takes place as the rocket breaks free of Earth's atmosphere. The camera points backward as the first stage separates and falls away with the Earth framing the shot in the distance.[1] Both exact sequences can be found in Al Reinert's 1989 documentary *For All Mankind* which uses a large selection of NASA's own footage, and also in a collection of launch clips on the NASA website.[2]

Referencing of this 'original' (documentary) footage is designed to dissolve the boundary between 'reality' and representation. Original documentary footage in itself, however, cannot claim to be unmediated truth. The very process of filming adds a creative subjectivity and can't replicate what we might tentatively call the aura of direct experience. Documentary as a form is just as problematic as fiction film in asserting a notion of 'truth' (Winston, 1995). The use of 'documentary' footage as an intertextual guarantor of authenticity, I suggest, transmutes a postmodern historicity reliant on the perpetual copying of a copy. For Baudrillard such endless reproduction constitutes a realm of absolute simulation in which the real collapses into a hyper-reality of signs:

> It is no longer a question of imitation, nor duplication, nor even parody. It is a question of substituting the signs of the real for the real, that is to say of an operation of deterring every real process via its operational double, a programmatic metastable, perfectly descriptive machine that offers all the signs of the real and short-cuts all its vicissitudes (2001: 522).

Cinematic representation has become the arbiter of history, sublimely creating a past through the reproduction of aesthetics that are themselves copies of the real. *Capricorn One* (Hyams, 1978) tells of a faked mission to Mars and the conspiratorial dangers of manufacturing history. *Apollo 13* revels in its mastery of such artifice. The result of this visual inveiglement collapses history where distinctions between past, present and future become annulled.

The very visual immediacy of postmodern cinema is inherently seductive in working to replace the materiality of history with sublime myth. This undoubtedly has ideological implications. A film such as *Apollo 13* becomes a nostalgic artefact in which a utopian view of the past is woven into social fabric as cultural memory. Jameson asserts that, 'In the nostalgia film, the image – the surface sheen of a period fashion reality – is consumed, having been transformed into a visual commodity' (1986: 303). The production of such a consumable history is not solely an effect of the surface aesthetics, however, but extends to the film's depiction of wider formations concerning American society. As McCrisken and Pepper point out, 'The displacement of the historically "real" into myth, therefore, is part of a wider process whereby cultural forms avail themselves to the task of re-inscribing the status quo' (2005: 17). In *Apollo 13* the rendering of 1970s America epitomizes an ideological mythologizing through its presentation of a utopia of the past: a retrotopia.

'Retrotopia' and the manufacture of ideology

The film's production uses a range of familiar visual markers, including relevant cars, clothes, hairstyles and set design to elicit the 'feel' of the period. More important than these historical artefacts, however, is an allusion to an idealized sense of community which emanates from the character's shared ideological values. Elements such as teamwork, friendship and duty are bound together by the seemingly interminable glue of family, nationhood and bravery. This is established early in the film when Jim Lovell's (Tom Hanks) family and a large group of fellow astronauts and friends gather to watch Neil Armstrong set foot on the moon. The collective gathering to witness a seminal moment in American history calls to an imagined yet sincere sense of community and national identity (Anderson, 1983). This depiction of historical context, I suggest, invokes a nostalgic idealism emptied of any political or cultural dissent.

Vietnam, the civil rights movement and women's liberation are collectively an absent presence alluded to only fleetingly. The entire counter-culture is symbolized by Lovell's teenage daughter having a tantrum about the break-up of the Beatles. Lizzie Francke attests to this unsophisticated appropriation of social background:

> The political context is conspicuously disregarded here. Instead, director Ron Howard shows us a bright and cheerful America, blooming with vibrant flower prints and grooving to Jimi Hendrix and James Brown. Only the comment about the Beatles indicates that the 60s dream is about to turn sour (Francke, 1995: 43).

The negation of such social aspects, I argue, deliberately undermines the possibility of critical interrogation. What is created is a Disneyland of harmless adventure, whitewashed of any thematic which would disturb the coherence of its flawless model. A review in the *New York Times* suggests that the spectre of political context augments the positive aspects of the narrative, '*Apollo 13* doesn't mention Vietnam, but it doesn't have to. The war-weary climate of that time enhances this film's wishful, stirring faith in American know-how' (Maslin: 1995). The suggestion here is that an *a priori* understanding of such social context automatically frames how the film will be understood. Yet the sophistication of the simulated artifice destroys any direct or subconscious connection to wider political discourse and creates a historical document free from contradictory anxiety.

This is reflected in the way *Apollo 13* was utilized as a template for the discussion of social issues in the United States. Reverence for the philosophical and ideological aspects of the space race became a metaphor for a re-branding of American achievement. Martin Walker in *Sight and Sound* commented at the time of the film's release:

> There is something about the current American mood which makes the 25-year-old success of the Apollo missions and the Apollo rescue politically important. The first full screening of *Apollo 13* took place at the White House, at the President's request. Then in a long speech to his old university, Georgetown, on 'Responsible Citizenship and the American Community', Clinton cited *Apollo* 13 repeatedly. It was an example of the American ability to overcome mortal challenge (Walker, 1995: 7).

In this context the film is defined as an authentic benchmark for a conception of idealized American identity. Yet this is again indicative of a postmodern dissolving of reality into representation. The nostalgic construction of the 1970s is reflected through a 1990s lens which symbolizes an imaginary utopia of the past cleansed of complex ideological oppositions. Tom Crouch, in the *Sight and Sound*, states:

> Whatever his commitment to accuracy in the presentation of technical detail, Ron Howard clearly intended to reproduce a fable for the 1990s, a nostalgic reminder of a time, not so long ago, when Americans accepted a difficult challenge and saw it through to a triumphant conclusion (Crouch, 1997: 1181).

This unqualified acceptance of *Apollo 13* as an authentic historical document imbues its cinematic vision as a template. Utopia lies not in reaching for an increasingly indefinable future but returning to an imagined ideal of the past: a 'retrotopia'. This concept is epitomized by the retro-film, 'which recreate the feel, shape and tone of older films while remaining incontestably up-to-date' (Brown *et al.*, 2001: 58). *Apollo 13* relies on the stimulation of recognizable symbolic markers which authenticate its representation of the space race. But this, in turn, is produced through the visual technologies and stylistic language of the postmoden era which reveal the film's very up-to-date-ness.

Retrotopia here isn't merely a postmodern 'take' on what has gone before but an ideological affirmation of a constructed historical ideal which incorporates elements of the past and future. As Brown *et al.* outline:

> The present is characterized by material progress and moral decline, the past by moral probity and material deficiency. Utopia, therefore, does not lie in the future, because material advance will come at moral cost. Nor does it lie in the past, since a material

price has to be paid for moral worth. It resides rather in the interaction of the two – retrotopia – where the best of the past meets the best of the future, where handicraft embraces high technology, where form and content combine (Brown *et al.*, 2000: 174).

Retrotopia not only defines the film's visual aesthetics and social context but also underpins the construction of identity in terms of the astronaut's idealized masculinity. Friedberg suggests that contemporary cinema's historicizing produces 'detemporalized subjectivities', indicative of a 'postmodern condition' which fosters, 'an increasingly derealized sense of 'presence' and identity' (1993: 2). On the one hand, *Apollo 13's* astronauts embody an un-reconstituted version of the astronaut myth. Yet, on the other hand, the text rearticulates elements of masculinity derivative of a postmodern sensibility. In these terms the postmodernism of the film authenticates constructions of masculinity that are inevitably influenced by contextual shifts of postmodernity. The outcome of this, which I discuss in the following section, is the authentication of a masculinity defined in a nexus between past and future, traditional and progressive, modern and postmodern.

Re-articulating homosocial enactment

In one early scene, Lovell returns home to tell his wife Marilyn (Kathleen Quinlan) that his reserve crew has been promoted to prime crew for the Apollo 13 mission. His excited demeanour at the misfortune of fellow astronaut Alan Shepard's ear infection, which has prevented him from commanding the mission, demonstrates the competitive, individualist underpinning of the astronaut myth. Lovell's joke that he 'wouldn't want to be around Alan Shepard tonight', exemplifies an individual drive and ruthlessness definitive of the astronaut's (hegemonic) identity. Masculine power and competitiveness effectively, 'facilitates hierarchy in relationships' (Bird, 1996: 122), a factor epitomized by how the astronaut is dependant on the subordination of others (engineers, ground crew, wives and fellow astronauts) for their own symbolic ascendancy. Lovell epitomizes how for heroic men, 'the enterprise of winning is life-consuming and this form of competitiveness, "an inward turned competitiveness focussed on the self" creates, in fact, an instrumentality of the person' (Donaldson, 1993: 655).

Lovell's internalized competitiveness becomes even more acutely defined when he cuts one of his own crew from the mission, command module pilot Ken Mattingly (Gary Sinise), as he is diagnosed with measles. When Mattingly learns that he is to be replaced, his reaction is anger and frustration yet his realization that it was Lovell's personal decision to cut him from the crew, rather than a bureaucratic choice by NASA, changes his perception. Mattingly says to Lovell, 'This was your call? It must have been a tough one', a statement which implies a mutual understanding and even empathy between the two men that belies their competitive masculinity. Lovell feels guilty for making the ruthless decision and Mattingly understands that he would have done exactly the same thing. This is one in a series of subtle moments in which the film effects a re-articulation of the competitive, individualized masculinity definitive of these iconic heroes. Out of the discourses that underpin the astronaut's gendered and hegemonic cultural repertoire, emerges an empathic, mutually-reliant masculinity borne out of a progressive homosociality.

Michael Kimmel defines 'homosocial enactment' as a process through which 'we (men) test ourselves, perform heroic feats, take enormous risks, all because we want other men to grant us our manhood' (2001: 275). In *Apollo 13* this is explicitly realized through the relationship between the three crew members Lovell, Haise (Bill Paxton) and Swigert (Kevin Bacon). As the 'rookie', and Mattingly's replacement, Swigert initially finds it difficult to be accepted into the homosocial framework. His abilities are questioned throughout practice simulations and this is crystallized when he 'stirs' the oxygen tanks which inadvertently causes the capsule's crippling explosion. At one point Haise blatantly implies that the explosion is Swigert's fault. Swigert's deficiency as an astronaut, I suggest, is symbolically underpinned by a discourse in which his status as a bachelor invokes a sexually and socially 'dangerous' masculinity.

The conception of the astronaut as a family man is central to his mythology as it links to ideologies of national identity, heterosexuality and 'American values'. Swigert's bachelorhood marks an ambiguity which Ehrenreich (1983) suggests has traditionally been linked to lack of maturity, responsibility and even latent homosexuality. Any allusion to Swigert's character breaking the homosociality/homosexuality boundary however, is strictly policed in the film. In the opening party scene, Swigert flirts overtly with his date. Holding a beer bottle and a glass end to end he playfully describes the docking manoeuvre in space while mimicking sexual penetration:

> This is me here in the command module (he holds up the bottle) and this is you in the LM (holds up the glass). This thing that sticks out in front is the probe. Tracy, when you feel that thing slide in, everything's clicking, it's like no other feeling in the world (*Apollo 13*: 1995).

There is no ambiguity here as to Swigert's heterosexual orientation. Such a characterization simultaneously sets up a dichotomy between Swigert's, unrestrained and dangerous sexuality, and the 'safe', ideologically sanctioned sexuality of his two colleagues.

Lovell and Haise epitomize what Sobchack calls 'virginal astronauts', who engender a bland, mechanical competence that is devoid of all corporeality:

> They are never 'sexy'. Their wooden postures and – dare I say it – tight assed competence disallow any connection with the sexual and sensuous. *2001's* astronaut Poole, basking nearly naked under a sunlamp, is hardly a piece of beefcake. Thus, whether named Buzz or Armstrong, Buck, Flash, or Bowman, our public astronauts reek of locker-room camaraderie, but hardly of male sweat or semen (1990: 108).

The casting of Tom Hanks in particular is key here. Despite winning two Oscars for roles that, on the surface, problematize aspects of masculinity in contemporary culture, namely gay lawyer Andy Becket in *Philadelphia* (Demme, 1993) and the intellectually challenged *Forrest Gump* (Zemeckis, 1994), Hanks arguably brings an everyman persona that negates the development of potent oppositional anxieties. Fred Pfeil conceptualizes this as Hanks's 'politics of the American "nice" ', through which he embodies an acceptable, but no less hegemonic, alternative to the rampaging 'angry white men' of 1980s and 1990s Hollywood cinema. Hanks himself has recounted his contribution to the role of astronaut:

> I can't do what (Mel) Gibson and (Kevin) Costner do. But they can't bring to their roles what I can bring. People relate to me as a regular guy. If Costner had played Jim Lovell (as was considered) it would have been a completely different focus on that story. It would have been about him. I'm just one of three guys in the pod. That's how it was (Hanks in Gardner, 2007: 199).

Hanks' persona is designed to engender the 'ordinariness' of the astronaut which, rather than dramatizing the role, supposedly adds to the historical authenticity.

One of the key traits that Hanks displays across his roles, according to Pfeil, is sexual passivity or muteness. This is defined in his early films in terms of the boyishness or lack of experience which undermines his accession to manhood (*Splash*, 1984; *Big*, 1988) and in his later films through physical or symbolic separations from female characters (*Sleepless in Seattle*, 1993; *Forrest Gump*, 1994; *The Green Mile* 1999; *Cast Away*, 2000). Even in *Philadelphia* the role of a gay AIDS sufferer, which would seemingly constitute quite a departure, is rendered non-threatening due to, 'not only Hanks's charmingly arrested boyishness but the Hanks persona's equally consistent indifference and disinclination to any politics' (Pfiel, 2002: 2007). The casting of Tom Hanks as Jim Lovell is therefore ideologically perfect for the apolitical, overtly nostalgic construction of an idealized, non-threatening masculine hero.

The 'tight assed competence' of Lovell and Haise contrasts markedly with Swigert's unconcealed sexuality. Yet such oppositions become increasingly negated as a more inclusive homosocial framework emerges. After Swigert completes the tricky power-up procedure ready for re-entry into the Earth's atmosphere, Haise, filmed from above so he appears in a submissive position, nods his head at Swigert and says, 'way to go Jack'. Swigert nods his head back in recognition. This understated exchange validates Swigert's status as a competent astronaut, which has been questioned throughout. As all three astronauts take their seats for the re-entry phase, Lovell, after realizing he has accidentally sat in Swigert's chair, the emblematic pilot's seat, says: 'Sorry Jack, old habit, I'm used to the pilot's seat, she's yours to fly'.[3] Swigert, through processes of homosocial enactment, affirms his status within the crew and his dangerous 'masculinity' is progressively incorporated into a sphere of acceptance.

Further re-articulations of masculinity at times do actually begin to blur what Sedgwick (1985) defines as the traditionally unbroken separation between homosociality and homosexuality. Typically, *Apollo 13* employs various strategies to enforce the astronaut's unquestioned heterosexuality as a counterpoise to the physical closeness and lack of privacy in the capsule. The use of close-up, tight editing and hand-held cameras shooting from awkward angles again attempts to relay the confines of the environment authentically. Any perceived anxieties concerning bodily closeness and functionality however, are regularized through humour. As Lovell detaches the 'relief tube' that is connected between his legs he quips, 'it's a pity we can't show this on television.' The camera cuts to a trail of urine floating off into space. Haise jokes, 'the constellation urine'. Here bodily functions and physical proximity are treated with a knowing irony that serves to preclude any drift into sexual ambiguity.

Such proprieties start to become destabilized, albeit in very subtle ways, as the emotional effects of the crisis begin to take their toll on the crew. Emotional detachment has often been conceptualized as intrinsic to the 'rationality' of masculine identity. For Stephen Whitehead, 'the idea that emotional maturity is the province of the female, and that men are emotionally incompetent, only serves to further reinforce the gendered public and private dualism at the heart of most societies, modern or otherwise' (2002: 175). I suggest that the traditional construction of the astronaut's identity epitomizes a post-enlightenment rational masculinity whose emotional repression underpins individuality, competitiveness and heterosexual stability. Yet the crisis of *Apollo 13* reveals a latent internalization of physical pain and psychological anxiety as the crew look to each other more directly for emotional support.

As Haise develops a fever the plummeting temperatures of the capsule begin to affect him. He and Lovell discuss getting home to their families. Haise suddenly says, 'it hurts when I urinate.' Lovell is seemingly surprised by this but displays empathy and concern. 'You're not getting enough water' he suggests as the two men share a look of understanding and empathy. This simple revelation and interchange, I argue, depicts an intimacy between the two characters which subverts emotional detachment. Haise, however, jokingly suggests, 'I think old Swigert gave me the clap, he's been pissing in my relief tube'. This restores the sanctioned homosocial boundary by again referencing Swigert's 'dangerous' sexuality. Yet as Haise's health gets progressively worse, all three astronauts increasingly display moments of intimacy, emotion and empathy. At one point Lovell sees that Haise is shivering. He hugs him, rubbing his shoulders to increase the circulation, and reassures him saying, 'Just a little while longer, we'll be in that water in the south pacific. We'll open the hatch, it's 80 degrees outside.' Such glimpses of emotional vulnerability invoke wider 'transformations of intimacy' (Giddens, 1992) which infuse the traditional astronaut mythology with elements of gender expression that could be considered contextually postmodern. Yet these 're-articulations' of masculinity do not totally reject the hegemonic archetype or the markers that make the astronaut recognizable.

Apollo 13 finds ways of fusing dualities to create an idealized masculinity that, both in terms of form and content, is transcendent. This is reinforced when hierarchies that structure masculine relationships are transformed into a more egalitarian form, specifically in terms of the binary opposition between astronaut and scientist. At various points the ingenuity and dedication of the engineers at mission control is foregrounded as the central construction of masculine heroism. When a makeshift air filter is required to combat the ship's rising carbon dioxide levels, a group of 'geeky' boffins build the device from any available materials. The procedure for construction is then relayed to the astronauts by the capcom.[4] When the crew attach the device to the life support system, the carbon dioxide levels immediately fall saving the astronauts' lives. Back at mission control the capcom turns to the short, balding chief engineer and exclaims, 'You, sir, are a steely eyed missile man.' The scientist's performance of the heroism at the centre of the narrative subverts the role normally reserved for the protagonists who, in turn, become passive subjects stripped of hegemonic agency.

I suggest that such shifts in definition of what constitutes a masculine hero mirrors changes in perspectives illustrative of the transition from the 1970s era of human space exploration to the 1990s era of travelling in cyberspace. *Apollo 13* depicts a time when Neil Armstrong was idolized but was produced in the era of Bill Gates. For Jodi Dean:

> Like and indeed part of the technological transformations that made spaceflight possible, those in computing and networked communications effect more than a revisioning of the active/passive, spectacle/spectator binaries of astronaut/audience citizenship (1998: 69).

With the astronaut defined as the ascendant and often sole protagonist of the space-age dream, the scientist is traditionally marginalized from what Connell (1995) describes as the 'hegemonic circle of legitimacy'. Yet the rise of computer and communication technology, indicative of postmodern culture, has altered this dynamic. *Apollo 13* in its centralizing of the role of the engineers and scientists reflects this change.

An embodiment of a retrotopian fusion of the astronaut and scientist emerges in the figure of the previously emasculated Ken Mattingly. Cut from the original crew by Lovell, Mattingly returns to play a pivotal role in returning the astronauts to Earth and in doing so represents a masculine ideal transcendent of past and present, modern and postmodern, dominant and benign. He is called in to help devise the power-up procedure by running a series of tests in the capsule 'simulator'. As he discusses the procedure with engineer John Young (Loren Dean) an embodied 'simulation' becomes the tool through which masculinity is redefined:

Mattingly: Have you started on a procedure?
Young: The engineers have tried but it's your ship. We gotta get you in there.
Mattingly: Ok, I need the same cold and dark, gimme the exact same conditions they've got in there now and I need present status of every instrument. I need a flashlight. (*Young hands him a large yellow torch.*) That's not what they have up there. Don't give me anything they don't have on board.
Young: Let's get this show on the road, put him in space fellas.

On a practical level, Mattingly is attempting to recreate the exact conditions the astronauts in space are experiencing so that the procedures he develops will be able to be carried out.

This 'simulated' role as astronaut however, rearticulates the masculinity that was taken away when he was cut from the mission. Yet it is no longer derived from the intrinsic competitiveness or individuality of the astronaut myth. Mattingly, in essence has to reject these elements in favour of re-constituting his identity through support, empathy and acceptance of what is traditionally considered a supporting role. The simulation however allows him to enact the central role. Idealized masculinity at this point deconstructs the boundary between astronaut and engineer, and therefore the hegemonic and subordinate hierarchy. After solving the problems of the power-up procedure, Mattingly takes over the Capcom to relay the instructions to Swigert. In the final scenes these two previously oppositional characters personify a 'retrotopian' ideal which has merged the astronaut's traditional symbolic repertoire with a pluralized and less hierarchical gender identity indicative of a postmodern context.

Conclusion

The seductive power of *Apollo 13*'s 'retrotopia' amalgamates images, themes and narratives of past and present, to create an ideological milieu, which is historicized as 'authentic'. At the centre of this the astronaut embodies a transition, in terms of both form and content, which is expressive of a postmodern *zeitgeist*. The film offers a deconstruction of hegemony and perhaps even represents a glimpse of what a more progressive egalitarian form of masculinity might look like. Traditional masculine subjectivity, which underpins a power and dominance men are often unwilling to relinquish, is re-imagined and re-articulated through aesthetic and thematic processes that I characterize as 'retrotopian'. The masculinity produced implies a transcendence which effectively negates the figure's underlying hegemonic potential. Such a 'historicizing' process infers a notion of idealized masculinity that is imbued as a 'reality' outside of specific, socially constructed contexts. In this sense, rather than negating or subverting the ideological dominance of the astronaut's identity, hegemonic masculinity is perpetually replayed. The transcendence of male power, which occurs through aesthetic form, thematic content and social context, is arguably facilitated through the very postmodern malleability of identity representation.

My reading of *Apollo 13* necessarily acknowledges the uncertainty of definitive constructions of the past, present and future. In this regard, retrotopias can morph into futuretopias at any given point. Yet the representations of the idealized male hero, in transcending such shifting contexts, epitomizes the transformative power of hegemonic masculinity. In order to decipher mythologies, particularly of masculine identity, the ways in which traditional, coherent formulations retain their cultural potency, despite myriad shifts in the dynamics of stylistic representation and social contextualization, remains a key avenue of analysis.

Notes

1 A photo still of this shot can be found at http://www.antiquark.com/img/saturn-v-separation. jpg
2 This an array of short clips of the Saturn V launch (and other launches such as the Space Shuttle), the composition, angle and framing of which are replicated with quite striking similarity in *Apollo 13*. See http://spaceflight.nasa.gov/gallery/video/apollo/apollo11/html/launch.html.
3 Even though during re-entry no actual 'flying' takes place, the Command Module pilot traditionally sits in the pilot's seat, rather than the Mission Commander, giving him symbolic control of the landing.
4 Capcom is the capsule communicator. He is the only one allowed to talk directly to the crew and the role is always fulfilled by another astronaut.

References

Anderson, B., (1983), *Imagined Communities,* London: Verso.
Barthes, R., (1957), translated by A. Lavers (1972), *Mythologies,* New York: The Noonday Press.
Baudrillard, J., (1981, translated 1994), *Simulacra and Simulation,* Michigan: University Press.
Baudrillard, J., (2001), 'The Precession of Simulacra' in M.D. Durham and D.M. Kellner (eds), *Media and Cultural Studies: Keyworks,* Oxford: Blackwell.
Bird, S.R., (1996), 'Welcome to the Men's Club: Homosociality and the Maintenance of Hegemonic Masculinity', *Gender and Society,* Vol.10 No.2. April.
Brown, S., Hirschman, E. C. and Maclaran, P., (2000), 'Presenting the Past: On Marketing's Reproduction Orientation', in S. Brown and A. Patterson (eds), *Imagining Marketing: Art, Aesthetics and the Avant-Garde,* London and New York: Routledge.
Brown, S., Hirschman, E.C. and Maclaran, P., (2001), 'Always Historicize!: Research Marketing History in a Post-Historical Epoch', *Marketing Theory,* Vol 1(1).
Connell, R. W., (1995), *Masculinities,* Cambridge: Polity Press.
Crouch, T. C., (1997), 'Apollo 13: Review', *The Journal of American History,* Vol. 84, no. 3 December.
Dean, J., (1998), *Aliens in America: Conspiracy Cultures from Outerspace to Cyberspace,* Cornell: University Press.
Donaldson, M., (1993), 'What is Hegemonic Masculinity?' *Theory and Society,* Volume 22 no 5, October.
Ehrenreich, B., (1983), *The Hearts Of Men: American Dreams and the Flight from Commitment,* London: Pluto Press.
Francke, L., (1995), 'Apollo 13: Review', *Sight and Sound,* Vol 5 No 9, September.
Friedberg, A., (1993), *Window Shopping: Cinema and the Postmodern,* California: University Press.
Giddens, A., (1992), *The Transformation of Intimacy: Sexuality, Love and Eroticism in Modern Societies,* Cambridge and Oxford: Polity Press.
Jameson, F., (1984), 'Postmodernism, or The Cultural Logic of Late Capitalism', *New Left Review,* No 146, July–August.
Jameson, F., (1986), 'On Magic Realism in Film', *Critical Enquiry,* Vol. 12, No.2, Winter.
Kellner, D. and Ryan, M., (1990), *Camera Politica: The Politics and Ideology of Contemporary Hollywood Film,* Indiana: University Press.

Kerfoot, D., (2001), 'The Organisation of Intimacy: Managerialism, Masculinity and the Masculine Subject', in S. M. Whitehead and F. J. Barrett (eds), *The Masculinities Reader,* Cambridge: Polity Press.

Kimmel, M. S., (2001), 'Masculinity as Homophobia' in S. M. Whitehead and F. J. Barrett (eds), *The Masculinities Reader,* Oxford and Cambridge: Polity Press.

Maslin, J., (2007), '*Apollo 13*: Review.' *New York Times* June 30, 1995. http://movies.nytimes.com/ movie/review?res=990CE0D7123FF933A05755C0A963958260 [accessed 9 August]

McCrisken, T. and Pepper, A., (2005), *American History and Contemporary Hollywood Film,* Edinburgh: University Press.

Mailer, N., (1970), *A Fire on the Moon,* London: Weidenfeld & Nicholson.

Prokop, T., (1995), 'Launching Apollo', *Cinefex* 63: 58–89.

Rynning, R., (1995), 'Ground Control to Major Tom', *Film Review,* October 19.

Sedgewick, E. K., (1985), *Between Men: English Literature and Male Homosocial Desire,* New York: Columbia University Press.

Sobchack, V., (1990), 'The Virginity of Astronauts: Sex and the Science Fiction Film' in A. Kuhn (ed.) *Alien Zone: Cultural Theory and Contemporary Science Fiction Cinema,* London and New York: Verso.

Walker, M., (1995), 'Apollo and Newt', *Sight and Sound,* Vol 5 No 9, September.

Whitehead, S., (2002), *Men and Masculinities,* Oxford and Cambridge: Polity.

Winston, B., (1995), *Claiming The Real: The Documentary Film Revisited,* London: BFI Publishing.

Wolfe, T., (1979), *The Right Stuff,* London: Jonathan Cape.

Middle America, the moon, the sublime and the uncanny

Darren Jorgensen

A contradiction haunts cultural histories of Apollo 11. This is the contradiction of an American public that, for the most part, did not support the expense of the moon landing, but did turn it into the most popular television broadcast in history. Here I want to argue that the 55 per cent of viewers who opposed the expenditure of the landing were nonetheless compelled to watch it because it represented their own alienation from a certain version of America (Nye, 1996: 71). Rather than an heroic victory for the American way of life, the broadcast represented the kinds of disorientation and self-doubt that this society was experiencing during the 1960s. Shots of the bleak darkness of space and an inhospitable moon were as estranging as the astronauts themselves, who spoke in an impersonal, technocratic language to describe the flight. It is useful to think of the public's experience of Apollo aesthetically, as the sheer strangeness of the mission contradicted the imperatives of this government project to sell space travel to the American public. Here I turn to the aesthetic ideas of the sublime and uncanny in order to think through this strangeness. These ideas are useful for thinking about the way in which the landing was compelling viewing for many Americans who nonetheless disapproved of it. The sublime is useful in making sense of this compulsion, as it describes the combination of discomfort and elation in witnessing a newly unfolding cosmos. The uncanny brings the sublime into the 20th century, situating its discomfort in the home, where Americans witnessed the moon landing on television. The landing turned the homely into the unhomely, as viewers saw the familiar ideals of American life displaced onto the hostile lunar surface.

Kant's sublime

Immanuel Kant originally wrote on cosmography, speculating on the meaning of the starry heavens as they appeared through the early telescopes of the 18th century (Kant, 1755). When, later in life, he came to philosophize about the sublime, he turned to these starry heavens to illustrate his experience of elation. The sight of outer space brings about elation for Kant because it implies an infinitude that lies not only in nature but also in one's own mind (Kant, 1790:

95). Gazing at the stars, Kant knows that they are far away, and yet in being able to think this distance, to hold this greatness in his mind, grasps the dimensions of the universe. Thought agrees with this immensity that produces a pleasure that exceeds the bodily senses, this being a supersensible pleasure (Kant, 1790: 97). Such is the pleasure of thinking about Apollo 11, which brings about a supersensible pleasure because it demonstrates that the human mind has mastered the infinite. The mind appears all-powerful in its ability to configure a spacecraft that will travel from Earth to the moon and back again. Yet this is not an unproblematic pleasure. Georg Hegel's critique of Kant, for one, argues that such cognitive pleasures domesticate the vast and incommensurable. He describes Kant's mathematical sublime as a bad infinite because it makes vastness amenable to a human mind that, in truth, does not really grasp the totality of infinity. Hegel's bad infinite is constituted by a repetition of the same, in an endless reproduction of the identical to itself (Hegel, 1830: 137–8). The infinite does not incite pleasure for Hegel but boredom instead, as it turns a series of differences into similitude.

Hegel's critique of Kant can be seen in the American media's representations of the Apollo 11 mission. *Life* magazine was the official NASA media organ, and it attempted to humanize the space programme. The August 1969 *Life Special Issue*, released to commemorate the landing, wants to produce sympathetic accounts of the astronauts. It is filled with glossy, high colour photographs of the astronauts mastering not only outer space, but their domestic spaces as well. Neil Armstrong bakes pizza, Buzz Aldrin jogs through the suburbs, and Mike Collins prunes his garden. These images resonate with outer space itself, as the astronauts use tools in both terrestrial and extraterrestrial environments. The spatula and shears the astronauts use to cook lamb curry and prune roses with resemble the objects they hold while walking the moon, these being a laser reflector, seismometer and solar wind sheet. The masculine mission to conquer the moon is feminized by the tools of kitchen and garden. As Jean Baudrillard writes of a later space mission:

> The conquest of space that follows that of the planet is equal to derealizing (dematerializing) human space, or to transferring it into a hyperreal of simulation. Witness this two-bedroom/kitchen/shower put into orbit, raised to a special power (one could say) with the most recent lunar module. The everydayness of the terrestrial habitat itself elevated to the rank of cosmic value, hypostatized in space . . . (Baudrillard, 1981: 124)

Media representations of space travel turn the vastness of space into the similitude of domesticity, as human familiarity comes to stand in for the infinite. At the same time, the domestic attains the dimensions of this infinite, and in turn becomes strangely unfamiliar to the television viewer.

This estranging combination of domestic and outer space is elaborately imagined by science fiction. At the end of the film *2001* (1968), released a year before Apollo 11, invisible superbeings who have manipulated human evolution welcome the astronaut Dave by reproducing a spacious but weird simulation of a Western living space. Dave wanders cavernous, shiny rooms that echo with the fragmented sounds of Earth, waiting for the aliens to make themselves known. A later story by J.G. Ballard, 'Report on an Unidentified Space Station' (1982), also simulates the strangeness of the modern human habitat in outer space. In this story a spaceship makes an emergency landing on an unidentified space station. It is uninhabited, and the crew of the ship begin to explore. They describe its interior as 'a series of open passenger concourses, with comfortably equipped lounges and waiting rooms' (Ballard, 1982: 96). At first they estimate the station's diameter to be five hundred meters. Upon wandering the many spaces of the station, each of which appears to be identical to the one before, the crew realize the station must be much larger than it appears from the outside. By the end of the story they estimate the station's size to be fifteen thousand light years. They wander indefinitely across this infinity of concourses and decks that extend infinitely up and down so that:

> Our instruments confirm what we have long suspected, that the empty space across which we have travelled from our own solar system in fact lies within the interior of the station, one of many vast lacunae set in its endlessly curving walls. Our solar system and its planets, the millions of other solar systems that constitute our galaxy, and the island universes themselves lie within the boundaries of the station. The station is coeval with the cosmos, and constitutes the cosmos. Our duty is to travel across it on a journey whose departure point we have already begun to forget, and whose destination is the station itself, every floor and concourse within it. (Ballard, 1982: 101)

This incredible image, of an endless series of transit lounges and concourses, captures the conjunction of the infinite with the historically specific space of the foyer or waiting room. Ballard's fantasy is sublime because it describes the infinite, yet does so as a repetition of the same, as a Hegelian bad infinite.

While Kant categorizes pleasure in the infinite as the mathematical sublime, the second type of Kant's sublime is the dynamical, which is impressed not by the capacity of the human mind but by the immensity of nature. Threatening rocks, volcanoes, spectacular clouds and mighty rivers inspire our fear and respect (Kant, 1790: 100). So it was that the moon appeared dynamically sublime as it loomed disconcertingly into view during the Apollo mission. In his book on the moon landing, Norman Mailer describes the way in which 'a reductive society was witnessing the irreducible', its rational, bourgeois lifestyle exposed to an alien mass (Mailer, 1970: 103). The living room, once the secure space of middle America – clean, well ordered, and a place to grow old in – was exposed to fearful immensity. Mailer finds an analogy for the defamiliarization that the moon engendered in an unidentified Rene Magritte painting. It shows a rock inside a room inside a house:

> In the foyer was a painting by Rene Magritte, a startling image of a room with an immense rock situated in the centre of the floor. The instant of time suggested by the canvas was comparable to the moon of a landscape in the instant just before something awful is about to happen, or just after, one could not tell. The silences of the

canvas spoke of Apollo 11 still circling the moon: the painting could have been photographed for the front page – it hung from the wall like a severed head (Mailer, 1970: 108)

Like the painting, the Apollo mission placed the incomprehensible inside televisions inside living rooms inside houses throughout middle America. Closer than ever before, the moon asserted its alien magnitude. While the laws of the universe are unravelled and manipulated by science, such laws do not explain the existence of this natural mass. Looming in the Apollo television footage is this repressed question of the moon's mysterious immensity. The Apollo programme, then, encountered Kant's doubled typology of the sublime: infinitude, in the mathematical pleasures of thinking outer space after its calculated conquest; and magnitude, represented by the natural mass of the moon itself. Yet these aesthetic affects are also curtailed by the banality of the American media's representations of the Apollo mission, as the astronauts carried with them an association with the domestic spaces and lifestyles of middle America.

Television

In 1960 televisions were in about 90 per cent of American homes, and switched on for an average of five hours a day (Spigel, 2001: 33). The rise in the medium's popularity coincided with the popular rise of family values in America over the course of the 1950s (Spigel, 2001: 31). In this decade, the American middle classes moved out of inner city communities and grouped themselves in nuclear family housing in the suburbs. Television brought a wider sense of social cohesion to these families, selling a national ideal that substituted for actual contact with wider society (Spigel, 2001: 43). Yet the social demographics of the country began to change over the course of the 1960s, with rising divorce rates and deaths in the Vietnam war. By 1969 many of the most popular sit-coms, such as *Family Affair* (1966–1971), *Here's Lucy* (1968–1974) and *Julia* (1968–1971), were about widows and widowers attempting to hold their families together. Despite this unprecedented representation of different family types, the living spaces of these programmes remained comfortably middle class, set as they were in spacious apartments and suburban homes. This standard of living contradicted the reality for many broken families in the US, who lived in much less affluent surroundings. American television continued to effect a 'social sanitization' of the American ideological landscape, maintaining this image of an affluent middle American lifestyle (Spigel, 2001: 53).

While not achieving the popularity of the sit-com, science fiction was also a part of the 1960s television experience. Shows such as *The Twilight Zone* (1959–1964), *The Jetsons* (1962–1963) and *Lost in Space* (1965–8) juxtaposed images of suburban and outer space. The characters use everyday artefacts such as cutlery and crockery, chairs and tables, in homes of the interstellar future. The limits of suburban objects give way to the vastness of their own beyond, imply-ing the infinite in the finitude of the everyday. An episode of *The Twilight Zone*, 'The Monsters are Due on Maple Street' (1960), anticipates Apollo 11 in imag-ining suburbia on the lunar landscape. Evil aliens, humanoid but for their pointed ears, lift an average American street from its neighbourhood and place it on the surface of the moon. The street's residents do not notice that they have been transported beyond the Earth and instead bicker with each other inces-santly. The aliens watch from a nearby spacecraft as petty conflict between the residents grows violent. The aliens conclude that to conquer the Earth all they need to do is leave the planet alone, since its inhabitants will end up killing each other anyway. Such science fiction television anticipated the Apollo 11 broad-cast. In *The Jetsons* and *Lost in Space*, suburban lifestyles are displaced. In *The Monsters are Due on Maple Street*, an entire suburban block, with its intact houses, letterboxes and parked cars, is placed upon the moon's wasteland and before the black void of space. This 1960 scene is a precursor to the images of astronauts on the moon. In both, a small group of people go about their busi-ness on a barren lunar surface, swimming in the cold void of space. Busy with their own anthropocentric purposes, Aldrin and Armstrong, like the residents of Maple Street, avoided an encounter with the extraterrestrial void that sur-rounded them.

The cold war

It is instructive to turn to the Soviet Union, whose media were also interested in promoting their own space programme with images of astronauts and outer space (see Kohonen, this volume). Images from Yaroslav Golovanov's *Our Gagarin* (1978) are in striking contrast to those of the 1969 *Life* Special Issue. This book promotes the cosmonaut Yuri Gagarin as a peasant made good, a man of the Earth who has not forgotten his roots in the planet's living soil. The black and white images of Gagarin strapped into his spaceship are in great contrast to the colour photographs of a home village that is lush with vegeta-tion. When he returned to Earth, Gagarin's parents met him dressed in poor, peasant clothes. The emphasis here is on Gagarin's roots, on the material, organic world from which he came. *Our Gagarin* works to humanize cosmonau-tics by tracing Gagarin back to the organic world, to family and the history of the Soviet Union's scientific endeavours. His orbit is also symbolic of the unity of the Earth itself, of this living planet that the old Soviet Union wanted to turn into a communist utopia. The early autobiographies of the cosmonauts are also instructive of just how the symbolism of cosmonautics differed from that of astronautics. As he passes over Africa, Second Cosmonaut Titov greets those struggling against colonialism. As Titov flies over the Soviet Union he envisages the great industrial apparatus that sent him into space, his ship symbolizing its achievements as 'the sun is reflected in a dewdrop' (Titov, 1963: 107). When the cosmonauts returned, they did not seek to individuate themselves from the

Soviet space programme, instead talking of their flights as 'our' flight that was shared with the nation (Burchett and Purdy, 1961: 120).

Gagarin's flight was broadcast on radio, but in 1973 the Soviets reached the moon with an unmanned rover equipped with a television camera. The footage of the moon broadcast home by Lukokhod 2 is less contaminated by the human figure (*Tank on the Moon*, 2008). This mission shows a barren, desolate and spectacular world. While Apollo 11 aligned a particularly human cognition with the structure of the universe, placing technology in a submissive relation to its human operators, the Soviet buggy demonstrated that technology can function independently of its creators. The absence of human crew on this Soviet mission points the way to a fully automated lunar programme that is independent of human control and presence. The most ambitious plans for such automation are machines that would reproduce themselves in space, mining and processing materials for their own exponential expansion. Physicist John von Neumann thinks that this would be the best way to mine the moon and the asteroids (Baxter, 2000: 13). Whether humans would ever follow is another question, and one that is largely irrelevant to the operation of the machines themselves. Such machines do not presume that the human species have an unrivalled claim to the universe. As science fiction writer Arthur C. Clarke writes, the existence of the machine in space suggests that 'a given problem must evoke the same kind of solution from any group of engineers' (Clarke, 1954: xvii). This is why the UFO appears plausible to the Western imagination. An alien intelligence will, according to machinic reason, come to the same technological conclusions as the human race. It will broadcast on radio waves and build metal spacecraft because the laws of the universe are essentially the same all over. The machine carries with it the extension of human cognition and a universal cognition that is also independent of the human.

New journalism and the astronauts

Commissioned by NASA to commemorate and celebrate Apollo 11, Mailer's *A Fire on the Moon* (1970) turns instead to the estrangement the author felt from the impersonal, technocratic sensibility that enveloped the astronauts, a sensibility that turned them into zombies of a greater Apollo machine. He attributes the melancholy he feels in confronting the astronauts, who have been rigorously trained to repress their emotional lives, to the loss of romantic heroism in modern life. The rugged qualities that once characterized the American male, who proved himself in the Wild West and on the front lines of World War Two, have been superseded by a coldness of character. Apollo turned the astronauts from heroic test pilots, depending on their manual skill and reaction time, into technocrats obsessed with the machines and routines that would achieve mission success. NASA feminized its astronauts, requiring them to have college degrees and an engineer's mind. Mailer thinks engineers better represent the spirit of the Apollo space programme than astronauts. For Mailer, the astronauts are themselves impoverished engineers. Full of technical talk about the mission, the spaceship, and the scientific goals of Apollo, they have forgotten the sublime experience of flight.

Even Louden Wainwright, appointed as *Life* magazine's official journalist to the astronauts and their families, and unofficial spokesperson for the NASA publicity line, complains that these men have little of interest to say. He quotes Neil Armstrong's answer to a question:

'I think we understand the nature of the difficulty that came up with the Apollo 10, even though we cannot precisely ascribe the difficulty to a certain failure. Our procedure is one where we have procedurally implemented methods of circumventing the problem and, should it occur, we have procedures that will be able to cancel the kind of problem we get in.' (Armstrong cited in Wainwright, 1969: 71)

Mailer dubs this kind of talk 'computerese', which is inaccessible to the 'average guy' (Mailer, 1970: 33, 11). Of all the astronauts, Neil Armstrong is the most uncompromising figure of Apollo efficiency. Unlike Aldrin and Mike Collins, Armstrong never released a book of his subjective experience of the flight. *Life* magazine compares him to a machine, declaring that he 'finds people far less efficient than aircraft and their performance generally short of their capacity' (Hamblin, 1969: 36). Aldrin, who walked beside Armstrong on the lunar surface, reports on his own repression of emotion in his account of the mission:

My strongest memory of those few hours as the first men on the lunar surface was the constant worry that we'd never accomplish all the experiments we were scheduled to do. Philosophy and emotion were not included and, in fact, were discouraged. (Aldrin, 1973: picture caption)

Yet even Aldrin was not efficient enough for Collins, who in *Carrying the Fire* (1974) confesses that he was irritated with Aldrin's introspection during the mission, judging him harshly for deviating from the set parameters laid down by NASA (Collins, 1974: 367–8). Collins also condemns an earlier astronaut, Scott Carpenter, who expressed his feelings on a mission, as 'kind of out of it' (Collins, 1974: 59). Carpenter nearly ran out of fuel orbiting the Earth because he was so enthusiastic about the flight. 'It seemed a pity that I was having to spend so much time worrying about a man-made object,' Carpenter writes, 'when God's own creations, just outside the window, were much more mysterious and challenging' (Carpenter, 1962: 337). The very first American astronaut, Alan Shepard, also appeared to have a more subjective experience of outer space. Although in orbit for just fifteen minutes, his voice trembled when he spoke of the flight (Wainwright, 1969: 73). Throughout the 1960s, NASA tightened its training regimes with a view to safety and mission success. Shepard and Carpenter are earlier exceptions to the efficient cognition that, by the late 1960s, NASA had ensured would come to define the experience of astronautics.

Tom Wolfe answers Mailer's complaint that the astronauts had been trained out of having emotions, even personality, in a series of *Rolling Stone* essays in 1973. He goes drinking with the astronauts just as the Apollo programme is being shut down, their future missions to the moon cancelled. He finds they are not so much technocrats as hard drinking, fast car driving, all male heroes. He accuses NASA of constructing a clean, all-American image of astronauts in order to sell the space programme. Like Mailer, Wolfe styled his writing after a so-called New Journalism that wanted to keep up with the cultural revolution taking place in America in the 1960s (Weber, 1975: 49). While Mailer employed New Journalism as a language of resistance to the ideologies of middle America, Wolfe is able to fashion its vernacular around the very conservative idea that astronauts are tough, all-male and all-American heroes after all. Wolfe describes the suburban family image of these men as the '*Life* screen', a charade played out for the good of the space programme. He cites one astronaut as saying that without *Life* 'we doubt that NASA could have ever succeeded in preserving the image of us as a bunch of God-loving crewcut Explorer Scouts' (Wolfe, 1973: 23). The jovial prose restores a certain virility to these astronauts whose missions were being grounded at the time of writing. Theirs was the problem of having what Wolfe calls 'the Right Stuff' with nowhere to express it (Wolfe, 1973: 23). They were the elect survivors of fatalities during the Korean war, in rocket plane tests and street racing accidents. They had proved themselves exceptionally gifted and capable, demonstrating a knack to survive at the limits of man's encounter with technology.

To show how manly they are, Wolfe turns to contrasting examples of feminine behaviour. As Wolfe gleefully reports, reporters for *Life* magazine were so nervous about Apollo missions that one had a heart attack and another threw up while watching the astronauts on television (Wolfe, 1973: 24). These reporters are from a booming white collar America. Caught up in the wealth of the post-war economy, American men were losing their virility to the paper professions. Even the astronaut's wives are tougher than the new American man, as they take care of these sick reporters while their husbands are in danger in outer space. Wolfe speculates that the wives are laughing from behind the curtains as reporters gather fearfully around their houses during missions (Wolfe, 1973: 26). Like the astronauts, they carry on the publicity charade for the sake of astronautics, but are not defined by it. Wolfe works hard to undermine NASA's careful illusion of middle American harmony, in an attempt to recreate America as a home for the brave. Aldrin's biography, also released in 1973, similarly criticises the media charade around Apollo 11. Confessing that he and many other astronauts were not the perfect model of middle America, Aldrin tells of extra-marital affairs and of a deep depression he experienced after Apollo 11. Aldrin wanted to 'stand up and be counted' as a real human being after being caught up in NASA's sanitized media programmne (Aldrin, 1973: 338).

Wolfe's later book, *The Right Stuff* (1979), recycles material from his *Rolling Stone* essays to describe the era of test piloting rocket planes in the 1940s and 1950s. He constructs this period as one in which these pilots had a certain boyish charm, and before the space programme became a more political and expensive part of the cold war. Wolfe portrays an ideal of American innocence, depicting young men in love with flight for its own sake. The astronauts measure themselves and each other with tests of '*Manliness, manhood, manly courage* . . . there was something ancient, primordial, irresistible about the challenge of the stuff, no matter what a sophisticated and rational age one might think he lived in' (Wolfe, 1979: 29). It is as if Wolfe wants to peel back the layers of technocracy and publicity that surrounded the NASA astronauts to reveal the tough, sexed identity that originally defined this generation. Perhaps by 1979, he felt that his battle to recover their heroic identity had been lost to NASA's mass media campaign to construct them as good rather than bad boys.

The uncanny

If the publicity campaign that accompanied the Apollo programme succeeded in domesticating outer space by subjecting it to technocratic principles, this had the reverse effect on domestic space itself. The clean spaciousness of the middle American home, its compartmentalization and efficiency, resonated uncannily with the interior of the Apollo spacecraft. The home was invaded by an extra-terrestrial image, of a small bubble of life hurtling through vast expanses to a hostile moon. Twentieth century theory would come to define this transformation of the sublime into the banal and disconcerting as the uncanny. Instead of being located elsewhere, in the vastness of the unconquered, the uncanny situates its estranging effects firmly within the known. Anthon Vidler writes that the uncanny is effected by a:

> contrast between a secure and homely interior and the fearful invasion of an alien presence; on a psychological level, its play was one of doubling, where the other is, strangely enough, experienced as a replica of the self, all the more fearsome because apparently the same. (Vidler, 1992: 3)

Apollo 11 was this very disconcerting repetition in the home, a repetition of middle America that was made strange by its mission to the moon. The vast stretches of sublime territory that revealed themselves to the European explorers of Kant's era had become, by the time of the space programme, a deterritorialized conquest, with no mountains, rivers or valleys to welcome the imagination. The interest in settlement that follows in the wake of conquest, the concept of a homestead or settlement, could not be established in an environment so hostile to life. Human beings, suited up and in danger, appeared uncannily out of place in this environment, repeating the old historical idea of conquest, but not welcomed by this hostile, unliving environment.

Sigmund Freud has had the most influence on the thinking around the uncanny. He tells of walking around an unnamed town in Italy, where he repeatedly runs across the same district of 'painted ladies' (Freud, 1919: 359). What disconcerts Freud is not only the repetition of this discomforting situation, but his own inability to find his way beyond it, as his unconscious drives him to return and return again to the scene of discomfort. Such repetition is also on the cover of the *Life Special Edition* of 1969 that commemorates the landing.

The cover shows the famous photograph of Aldrin standing on the moon, and Armstrong is reflected in his helmet's visor. Armstrong's own visor is itself reflecting Aldrin, and in his visor is Armstrong, in an infinite regress of astronauts. The repetition of the human figure in this strange, inhuman environment displaces Kant's supersensible identification with the universe, the scientific gaze upon the unknown becoming a repetition of the known. It supersedes the sublime with the grotesque uncanny, in a distortion of the human figure that is itself distorted by spacesuits, in anamorphic reflections of men costumed against their own vulnerability.

Such repetitions are in play as the astronauts, like boys, leave home to explore the vast universe. The home quickly turns into the unhomely, as this vastness makes the familiar strange. Despite their attempts to sanitize the mission, to make it familiar to television viewers, the media's representation of Apollo 11 could not cover over the contradictions that outer space presented to Americans. As moon dust coated the interior of the returning spacecraft, so the anxieties attendant upon encountering the void haunt representations of this journey into outer space.

For the psychoanalytic thinker Joan Copjec, working from Freud's models of the human psyche, the uncanny is symptomatic of man's encounter with woman. Copjec claims that, for man at least, woman does not exist, but instead shifts between different representations of woman. Man on the other hand is a transcendent, definite idea, which finds its way outside the series of feminine reflections by sitting beyond the regression of its own representations (Copjec, 1994: 217–227). The feminine is uncanny because it multiplies such representations, and enfolds everything it encounters within a series of distorted reflections of itself. The photographs of humans on the moon changed the masculine gaze upon an objective universe into a feminine regress, as these human figures repeat themselves in different, distorted variations. In grotesque spacesuits and reflected in convex visors, these figures displaced the sublime pleasures to be had in thinking about outer space. The ideologies of conquest, that had served European and American nations so well, turned uncanny as this conquest encountered the limits of the Earth, and the nothingness beyond. Human beings, or at least their figuration, were transformed by the alien environment and rendered unrecognizable by an infinite regression of distortion and reflection. What was to be a heroic arrival on an alien world was caught up in the sexed pathologies of human beings, the endless depths of outer space precluded from view by the bulky spacesuits of Armstrong and Aldrin.

Following his speculations on the uncanny, Freud published a longer essay suggesting that the body is itself attracted to repetition, that the drive to repeat and return is a biological compulsion. In *Beyond the Pleasure Principle* (1920), written amidst the horrors of World War One, Freud describes this drive as a morbid one, embedding an attraction of the body for its own death. The uncanny is a sign of the death drive, an attraction for the unchanging and inanimate that is written into the matter of cells, and which produces repressive structures of social and cultural life (Freud, 1920: 43–51). In the Apollo mission the inert, dead mass of the moon exerts such gravitation upon the body, which acts out the repetitions of a rigorous training programme. The astronauts were trained to repeat, rather than to experience that which had never been experienced before. In his biography Aldrin describes his time on the moon as identical to the training simulations, and the simulations to the experience of space travel itself (Aldrin, 1973: 232). Even to those who lived it, Apollo 11 was strange, removed from itself by its own compulsions. The heroic, masculine imperative that usually determines conquest turned into a feminine compulsion-repetition. After Freud, Apollo reveals an America that entertains a drive toward death, as it takes on repetitions that empty it of humanizing qualities. After Hegel, Apollo 11 represents a middle American domestication rather than a celebration of human beings in the universe. Rather than the pinnacle of American accomplishment, criticisms to do with the sublime and the uncanny point out just how much Apollo 11 represented an America that had become unhinged by its own technocracy, its middle class lifestyle, and television.

References

2001: A Space Odyssey, Dir. Stanley Kubrick. Screenplay by Arthur C. Clarke and Stanley Kubrick. Metro-Golden-Mayer, 1968.

Aldrin, B., (1973), *Return to Earth*, London: Random House.

Ballard, J.G., (1982), 'Report on an Unidentified Space Station', in J.G. Ballard (ed.), *War Fever*. London: Paladin: 96–101.

Baxter, S., (2000), *Space*, London: Voyager.

Baudrillard, J., (1981), *Simulacra and Simulation*, translated from French by Sheila Faria Glaser, Michigan: University of Michigan Press, 1994.

Burchett, W. and Purdy, A., (1961), *Cosmonaut Yuri Gagarin: First Man in Space*, London: Anthony Gibbs and Phillips.

Carpenter, M.S., (1962), 'The Confirmation', in *We Seven: The Astronauts Themselves*, New York: Simon and Schuster: 329–346.

Clarke, A.C., (1954), *Prelude to Space*, London: Pan.

Collins, M., (1974), *Carrying the Fire*, New York: Farrar Strauss Giroux.

Copjec, J., (1994), *Read my Desire: Lacan Against the Historicists*, Cambridge: MIT.

Family Affair (1966–1971), CBS.

Freud, S., (1919), 'The Uncanny', in *Penguin Freud Library: Art and Literature*, translated from German by J. Strachey, London: Penguin, 1953: 339–376.

Freud, S., (1920), *Beyond the Pleasure Principle*, translated from German, by J. Strachey, New York: W.W. Norton, 1961.

Golovanov, Y., (1978), *Our Gagarin*, Moscow: Progress.

Hamblin, D.J., (1969), *Neil Armstrong: He Could Fly Before He Could Drive*, Life Special Edition: To the Moon and Back, 10th August: 35–40.

Here's Lucy (1968–1974), CBS.

Hegel, G.W.F., (1975), [1830], *Hegel's Logic: Being Part One of the Encyclopaedia of the Philosophical Sciences*, translated from German by W. Wallace, Oxford: Clarendon.

The Jetsons (1962–1963), Hanna-Barbera.

Julia (1968–1971), Twentieth Century Fox.

Kant, I., (1755), [1970], *Cosmogony: As in his Essay on the Retardation of the Rotation of the Earth and his Natural History and Theory of the Heavens*, translated from German by W. Hastie, New York: Johnson.

Kant, I., (1790), [1987], *Critique of Judgement*, translated from German by W.S. Pluhar, Indianapolis: Hackett.

Life Special Edition: To the Moon and Back (1969), 10th August.

Lost in Space (1965–8), Twentieth Century Fox.

Mailer, N., (1970), *A Fire on the Moon*, London: Weidenfeld & Nicolson.

Nye, D., (1996), 'Don't Fly Us to the Moon: The American Public and the Apollo Program', *Foundation* 66, spring: 69–81.

Spigel, L., (2001), *Welcome to the Dreamhouse.*,Durham: Duke University Press.

Tank on the Moon, (2008), Science Channel.

Titov, H., (c1963), *700,000 Kilometres Through Space: Notes by Soviet Cosmonaut No. 2*, translated from Russian by S. Borzenko. Moscow: Foreign Languages Publishing House.

The Twilight Zone: The Monsters are Due on Maple Street (1960), Metro-Goldwyn-Mayer.

Vidler, A., (1992), *The Architectural Uncanny: Essays in the Modern Unhomely*, Cambridge: MIT.

Wainwright, L. (1969), *The Dawn of the Day Man Left his Planetary Cradle*. Life Special Edition: To the Moon and Back, 10th August: 73–74.

Weber, R., (1975), 'Moon Talk'. *Journal of Popular Culture: Special Issue on New Journalism*, 9 (1): 44–54.

Wolfe, T., (1973), *Post-Orbital Remorse Part Two: How the Astronauts Fell from Cowboy Heaven*, Rolling Stone, 18th January, 1973: 22–27.

Wolfe, T., (1979), *The Right Stuff*, London: Jonathan Cape.

Re-thinking Apollo: envisioning environmentalism in space

Holly Henry and Amanda Taylor

The Apollo programme's impact on the ecology movement in the US provides a powerful analogue of current astroenvironmental initiatives for future manned planetary exploration. Those now famous Apollo 8 images of *Earthrise from the Moon* and Apollo 17's image of the *Whole Earth* in the black abyss of space profoundly focused the US – and ultimately the world – on ecocritical concerns and called into question the rhetoric of Manifest Destiny that in part fuelled the Apollo era. As humans continue their journey across the solar system, imaginative artistic renderings of planetary landscapes also often suggest, like the Apollo photos of Earth, the need for greater ecocritical awareness. A cultural analysis of the impact of widely distributed Apollo photographs on an emerging environmental movement, and of artistic renderings by Chesley Bonestell, David Hardy, and Chris Butler, suggests that continued exploration of the solar system must proceed with the environmental awareness gained from Apollo.

Twenty-seven astronauts travelled to the Moon. Twelve spent a total of 300 hours on the lunar surface. These men captured on film, often by sheer chance, 'some of the most spectacular snapshots in the history of photography' (Crouch, 1999: 226). The Apollo 8 image of *Earthrise* as well as Apollo 17's photo of *Whole Earth* appeared on the walls of corporate offices and powerfully provoked a sense of humanity's inherent responsibility to one another. Set against the black wastes of space, these two Apollo photos galvanized the ecology movement in the US and sparked a radical rethinking of our dependence on, and responsibility to, sustaining Earth's ecosystems and the diversity of life on our fragile biosphere. In an analysis of the Apollo photo archive, cultural geographer Denis Cosgrove has eloquently argued that *Earthrise* and *Whole Earth* have defined Apollo's legacy, at least in the popular imagination.[1] Surprisingly, those two images were neither specifically planned nor particularly prioritized by NASA. Yet, as Cosgrove points out, 'it was [NASA's] low priority targets of opportunity that would yield some of the most enduring images of the entire Apollo program' (1994: 274).

Cosgrove has meticulously demonstrated that the Apollo photographs are multivalent. *Earthrise* and *Whole Earth*, Cosgrove rightly argues, are deeply embedded within a western imperialist global imagination that dates back to at least Constantine; the photos are situated within a variety of imperialist discourses and their armature of cartography, globe making, and of commodifying the Earth and its populations as resource (1994: 272). Yet, as Cosgrove admits, the cultural impact and resonance of the Apollo photographs far supersede even hundreds of years of imperialism, as the photos equally connote a sense of Earth's biodiversity and inherent agency. Such a perspective reflects the work of science studies theorist Donna Haraway, who contends that scientific narrative must provide responsible accounts of the world to afford nature, which cannot speak for itself, a voice. For Haraway, both 'scientists and organisms are actors in a story-telling practice,' which suggests that investigating what narratives are told about the Apollo photos of Earth, and why, matters (1989: 5). Whatever the motive in planting the American flag on the Moon, if only to trump the Soviets in the space race, the Apollo images resist being narrated as merely conquered frontier and instead powerfully revealed Earth's agency as an autonomous, self-regulating biosphere.

Capturing the first earthrise

Mark Williamson posits that 'the most significant legacy of the Space Age is the image of the Earth rising above the surface of the Moon' (2006: 11). *Earthrise* was captured on film in December 1968 by Apollo 8 Commander Frank Borman and crewman William Anders. During this first manned mission to the Moon, Anders was to photograph the lunar surface in search of a landing site for Apollo 11 and obtain photos of the far side of the Moon, which never faces the Earth. On their fourth orbit, as Apollo 8 emerged at the equator from behind the Moon, Borman repositioned the spacecraft to regain radio contact with mission control. Unexpectedly, he caught a glimpse of the Earth just beyond the Moon's limb, grabbed Anders's camera loaded with black-and-white film, and shot a photo. The crew were the first ever to observe an Earthrise and instantly knew they needed to photograph the event in colour. Jim Lovell scrambled to find a colour cartridge, which Anders subsequently loaded into the camera. Anders then took two more photos, including the now famous image of the blue, half shadowed Earth above a desiccated lunar landscape.[2]

Though NASA listed among its photographic objectives for Apollo 8 'long distance Earth photography,' including analyses of Earth's atmosphere, weather, and terrain, Cosgrove suggests that photographs of Earth were 'almost an afterthought in mission planning' (1994: 274). In fact, when Borman rolled the spacecraft and declared, 'Oh, my God! Look at that picture over there! Here's the Earth coming up,' Anders jokingly responded, 'Hey, don't take that, it's not scheduled,' upon which the crew burst into laughter.[3] Later during their ninth orbit of the Moon, the crew presented a live TV broadcast that began with a blurry glimpse of Earth above the lunar surface. While describing the lunar terrain, the crew turned the camera to the forbidding landscape scrolling beneath the Command Module and read the opening of Genesis. Earth was seen in deep

Figure 1: *This is the orientation and view of Earthrise first glimpsed by humans, as the Apollo 8 command module emerged from the dark side of the Moon. Photo credit: NASA.*

time as well as in deep space. Robert Poole writes of the Earthrise images, 'the view seemed eternal, like a snapshot of the creation' (2008: 195).

Published just two days after Apollo 8 returned, '*Earthrise* was the subject of immediate commentary and speculation about a reformed view of the world' (Cosgrove, 1994: 273). Though most publications of *Earthrise* usually present the lunar surface as horizontal, Bill Anders points out that the accurate orientation of the photograph should be with the Earth to the left of the Moon's vertical limb, as that was the astronauts' view from the Apollo 8 spacecraft.[4] Either way, the photo was a sensation, and had, as astronomer Fred Hoyle anticipated in 1948 regarding the eventual first widely disseminated photo of Earth, confronted humankind with 'a new idea as powerful as any in history' (cited in Zimmerman, 1998: ix).[5] The Apollo astronauts themselves have reflected on the significance of *Earthrise*. Anders recalls,

> When I looked up and saw the Earth coming up on this very stark, beat-up lunar horizon, an Earth that was the only color that we could see, a very fragile looking Earth, a very delicate Earth, I was immediately almost overcome with the thought

that here we came all this way to the Moon and yet the most significant thing we are seeing is our own home planet, the Earth. (Ritsko, 1999)

Jim Lovell, also onboard Apollo 8 and later commander of Apollo 13, likewise has commented on the impact of *Earthrise* on the broader national imaginary: 'We learned a lot about the Moon, but what we really learned was about the Earth . . . and how insignificant we really all are. But then, how fortunate we are . . . to enjoy living here amongst the beauty of the Earth itself' (Sington, 2007).

The global impact of *Whole Earth*

If *Earthrise* took the astronauts and the American public by surprise, Apollo 17's *Whole Earth* image of the fully illuminated Earth in space stunned the world. Nobel Prize author and former US Vice President Al Gore contends that *Whole Earth* 'has become the most commonly published photograph in all of history' (2003: 15).[6] Yet, Cosgrove notes, the serendipity and rarity of the *Whole Earth* photos are little understood: Referred to by NASA as simply AS 17-148-22727, *Whole Earth* was taken in a series of 11 photos by astronaut Harrison Schmitt on December 7, 1972.[7] The photos were shot at approximately 28,000 miles from Earth as Apollo 17 raced toward the Moon at roughly 25,000 miles per hour. Given the orientation of the Earth and Sun during the nine Apollo Moon missions, only Apollo 17's crew could glimpse and photograph the fully illuminated globe of Earth in space. This was the only set of full-phase Earth images ever taken by an astronaut, and not a space probe. Though taken with a camera plagued with uneven exposure difficulties, *22727* for the first time in the history of our species allowed the human eye to register the Earth's full globe set against the empty wastes of space.[8] It is no wonder the image has become iconic.

22727 is not, however, the first photograph of the fully illuminated Earth. As early as 1966, 'Lunar Orbiter 1, an unmanned lunar vehicle, sent from lunar orbit a blank and white full-Earth photograph that had been processed in space and electronically recomposed back on the ground,' and in 1967 a US Navy satellite snapped a colour photograph of the full disc of Earth but, apparently due to their poor resolution, neither of these photos were widely circulated (Cosgrove, 1994: 275). Nor was *22727* the first widely distributed whole Earth image. As early as 1966, Stewart Brand, an early environmentalist from San Francisco, wondered why NASA had not released a satellite image of the whole Earth; he was convinced by Buckminster Fuller's theory that eco-awareness would become widespread once people perceived the Earth as a delicate biosphere (Tierney, 2007: F1). Brand later obtained a NASA satellite photo of the Earth in full phase and used it to illustrate the Fall 1968 cover of his newly self-published *Whole Earth Catalog*.[9] But at that point, humans had not yet traveled 28,000 miles into space, much less to a cratered lunar surface a quarter million miles away. Nor could they articulate what such a view evoked – that is, not until Apollo journeyed to the Moon.

The environmental movement and the Apollo photograph archive

As with *Earthrise*, the image of Apollo 17's *Whole Earth* became indelibly etched into the human imagination. Both photos revealed Earth as a fragile oasis, a biosphere of tremendous biodiversity. Apollo 15 Commander Dave Scott recently commented on the impact of Apollo in shaping a global environmental awareness: 'It [the Earth] truly is an oasis. . . . I think the elevation of that awareness is a real contribution [of Apollo] to saving the Earth, if we will' (Sington, 2007). Robert Poole's *Earthrise* offers a delightful, scholarly and detailed investigation of the Apollo programme's many contributors to environmentalism (2008). That Apollo forever altered the way we see ourselves in relation to our planet is indisputable, though its specific intervention in the environmental movement is nearly impossible to map. The environmental movement in the US existed long before the Apollo programme, dating to the 1890s with the establishment of Sequoia and Yosemite National Parks in 1890, the Forest Reserve Act of 1891 that preceded the formation of a national forest service, and the founding of the Sierra Club in 1892. By the 1960s, multiple events in the US, including the emergence of NASA in 1958, nuclear weapons testing, publication of Rachel Carson's *Silent Spring* (1962), the Civil Rights Movement, and the Peace Movement converged in sparking widespread and various responses to environmental concerns. However, it is widely conceded that with the first Earth Day in 1970, 'a truly national ecology movement took shape' (Giugni, 2004: 39). According to Flight Director Gene Kranz, 'Apollo 8's stunning images of the Earth in vibrant color' became for the environmental movement in the US 'a powerful visual expression of the concept of "Spaceship Earth"', a phrase coined by Buckminster Fuller to depict the Earth as a self-contained biosphere sweeping through the voids of space (2000: 247). Nature photographer Galen Rowell declared in 1995 that Anders's colour photograph of *Earthrise* has been 'the most influential environmental photograph ever taken' (cited in Zimmerman, 1998: 242). Likewise Apollo 17's *Whole Earth* image was immediately taken up in environmental discourse. 'In the 1970s, photo *22727* quickly became the Earth Day logo in the United States, while the environmental lobby group Friends of the Earth used it effectively to convey a message of global dwelling, care, and fragility,' explains Cosgrove (2001: 263).[10] Aarguably the most important recent contribution to the environmental movement by a single individual, Al Gore, in both his text and film *An Inconvenient Truth*, has powerfully used *Earthrise* and *Whole Earth* rhetorically to frame his appeal for greater eco-awareness and global action. Of *Earthrise*, Gore writes: 'The image exploded into the consciousness of humankind . . . In fact, within two years of this picture being taken, the modern environmental movement was born. In the US, the Clean Air Act, the Clean Water Act, the Natural Environmental Policy Act, and the first Earth Day all came within a few years of this picture being seen for the first time' (2003: 12).[11]

Apollo afforded Earth a voice

By sheer coincidence, Cosgrove observed, Apollo 17's *Whole Earth* frames Africa, the origin of humankind, not the US or western Europe; its image of a blue planet swirled in clouds, he further contended,

> strips away the graticule, principal signifier of Western knowledge and control, radically challenging a global image dominant over four hundred years. Thus liberated, and with no signs of meaning, boundary marking, or possession, Earth appears to float free as a *sui generis* organism. (2001: 261)

The cover of James Lovelock's text *Gaia* (1979) was illustrated with the *Whole Earth* image, precisely to make the point that Earth is an autonomous, life-sustaining organism (Cosgrove, 2001: 263).[12] Centuries before Apollo, Immanuel Kant had intuited that Earth is not, in actuality, the property of nations or individuals. In his 1795 essay 'Toward Perpetual Peace,' Kant argued that the right to travel belongs to all humans as they share 'in common of the earth's surface on which, as a sphere, they cannot disperse infinitely . . .' (1996: 329). The Earth in principle cannot be owned, claimed Kant, as all people have 'a common right to the face of the earth' (1986: 284–5). After Apollo 8's *Earthrise*, Robert Zimmerman claims, Earth could 'no longer be seen as land over which nations could claim control' (1998: 245).

Many space historians have observed that the Apollo photos of Earth afforded humankind the opportunity to see our planet in context, to see just how fragile our world, and all life on Earth, really is. Wyn Wachhorst speculates, 'If the essence of exploration is to touch the boundary – the beach, the mountaintop, or the moon – the core of the human condition is the attempt to see the self in context. To stand on the moons of Saturn and see the Earth in perspective is to act out the unique identity of our species' (2001: 78). Standing on the surface of our Moon, Apollo 17 commander Eugene Cernan recounts seeing Earth turn on its axis, with multiple time zones visible at once, and realizing how our finite constructs, such as standardized time, do not translate well in the larger context of space. 'Another hundred years may pass before we understand the true significance of Apollo,' predicts Cernan, 'Lunar exploration was not the equivalent of an American pyramid, some idle monument to technology, but more of a Rosetta stone, a key to unlocking dreams as yet undreamed' (Cernan and Davis, 2000: 344). Apollo seems to have been the Rosetta Stone by which not just the American public but all of humankind could see itself in context and decipher our own situatedness and need for ecocritical awareness. Apollo invited us to think beyond ourselves, to think environmentally about the worlds we yet dream of exploring: Mars, Europa, the moons of Saturn.

If the Apollo programme can be thought of as a Rosetta stone as Cernan suggests, its decryption began with its iconic Earth photographs, which illustrated, first, Earth as a fragile environment in need of protection and, second, space as a natural extension of the Earth's environment. Realistic space art builds particularly on the second concept and helps us envision ourselves in the space environment.[13] Though space art arguably began with the first pictorial representations of the night sky, these representations did not enable viewers to envision themselves in space due to a lack of sufficient detail. Thus, artists relied more on their imagination than on available science to depict celestial bodies. Space artist Ron Miller posits that two things were necessary to alleviate this problem. We needed 'scientific knowledge about the actual conditions that existed beyond the Earth's atmosphere or on the Moon and other planets, and a realistic means of leaving the Earth' (1996: 139). Miller claims that the first condition was met when Galileo in 1610 provided the first detailed, scientific knowledge of other planets by 'turn[ing] a telescope toward the heavens' by which 'mankind realized for the first time that there were worlds other than this one' (1996: 139). Miller's choice of 'worlds' over 'planets' in this passage is significant. The use of 'planet' suggests distance and mystery where the use of 'world' suggests nearness and familiarity. While planets were known to exist well before Galileo, his telescope provided details about these distant, cold planets that transformed them into knowable worlds.

Space art and the alien-as-familiar

Though Galileo's telescope 'moved the heavens from the realm of the mystical into that of the physical,' technology, as Miller notes, did not make 'this new heaven accessible' (1996: 139) until 1783 with the invention of the balloon. With the balloon, humans could actually leave the ground and seem to touch the sky, hinting at the possibility of someday actually leaving Earth to visit new worlds. In the meantime, however, if 'it was not possible to reach these new worlds in the sky in reality,' art could make it possible 'by proxy' (1996: 140). This is particularly the case with realistic space art. Science writer and space art collector Andrew Fazekas claims that the work of realistic space artists requires knowledge of 'astronomy, geology, space technology, hardware, or even astrobiology' (2004: 79). Such knowledge allows realistic space artists to render alien environments as accurately as possible, enabling viewers more easily to imagine themselves as part of these environments. Fazekas writes, '[T]he artistic ability to . . . transform the coldness of science into a uniquely human experience makes space artists indispensable' (2004: 79).

Described as the 'father of astronomical art,' Chesley Bonestell is one of these indispensable artists (Miller, 1996: 142). As Wyn Wachhorst observes, 'Bonestell brought the edge of infinity out of the abstract and into the realm of experience' (2001: 58). We see this in Bonestell's now iconic 'Saturn as seen from Titan', which appeared in May 1944 in *Life* magazine.[14] This painting invited viewers into the possible planetary landscapes that exist on moons of the outer solar system. In Bonestell's depiction, Titan's landscape resembles that of the American Southwest or perhaps the craggy cliffs of the Rocky Mountains in winter. The deep blue of the sky recalls that of Earth; the view of Saturn is reminiscent of the view of the Moon we would expect in an Earth landscape. Miller argues that the 'almost intense believability' of Bonestell's paintings is 'far more important than any mere scientific facts they may [entail]' (1996: 142). Even if Bonestell's work was not completely accurate, viewers can imagine themselves standing on Titan viewing Saturn, an important quality considering that this particular Bonestell piece pre-dates spaceflight.[15] The painting had an undeniable impact on many engineers, astronauts, and civilians in what became the US space programme. 'For those who grew up with Bonestell's painstaking accuracy in light, shadow, perspective and scale, the reality of spaceflight seemed a foregone conclusion' (Wachhorst, 2001: 50).

Bonestell's ability to portray perspective and scale is evident in his placement of 'tiny space suited figures in most of his scenes' (Wachhorst, 2001: 49) not only as a type of signature, but also as a reminder of the immensity of space as compared to humans. Humans are almost incidental in Bonestell's work; rather, it is the landscape that dominates the view and invites contemplation. Bonestell's paintings allow us to view Saturn in the same way the Apollo images allow us to view Earth as part of a larger space environment. Mark Williamson contends that 'the space environment deserves at least as much consideration as the terrestrial environment' and that 'many aspects of the space environment are more fragile than the Earth's because they lack the Earth's capability for self repair' (2006: 244). Williamson further argues that both the general public and space professionals need to be educated, without being alienated, about astroenvironmental concerns such as the environmental impact of exploration on other planetary bodies.

Williamson suggests that this education could 'perhaps tak[e] the line of the 19th century wilderness painters' (2006: 257). These painters' landscapes had a significant impact on the eventual creation of the US national park system. Their paintings helped viewers to see inhospitable, even savage lands as 'places of natural beauty' (2006: 255–56), which fostered a sense of emotional attachment to these lands, ultimately leading to their protection. Williamson does not transfer this potential to space artists, however. Rather, he seems to privilege photography over art in raising astroenvironmental awareness. He writes, 'Whereas photographs of the Earth from space, particularly those resulting from the Apollo missions, had an important affect on society . . . images of the more distant planetary bodies are unlikely to provide such a fundamental boost to the planetary environment movement' (2006: 257). Williamson seems both to forget how Bonestell's art captivated the popular imagination and to minimize the effects that space art can have. It seems plausible that realistic space art could galvanize a planetary environment movement in the same way the Apollo images impacted the ecology movement. For example, astronaut and space artist Alan Bean's 'Kissing the Earth' deliberately reworks the *Earthrise*

Figure 2: *In 'Neighbours' by David Hardy, the terrain of the Moon and Mars appears as a natural extension of Earth's landscapes, even as the Moon and Mars seemingly comprise Earth's core and mantle. Photo credit: David A. Hardy/www.astroart.org.*

image so that Earth overwhelms the viewer, only to confirm Bill Anders's observation that it took traveling a quarter million miles to the Moon to understand Earth's fragility.[16] While Williamson includes space artwork with similar potential in his book, such as David Hardy's 1997 painting 'Neighbours', he does not give it adequate attention (2006: 274).

Seeing the Earth as analogue

Hardy describes 'Neighbours' as more abstract than his other work, which he says is typically 'purely realistic and representational'. Like Bonestell, Hardy offers us a view of a world in context. 'Neighbours' simultaneously recalls and complicates the *Whole Earth* image. As in the Apollo image, the Earth is central to the backdrop of space. Its vibrant blue ocean is interrupted by a wisp of cloud and surrounds not Africa as in *Whole Earth*, but Mars and the Moon. Intriguingly, Mars and the Moon seem to form Earth's mantle and core. Additionally, all three bodies are depicted in their 'relative sizes and terrains, with all their similarities and differences' (Hardy, 2008) This is in accordance with Hardy's determination to 'rende[r] pictorially as accurately as possible aspects of astronomy . . .' (Hardy, 1976: 95). In Hardy's work, Earth's landscapes become an analogue for its planetary neighbors.[17]

Whereas Hardy's piece focuses on planetary environments, artist Chris Butler primarily focuses on humans interacting with these environments. Heavily influenced by his personal attachment to the Apollo programme, Butler's artwork seeks to recapture a sense of discovery he feels has been lost in the post-Apollo years. Butler literally grew up with Apollo. His father, Robert E. Butler, worked on the development of the Apollo lunar spacecraft and later the Space Shuttle and introduced Chris to all of the Apollo astronauts, some of whom remain family friends. Butler comments that 'space was and is very real' to him and that, as a child, he expected the Apollo missions would evolve into Mars exploration. The discontinuation of the Apollo programme was a 'huge, crushing disappointment' and Butler turned to painting to recapture the world he had lost. Much of Butler's art shows a single astronaut or spaceship in the expanse of space or on a distant planet, evoking the possibility of engaging firsthand in these landscapes. This evocation contributes to the two main purposes his artwork serves. First, his art is meant 'to get people to think and feel about space' while accomplishing the second purpose, resuming planetary exploration. (Butler, 2008b)

Butler insists, however, that we must conduct this exploration responsibly, evidenced by his work 'Water, Water Everywhere'.[18] Inspired by a polluted Los Angeles beach, this painting depicts an astronaut in full space gear standing ankle deep in an alien ocean. We simultaneously sense familiarity and apprehension in the scene as the astronaut, poised to wade in further, more fully considers the new environment. The ocean *looks* like a terrestrial ocean, but only because

Figure 3: *'Water, Water Everywhere' by Chris Butler imagines an astronaut on the verge of wading into an alien ocean. Photo credit: Chris Butler/Science Photo Library.*

like Earth's oceans, it reflects the blue sky. An ocean of liquid methane, for example, could also reflect the blue sky and would have water-like properties. Having no idea what organisms or chemicals lurk in the water, and despite the initial thrill of discovering something familiar, the astronaut rightly hesitates. As Butler indicates, on a 'world very likely to have life, direct contact would be both irresponsible and extremely dangerous to all concerned [until] decades of study were made.' (Butler, 2008a)

While depicting the need to consider the environmental impact of future exploration, 'Water, Water Everywhere' illustrates more than just an environmental consciousness. Butler's use of a coastal landscape echoes Bonestell's work, which, as Wachhorst observes, often deploys the 'root metaphor' of 'the shoreline itself. The interface of known and unknown, civilization and wilderness, [. . .] the beach is [a] narrow band of equilibrium . . .' (2001: 54–5). Stepping off the shoreline into the ocean symbolizes an embrasure of the unknown wilderness. If space is humankind's 'new ocean' as President John F. Kennedy suggested, perhaps 'Water, Water Everywhere' reflects the fact that humans have only got our feet wet and need to pause to consider the ramifications of such a step for the sake of both humanity and the space environment.

Recent initiatives by the US, China, and Russia for return manned missions to the Moon, and American space enthusiasts' proposals for space tourism and possible terraforming of Mars, have raised concern about the protection of planetary wildernesses. This is especially relevant in light of the discovery of extremophiles thriving near deep-sea volcanic hydrothermal vents, which indicates that microbial or other life forms could survive in the oceans of Jupiter's moon Europa or in the permafrost of Mars.[19] Astroenvironmentalists argue that determining whether life exists, or existed, in these and similar locations in the solar system will require an even greater ecocritical awareness in planning missions to Mars, as well as sample-return missions, both robotic and manned, that could impact Earth's own ecosystems.

To mitigate this impact, Charles S. Cockell and Gerda Horneck propose a 'planetary park' system similar to a national park system.[20] A planetary park system would both preserve and protect planetary environments. Preservation would mandate certain areas of planetary bodies off-limits to human use; protection would mandate protocols for the responsible use of certain areas of planetary bodies. Cockell and Horneck offer four main arguments for this type of system.[21] First, they argue that 'we need wilderness areas' to help us define our culture and civilization (2006: 258). Second, like Earth, other planetary bodies 'exist independently of human valuation' and have 'value in [their] own right' (2006: 258). Third, a planetary park system 'expresses a respect for the options and choices' of future generations (2006: 258). Finally, Cockell and Horneck argue that we must preserve extraterrestrial lands for the potential, if currently unknown, resources or other benefits they may contain (2006: 258).

If space exploration and tourism are to increase in the coming decades, protection of the space environment must become a major objective for entrepreneurs and space agencies alike. Williamson reports that in 1963 President Kennedy approved a military test 'to detonate a nuclear weapon on the inner edge of the Van Allen belts'; 'the explosion,' Williamson notes, 'created 'a little Van Allen Belt of its own' (2006: 53).[22] Current estimates indicate that 'one tonne of uranium 235 and fission products' as well as roughly 100,000 pieces of space debris orbit our planet and subsequently threaten space missions, the space station, as well as the numerous satellites that sustain our world (Williamson, 2006: 55, 79). Those first amazing images of the blue Earth rising over a stark lunar surface sparked the public imagination and suggested the need for global ecocritical awareness. Though not as ubiquitous as the Apollo images, realistic space art has contributed to an emerging astroenvironmental consciousness that envisions space as a natural extension of Earth's environment and suggests ways we might encounter alien landscapes and not only survive, but thrive. With humanity poised to return to the Moon and venture on to Mars, envisioning and articulating our purposes in space will make all the difference regarding the protection of worlds we may someday inhabit.

Notes

1 There were, of course, multiple Apollo photographs of Earth in space, but *Earthrise* and *Whole Earth* were remarkable for reasons noted in this chapter.

2 To view the Earthrise images, visit the The Apollo 8 Flight Journal at <http://history.nasa.gov/ap08fj/14day4_orbits456.htm>. For years both Anders and Borman claimed they had taken the famous *Earthrise* image. Indeed they both had, Borman with black and white film and Anders with color film. For a detailed discussion of Apollo 8 and this debate, see Robert Zimmerman's *Genesis: The Story of Apollo 8*.

3 See the Apollo 8 Flight Journal at <http://history.nasa.gov/ap08fj/14day4_orbits456.htm>.

4 See the Apollo 8 Flight Journal at <http://history.nasa.gov/ap08fj/14day4_orbits456.htm>. The Earthrise, of course, was a result of the Apollo 8 spacecraft shooting around the side of the Moon, not a function of the Earth actually moving relative to the Moon.

5 See also Hoyle, F. (1950), *The Nature of the Universe*: 9–10.

6 To view the *Whole Earth* image, visit the Apollo 17 Image Library, Apollo Lunar Surface Journal at <http://www.hq.nasa.gov/alsj/a17/a17.html>. NASA archivist Mike Gentry also has speculated that *22727* is the most widely reproduced photograph *ever* (Monmaney, 2002: 19).

7 Schmitt recalls that he took the series of photos during translunar coast (Monmaney, 2002: 19).

8 There was apparently a problem with the film forwarding motor in the camera (Cosgrove, 1994: 275).

9 Robert Poole notes that the photo of the Full Earth used to illustrate the first *Catalog* was taken by NASA's ATS-III (Applications Technology Satellite) in 1967 (2008: 85). The *Catalog* offered reviews of hand tools, forestry gear, communication technologies, back to the land technologies, and information on alternative energy technologies (Turner, 2005: 488). Aimed at a readership spanning from naturalists to techno savvy entrepreneurs, the *Catalogue* in 1971 alone sold a million copies and won a National Book Award (Turner, 2005: 496). Zimmerman notes that besides images of Earth on the *Catalog*'s cover, each edition included *Earthrise* on the inside cover (1998: 242).

10 Friends of the Earth, founded in the US in 1969, is today a global confederation of organizations that promotes awareness of a variety of ecological and sustainability issues.

11 In 1969, the National Environmental Policy Act was passed and the Environmental Protection Agency was created. A Clean Air Act was passed in 1970; the Water Pollution Act was passed in 1972, and the Endangered Species Act in 1973.

12 Working with NASA's Jet Propulsion Lab to find evidence of life on Mars inspired Lovelock to theorize that Earth's atmosphere is a natural extension, and byproduct, of living organisms on our biosphere. Robert Poole's (2008) informative study, which also discusses the Apollo Programme's impact on Lovelock's Gaia theory, was published after this chapter was submitted for publication.

13 For a distinction between space art and science fiction art, see Hardy, D. (1976), 'Painting: The Impact of Astronautics and Science Fiction on My Work', *Leonardo*: 96–7.

14 To view the image, visit NovaSpace Art at: <http://www.novaspace.com/LTD/BONESTELL/Titan.html>.

15 For a more complete discussion of Bonestell's accuracy compared to that of predecessor Lucien Rudaux, see Miller's 'The Archaeology of Space Art': 142.

16 To view the image, visit The Alan Bean Gallery at <http://www.alanbeangallery.com/kissing-new.html>. Of this painting Bean writes, 'We were the second crew to attempt a landing on the Moon. . . . After returning to Earth, I had to paint my experience. But what would be a suitable title? I thought of a favorite painting by Winslow Homer, an American artist of the late 1800's depicting 3 fishermen in a small boat. In the distance was a faint full Moon just being touched by the Earth's horizon. Homer's title: "Kissing the Moon"'.

17 This is also the case for space artist Pat Rawlings, who depicts the discovery of past life in the canyons of Mars, most notably in 'Natives' and 'Mars Archeology'. In order to view these paintings and others related to Mars exploration, see the 'Mars Exploration' gallery at Pat Rawlings.com: <http://www.patrawlings.com/gallery.cfm.>

18 The allusion to Samuel Taylor Coleridge's poem *The Rime of the Ancient Mariner* is not accidental.

19 For more information on extremophiles, see Impey, C. (2007), *The Living Cosmos: Our Search for Life in the Universe*: 95.

20 For a more complete discussion of this issue, see Chapter 10 of Williamson, M. 2006, *Space: A Fragile Frontier*: 239–278.

21 For a more complete discussion of the basis for this proposal, see Cockell and Horneck's 'Planetary Parks – Formulating a Wilderness Policy for Planetary Bodies' pp. 158–159. See also Cockell, C. (2007), *Space on Earth: Saving Our World by Seeking Others*.

22 Between 1958 and 1962, the US and the USSR conducted more than a dozen high altitude nuclear explosions in Earth's upper atmosphere and in space. One US nuclear test, *Starfish Prime*, destroyed electronics in Hawaii and New Zealand as well as three satellites that passed through an artificial Van Allen Belt produced by the blast.

References

Bean, A., (2007), 'Kissing the Earth', The Alan Bean Gallery, <http://www.alanbeangallery.com/kissing-new.html> [accessed 5 December 2007].

Bonestell, C., (2008), 'Saturn as Seen From Titan', Nova Space Art, <http://www.novaspace.com/LTD/BONESTELL/Titan.html> [accessed 10 April 2008].

Brand, S., (1968), Whole Earth Catalog, Menlo Park, CA: Portola Institute.

Butler, C., (2007), 'Water, Water Everywhere.' NovaSpace Art, <http://www.novaspace.com/GICLEE/Butler/WaterPlanet.html> [accessed 26 October 2007].

Butler, C., (2008a), e-mail interview, 14 April 2008.

Butler, C., (2008b), personal interview, 3 June 2008.

Carson, R., (1962), Silent Spring, Boston: Houghton Mifflin.

Cernan, E. and Davis, D., (2000), *The Last Man on the Moon: Astronaut Eugene Cernan and America's Race in Space*, New York: St. Martin's Griffin.

Cockell, C., (2007), *Space on Earth: Saving Our World by Seeking Others*, New York: Macmillan.

Cockell, C. and Horneck, G., (2006), 'Planetary Parks – Formulating a Wilderness Policy for Planetary Bodies', *Space Policy* 22: 256–61.

Cosgrove, D., (1994), 'Contested Global Visions: One-World, Whole-Earth, and the Apollo Space Photographs, *Annals of the Association of American Geographers* 84(2): 270–94.

Cosgrove, D., (2001), *Apollo's Eye: A Cartographic Genealogy of the Earth in the Western Imagination*, Baltimore and London: Johns Hopkins UP.

Crouch, T., (1999), *Aiming for the Stars: The Dreamers and Doers of the Space Age*, Washington, D.C.: Smithsonian Institution Press.

Fazekas, A., (2004), 'Visions of Space', *Astronomy* 32(7): 78–81.

Giugni, M., (2004), *Social Protest and Policy Change: Ecology, Antinuclear, and Peace Movements in Comparative Perspective*, Lanham, MD: Rowman & Littlefield Publishers.

Gore, A., (2003), *An Inconvenient Truth: The Planetary Emergency of Global Warming and What We Can Do About It*, New York: Rodale.

Haraway, D., (1989), *Primate Visions: Gender, Race, and Nature in the World of Modern Science*, New York: Routledge, Chapman & Hall.

Hardy, D., (1976), 'Painting: The Impact of Astronautics and Science Fiction on My Work', *Leonardo* 9(2): 95–8.

Hardy, D., (2008) 'Neighbours', David Hardy AstroArt, http://www.hardyart.demon.co.uk/webimage/neighbor.jpg [accessed 10 April 2008]

Hardy, D., (2008), e-mail interview, 30 May 2008.

Hoyle, F., (1950), *The Nature of the Universe*, New York: Harper and Brothers.

Impey, C., (2007), *The Living Cosmos: Our Search for Life in the Universe*, New York: Random House.

Kant, I., (1986), 'Perpetual Peace', *Philosophical Writings*, E. Behler (ed.), New York: Continuum: 270–331.

Kant, I., (1996), 'Toward perpetual peace', *Practical Philosophy*. The Cambridge Edition of the Works of Immanuel Kant, translated by M.J. Gregor, Cambridge: Cambridge UP: 317–351.

Kennedy, J.F., (2008), 'Address at Rice University on the Nation's Space Effort.' 12 September 1962, John F. Kennedy Library and Museum <http://www.jfklibrary.org/Historical+Resources/Archives/Reference+Desk/Speeches/JFK/003POF03SpaceEffort09121962.htm> [accessed 27 June 2008].

Kranz, G., (2000), *Failure is not an Option*, New York: Berkley Books.

Lovelock, J., (1979/2000), *Gaia: A New Look at Life on Earth*, Oxford: Oxford UP.

Miller, R., (1996), 'The Archaeology of Space Art', *Leonardo* 29(2): 139–143.

Monmaney, T., (2002), 'No Place Like Home', *Smithsonian* 33(9): 19.

Poole, R., (2008), Earthrise: How Man First Saw the Earth. New Haven & London: Yale UP.

Rawlings: Pat Rawlings Art & Animation, <http://www.patrawlings.com/gallery.cfm> [accessed 1 December 2007].

Ritsko, A., Man. Dir., (1999), *Nova: To the Moon* Man, Lone Wolf Studios.

Sington, D., Dir., (2007), *In the Shadow of the Moon*, Perf. Harrison Schmitt, Alan Bean, Michael Collins. Velocity/THINKFilm.

Tierney, J., (2007), 'An Early Environmentalist, Embracing New "Heresies"', *New York Times* 27 February: F1.

Turner, F., (2005), 'Where the Counterculture Met the New Economy: The WELL and the Origins of Virtual Community', *Technology and Culture* 46(3): 485–512.

Wachhorst, W., (2001), *The Dream of Spaceflight: Essays on the Near Edge of Infinity*, Cambridge, MA: DeCapo P.

Williamson, M., (2006), *Space: The Fragile Frontier*, Reston, VA: American Institute of Aeronautics and Astronautics, Inc.

Zimmerman, R., (1998), *Genesis: The Story of Apollo 8*, New York and London: Four Walls Eight Windows.

Conclusion: to infinity and beyond?

Warren Smith

There is some disagreement about the date of the first powered flight by man. Let us settle on 1903, for it was then that Orville Wright flew 120 feet in 12 seconds. Sixty-six years later man had walked on the moon. We are now 40 years on. Of twelve human beings to have set foot there, nine still live. Men in their seventies and eighties it is perhaps unlikely that any will see another lunar landing. Certainly none will experience the technological leap of the Apollo years. I wonder about the expectations of those who watched these missions. What were their predictions for the future? Mars landings by 2000? Lunar colonization? Onwards and upwards? It's amusing, for example, to reflect on the compressed time horizons of much science fiction. In 1969, the year 2000 seemed way into the future. Time enough to achieve so much.

And yet Apollo 11 turned out to be the high point. Thereafter, despite periodic surges in interest, sadly some caused by dreadful failures, it is safe to argue that space programmes have failed to retain the public imagination. Whatever the lack of return on expenditure, it still seems somewhat startling that some simply got bored of moon landings after a mere six visits. Was there no more to see? When so much of what we enjoy in life derives from repetition of experience, why did space travel lose the capacity to engage?

This chapter wraps up the collection by reconsidering the pattern of public engagement with space programmes over the last 40 years. It is important to recognize that the moon landing was a great collective moment, received with great enthusiasm and with which millions strove actively to engage. Why then the falling away of interest? One explanation, as we will see, is that the moon provided a possibility to balance the transcendent, but intimidating and overwhelming, aspects of the space travel with an identifiable, achievable goal. The result was a degree of participation never seen again. Thereafter programmes, in turning towards the practical and the pragmatic and away from the sublime, tended to induce pacificity and disinterest. The possibility of space tourism in its various speculative incarnations offers some recovery of the transcendental. It should be recognized, however, that space, in its insurmountable vastness, throws us back on the essentials of our existence. This is a recipe as much for withdrawal as for exploration.

I have no clear recollection of the moon landings. The Apollo missions ended before I turned five. I have an impression of a bank of black and white monitors shown on a black and white television and an excited presenter relating the dreadful predicaments of the doomed Apollo 13 mission. But this is surely the memory of a recording; history's retelling. As the editors' point out in their introduction, personal biography does not explain everything about our engagement, or otherwise, with space travel. But it's certainly significant. It's hard to argue against the power of youthful memory, particularly where the images were so striking and were marshalled into some powerful narratives (see Jorgensen; Kohonen this volume). And expectations were, for the most part, satisfyingly realized. Conversely it would be perverse to suggest that the stuttering search for relevance of the last twenty years had no effect on the sentimental engagement of those so exposed.

So again I think some personal biography is important. I was a child of the post- Apollo, pre-Space Shuttle interregnum. Whilst without direct experience of the moon landings, it was easy to access and channel those experiences, to transform them into something new and exhilarating, some sense of progression. It was exciting to me that the Space Shuttle took off from the back of a jumbo jet, was called *Enterprise* and was to journey through space. Except that it turned out that none of this was true. *Enterprise* was just another model. And the functional shuttle looked like a space ship, but it didn't really behave like one. As Woods (this volume) shows, the Shuttle was never going to be able to fulfil all of the promises made about it. The vision presented to the public of an airliner in space was an attractive one which accorded with the sense of where space travel *should* go next, but the reality was different. Up the shuttle went; down (sadly, not always successfully) it came. I believe there were 'experiments' in between. It didn't seem to go anywhere like a space ship should.

It was all a little disappointing. I recall writing little dialogues with a school-mate in, appropriately, physics class. We would take the roles of the first Space Shuttle Astronauts. I can still remember their names; John Young and Robert Crippen. I think we found the name of the latter particularly appealing for what was a somewhat morbid pursuit, for what we composed was not accounts of daring-do, or mini space operas, but comedies in which things always were going wrong, bits of the shuttle kept dropping off and the astronauts laced their Tang with gin. This disappointment, soon metastizing into cynicism, prefigured many of the contemporary attitudes towards space travel. I was a generation that still had hopes and expectations about its future. Perhaps these expectations were fuelled rather more by the shiny speculations of science fiction, but, whatever, they were expectations unmet. The shuttle programme proceeded without, seemingly, any particular objectives or at least any that were clearly understood or shared. It appeared to have the misfortune of lacking cultural, ideological and commercial value. I recall the Russians were content to go up, stay a very long time, and then come down again. The international space station was intriguing, but did not evolve into the gyro-scoping form that one desired. The Hubble telescope didn't *quite* work. Returns to the moon, and onwards to Mars, are periodically announced but not really believed. Now gazing at the night time sky, is it hard to believe that we have been there?

I'm thinking here particularly of the generation lacking some experiential connection to events now somewhat buried in history. The editors suggest that more people in the globe know Neil Armstrong's name than that of the US president. Statistically this may be true, but I'm not sure that the details are as understood, and more importantly, felt, as these figures would suggest, most notably so in the nations and cultures once closest to this receding marvel. Of the moon landings, what is the youthful mind prepared to believe? Is it a plausible deed or a trivial one? Magnificent or mundane? Do they know that it actually happened? Freed from the moorings of possibility, do they take bearings from the improbable? The more you think of it, as you frame the numbers, the more distant becomes 1969. And, lacking comparable achievements, the more anomalous seems man landing on the moon. Simply to say man walked on the moon in 1969 produces an incredulous incongruity. One explanation for conspiracy explanations for the moon landings is that its simply easier to believe that they were faked in some Californian film studio than man was able to string together 1960's technology to achieve such unlikely results.

It is said that children no longer have ambitions to become astronauts. I didn't want to become an astronaut either. As an entirely sensible child, I realized that, so obviously lacking the right stuff, these were wholly unrealistic objectives and accordingly I set my goals much, much lower. Now I would have firmer criteria to assess my inadequacy since 'career entry' is more helpfully defined; it is possible to apply online for the European Space Agency Astronaut Corps as indeed one can for MI5 and the Coca-Cola graduate recruitment programme. This is not to suggest that there is any shortage of astronauts. Perhaps the reverse is true since there seems less for them to do.

NASA's Project Constellation envisages a lunar landing by 2019 to establish an outpost for future exploration, including in the distant future, to Mars. The Russians propose a permanent station on the moon by 2032. It says something about the development of space exploration over the last twenty years that these targets are regarded with rather more doubt than expectation. As with ambition, the development of technology seems to have adopted a resolutely earthbound trajectory. Of course, human 'progress' is far from linear and great inventions have many times been lost to the barbarian influence. Re-discovery and re-invention has always been central to innovation. Parker (2008) has noted the turn to the miniature technologies of 'inner space' and away from the grand designs of outer space. As the cliché goes, there is more technology in my refrigerator than in a Saturn rocket. Something of an exaggeration I'm sure, but fridge innovation seems to be doing its best to close any gap. Rather than our ambitions and our technology challenging the capacity of imagination, development seems directed to achieve the same goals a little better, a little faster, a little more efficiently. When we are surprised by what technology can achieve it is because we had failed to realize that we needed our refrigerator to text us to buy more milk. Of over 800 man-made satellites orbiting the earth only 40 point outwards, the rest provide for our internal communications. The geostationary orbit, as Collis (this volume) attests, is a valuable piece of 'real estate' which, as slots are filled, is being subsumed into an earthly legal environment.

But it's too easy to be cynical about the space programme. The arguments can be quickly rehearsed; the expense of the lunar landings and the influence of pork-barrel interests; the sheer wastefulness of it all in relation to more urgent issues of poverty and famine on Earth. One can also reflect on the commercial space junk (DeGroot, 2007: 184) produced by the process of 'selling the moon' (Smith, 1983). It may have been ridden with cold war paranoia and brute politics, but perhaps it's best to concede that it was a remarkable effort. The landing of man on the moon was the culmination of, outside war, the most impressive wielding of collective will. John F. Kennedy's Special Message to the US Congress, on May 25th 1961, was made only 20 days after the first US astronaut had reached outer space. At this point the nation had spent a little over 15 minutes in space.

It's also good to admit that, whatever the role and interests of the military-industrial complex, it was not war. One may forget that the space programme produced some great communal events. A crowd of 50,000 came to see John Glenn become the first American to orbit the earth and 4 million attended his ticker tape parade in New York. A million people were present at the Apollo XI lift off in 1969. With the Space Shuttle's rather sorry contemporary image, we might be surprised to learn that half a million saw its inaugural launch. The impression of the shuttle as a spluttering space jalopy rather neglects the fact that it moves at 17500 mph as it clears the earth's atmosphere and takes 20 minutes to travel from Florida to Spain.

And the space programme did once inspire. The Killian's committee's report in March 1958 into the viability of the US space programme was balanced towards the pursuit of the grand idea. Whilst the political dimensions were not neglected, the drive to explore and discover was strongly positioned. Again it's easy to view this as a convenient and politically expedient rhetoric, but at the risk of naivety I'm not so sure. It seems clear that the programme was the reframing of an established mythology, that of the frontier, which powerfully resonated with US sentiments (Wachhorst, 2000).

In shaping public commitment to the space programme in the 1960s, frontier rhetoric was critically important. John F. Kennedy's 1961 address to Rice University on the 'Nation's Space Effort' on September 12th was a prime example of the mobilizing of sentiment to produce public engagement, identification and, importantly, commitment to the mission. His strategy had two important intentions: firstly to draw upon the romanticism of the frontier rhetoric's mythological framework; secondly, to render the moon as a tangible goal. The rhetoric had to manage a tension between the transcendent and the pragmatic; in the American heritage the frontier was not simply about adventure, it was also a place of potential. Although it was beyond what was known, it also offered the possibility of ownership. Kennedy therefore had both to allow the public to access the frontier spirit through the space programme and also to convince them that it was a 'traversable frontier' and therefore worth the sacrifice (Jordan, 2003). Both dimensions were necessary to manifest the public support necessary to push through the required political and economic commitments.

This is the paradox of the frontier; it 'implies unlimited space on the one hand and encourages conquest on the other' (Rushing, 1986: 266). The paradox was the greater when faced with the infinite frontier of outer space. Kennedy attempted to juggle the practical with the sublime, or as Jordan (2003: 215) puts it, to balance 'awe with action.' Whilst the awesome proportions of space added something unparalleled to the frontier myth, it also could quickly overwhelm the pragmatics of achievement. What was there that could be conquered?

Here the Apollo programme had the benefits of being directed towards the moon. The moon provided a conceivable goal, a point within the infinite. But post-Apollo a new driving narrative was required. In the event, an emphasis on the technological benefits that were derived from space science and the accent on more 'economical' modes of transportation, through reusable rockets and vehicles, provided an instrumental rationale for the US programme's continuation. But in subjecting the enterprise to such cost/benefit calculus, in what might be neatly termed the Tang/Teflon justification, the public become disinterested beneficiaries, consumers if you like, of technological innovation rather than affiliating with a transcendent journey. An alternative is where space provides a well established international proving ground. Those nations jostling for global leadership may demonstrate their worth extraterrestrially. The recent Chinese space mission seemed to present a kind of audition for the role of 21st century superpower. It followed a well-established repertoire; all the necessary images were competently produced, the march of the astronauts to the launch tower and the flag-waving crowds, the phone call to the orbiting capsule, the re-entry sequence with the melodrama of the radio silence. But one couldn't help seeing it as rather a pastiche. The subsequent Indian unmanned mission to the moon triggered declarations of an 'Asian space race' and critical comparisons with extreme earthbound poverty. It was a familiar script but which nevertheless creates new circuits of danger (see Dickens, this volume).

The rebalancing of the rhetoric towards the pragmatic and accountable had adverse consequences for the extent of mass identification and connection with projects. If the emphasis on the achievable does not compel, what about the other side of the frontier paradox? What if the narrative is reoriented towards an experience of the sublime? The emphasis on experience suggests firstly the various versions of space tourism that have been proposed. I'm thinking here primarily of dedicated commercial ventures rather than the phenomenon of multi-millionaires paying for berths on scheduled missions. There have been, to date, 6 of these 'spaceflight participants' or 'independent researchers' and fees of up to $30 million dollars have helped offset the costs of the flight. In contrast, the so-called 'mass market' version of space tourism envisages sub-orbital flights in which passengers would experience 5 minutes of weightlessness and view the curvature of the earth. The cost is projected to be $200,000 a ticket.

It's relevant, in the context of the concept of the frontier, to consider the definition of space. The United States' definition of an astronaut is someone who has flown over 80 kilometres above mean sea level. The Kármán line lies at 100 kilometres above sea level and is used to define the boundary between the earth's atmosphere and 'outer space' by the Fédération Aéronautique Internationale. The Virgin Galactic craft, unsurprisingly the best publicized of the handful of space tourism ventures, aims to reach an altitude of 110 km. Surely it promises an exciting adventure, but I wonder how it should be placed, as a commercial proposition based on the provision of experience (perhaps even 'entertainment'), within the rhetoric and sensibilities, of space travel. As Kemp's (2007: 5) puff for Virgin Galactic has it, 'Space has become interesting again. And so much more fun'.

There didn't seem a place for fun in Kennedy's rhetorical call to action. Indeed, can the sublime be 'fun'? For Edmund Burke the sublime was characterised by vastness, darkness, infinity, vacuity, difficulty and danger. It confronts us with our mortality and our significance in relation to something much, much greater than ourselves. He contrasted the beautiful with the sublime. Beauty provoked feelings of tenderness and affection whereas the sublime produced an 'ecstasy of terror' which filled the senses completely (in Nye, 1994: 7). Outer space, and travel in it, seems to provide the purest imaginable manifestation of the sublime. It offers the sensations of agoraphobia, claustrophobia and vertigo in terrifying proportions. What this means for the prospects of space tourism is uncertain because if it is fun, surely it cannot be sublime. Perhaps because space tourism it is sub-orbital it is able to evade the problem of the frontier. It can be associated with some conceivable experience, deriving excitement from an extrapolation from some recognizable activity. But this diminishes its transcendent aspect.

Post Apollo, the paradox of the frontier could not be satisfactorily reconciled so as to arouse and engage. Only the moon provided a gravitational field strong enough both to attract and to convince. But a frontier traversed no longer produces the same stimulus, and so it proved here. The problem of contemporary space programmes is that they have not resolved this paradox. Thus they are rendered uninspiring by pragmatism (space research), somehow downgraded to a deluxe joyride (space tourism) or, finally, become abject in the face of insurmountable, endless space.

But it's this latter sense that, for me, always produced the most intoxicating effects. 'Space' is nothing, an absence. We might travel to the moon or orbit the earth (going around in circles it might be said). We might fly high to view the magnificence of our planet. Yet, space travel also suggests to me something different; space is simply nothing; the compulsion, and problem, of space travel is that is presents the frightening possibility of unfillable space where the sublime is not a vision to behold, but a sensation of relationship; there are unimaginable distances, populated (a word used carefully) with unimaginable things. It's a relationship that cannot be extrapolated and where the preposterous insignificance of self produces dread but, also, suggests an experience that defies narrative sensemaking.

For me, there was always something about the stride of the astronauts to the cockpit that evoked, not the march of heroes, but the walk of the condemned men. This was not due simply to the physical deprivation that they were to endure, although these are considerable. In fact, it could be argued that it is the primary function of the astronaut to bear suffering; incarceration, sensory deprivation, temporal and spatial dislocation was to be their lot. They were test subjects as much as pilots, their role to exist and provide evidence of their existence. But the metaphor of the condemned man does not simply summon the presence of suffering, but also the immediacy and purity of their existence, for as Camus (1955: 52) pithily put it, 'The divine availability of the condemned man before whom the prison doors open in a certain early dawn, that unbelievable disinterestedness with regard to anything except for the pure flame of life'. Here the spaceman was not just the subject of a physiological and psychological experiment, but perhaps also a philosophical one.

Whilst these notions do not form a strong part of the narrative on space travel practice, unsurprisingly so since they do little to inspire and offer the antithesis of a 'productive' engagement, the existential challenges of space travel have received some attention from fiction. Indeed around the time that the Apollo programme was reaching its fruition, Robert Altman produced an altogether more downbeat take on the consequences of the space race. In his little seen *Countdown* (1968), the Americans rush forward their moon landing to beat an impending Russian launch. They have the technology only for a landing, a one-way trip, so their solution is to locate a shelter on the moon's surface which the astronaut must locate and occupy until a rescue mission can be organized. The film plots a series of existential challenges. The physical deprivations of space flight makes taken-for-granted bodily functions unignorable; the ground crew are told to, 'Feed this boy into a sausage machine and tell him that it does not hurt.' The flight itself is simply to be endured. The astronaut simply has to commit to landing when the shelter beacon in located. However he refuses to obey instructions to sleep, not through any desire to experience the sublime pleasures of the universe, but through anxiety, fear of missing a malfunction or some other unspecified, and no doubt unknowable, danger. Ground control want him asleep; he has no reason to be awake, he can only do himself and the mission harm, but he dare not sleep.

When the time comes, he cannot locate the beacon. He reaches a position where he must either land, attempt to return to earth or continue into the void. This is the point of no return. Despite not seeing the shelter, however, he initiates the landing sequence. Mission control asks, 'Why would he land without being sure'. But the pull of land is too much. The last moments of the film are spent with the astronaut searching aimlessly on the surface for the shelter. He encounters a crashed Russian vessel with dead cosmonauts strewn on the lunar floor. He is not the first to step on the moon. He takes out a rubber mouse, a toy given to him by his son, and follows the direction that its tail unfolds. In the last moments, through sheer fortune, he locates the shelter. He pulls himself inside to hope for rescue. Throughout the film the great lunar adventure is steadily eroded to a random search for a tiny shelter secreted on moon's surface; faced with the immensity that surrounds him the spaceman is forced to choose between abandoning himself to the unknown or staying in his room.

Whilst *Countdown* is an entirely minor film, it is notable for presenting an aspect of the extraterrestrial sublime somewhat more dreadful than the earthrises and star fields of popular imagination. Not here the epiphany of connectedness that is sometimes reported as being experience by astronauts (see Henry and Taylor, this volume). Instead, the film evokes something of the opposite, the awfulness of displacement. It brings to the fore the possibility, inherent in every mission, of being stranded. In this respect, space travel produced the deferred sensation of being marooned in the same way that vertigo is derived from the possibility of falling. Each mission offers the chance of simply going too far, of passing the point of no return. Norman Mailer once defined an existential situation as one 'where we cannot foretell the end' (Coktin, 2005: 185). It's hard to see a persuasive political narrative being built around space travel as the definitive existential experience and abandonment as some sort of objective. But there is great power here. To be marooned is when every breath has value, every breath is measurably nearer the last, life has both shrunk to the confines of the capsule and expanded into the vastness of the infinite universe. At this point life becomes distilled into the experience of each breath and a terrifyingly direct engagement with the universe.

Beginning with the greatest of achievements, something that, even today, serves to symbolize the ingenuity of mankind, the last 40 years of space travel has seen some highs and rather more lows. The post-Apollo years are unlikely to have realized the advances predicted by those who saw a man set foot on the moon. Perhaps the future, whether we will return to the moon and onwards, find new modes and means of transportation that render 'space' a realm of experience or a territory for geopolitical wrangling, will produce entirely unexpected developments. But whatever is achieved, what will always remain is an unfathomable expanse that will, should we expose ourselves to it, instantly overwhelm everything.

References

Camus, A., (1955), *The Myth of Sisyphus and Other Essays*. New York: Vintage. International.
Cotkin, G., (2005), *Existential America*, Baltimore: Johns Hopkins University Press.
DeGroot, G., (2007), *Dark Side of the Moon. The Magnificent Madness of the American Lunar Quest*, Jonathan Cape: London.
Jordan, J., (2003), 'Kennedy's Romantic Moon and Its Rhetorical Legacy for Space Exploration', *Rhetoric & Public Affairs*, Volume 6, Number 2: 209–231.
Kemp, K., (1997), *Destination Space*, London: Virgin Books.
Nye, D., (1994), *American Technological Sublime*. Cambridge, MA: MIT Press.

Parker, M., (2008), 'Remembering the Space Age: From Apollo to Cyberspace', *Information, Communication and Society* 11/6: 846–860.

Rushing, J.H., (1986), 'Mythic Evolution of 'The New Frontier' in Mass Mediated Communication', *Critical Studies in Mass Communication* Vol. 3. No. 3: 265–296.

Smith, M., (1983), 'Selling the Moon', in R. Wightman Fox and T. Jackson Lears (eds), *The Culture of Consumption*, New York: Pantheon: 177–236.

Wachhorst, W., (2000), *The Dream of Spaceflight*, New York: Basic Books.

Notes on contributors

David Bell teaches geography at the University of Leeds, UK. Among his recent publications are the second edition of *The Cybercultures Reader* (edited with Barbara M Kennedy, Routledge, 2007) and *Science, Technology & Culture* (Open Uinversity Press, 2005). He still dreams of space.

Christy Collis is Senior Lecturer in Media and Communication in the Creative Industries Faculty, Queensland University of Technology, in Brisbane, Australia. Collis has published widely on the cultural and legal geographies of Antarctica, particularly Australia's claim to 42 per cent of the polar continent. Her work on the still-unsettled legal geographies of Antarctica led her to undertake work on the legal geographies of Space, which are directly derived from Antartican territorial laws. Just how these two unique legal geographies were developed, and how they might evolve in the future, are the focii of Collis's work.

Peter Dickens is Visiting Professor of Sociology at the Universities of Brighton and Essex, UK. He is also Associate Lecturer in Sociology, Faculty of Social and Political Sciences, University of Cambridge. Since the early 1970s he has published widely on social theory, psychoanalysis and the natural sciences within a critical realist perspective. His 2004 book, *Society and Nature: Changing Our Environment, Changing Ourselves* was given an Outstanding Publication Award by the American Sociological Association. In 2007 he published, with James Ormrod, *Cosmic Society, Towards a Sociology of the Universe*. He continues to work on the sociology of outer-space humanization and the changing relationships between cosmologies, societies and human subjectivity.

Alice Gorman is Coordinator of the Graduate Programme in Cultural Heritage Management in the Department of Archaeology, Flinders University, Australia. Her research involves the cultural heritage management of material culture relating to space exploration, including terrestrial launch sites like Woomera (South Australia), Kourou (French Guiana) and Hammaguir (Algeria), orbital debris such as the Vanguard satellite, and planetary landing sites. In 2005 she convened a symposium on the heritage of Woomera. She is also writing a book on the archaeology of body modification, based on her PhD research, to be published by Blackwell in 2009.

Editorial organisation © 2009 The Editorial Board of the Sociological Review. Published by Wiley-Blackwell Publishing Ltd, 9600 Garsington Road, Oxford OX4 2DQ, UK and 350 Main Street, Malden, MA 02148, USA

Holly Henry is Associate Professor of English at California State University, San Bernardino. Henry's interdisciplinary research is focused on modernist studies, the cultural studies of science, and the history of astronomy and space science. She is the author of *Virginia Woolf and the Discourse of Science: The Aesthetics of Astronomy* (Cambridge University Press, 2003).

Matthew H. Hersch is a PhD Candidate in the University of Pennsylvania's Department of History and Sociology of Science. He received his SB from the Massachusetts Institute of Technology and a JD from New York University School of Law. Mr. Hersch specializes in 20th-century American science, technology, labour, and popular culture, and was the 2007–08 Guggenheim Fellow of the Smithsonian's National Air and Space Museum. He is presently writing a labour history of astronauts.

Darren Jorgensen is lecturer in Art History in the Faculty of Architecture, Landscape and Visual Art at the University of Western Australia. He has recently published essays on science fiction, critical theory, Marxism and Australian Aboriginal art. He is currently researching the experiences of cosmonauts after the fall of the Soviet Union, and is preparing a manuscript on Science Fiction and the Sublime.

Iina Kohonen works as a researcher at the University of Art and Design Helsinki (School of Visual Culture/Photography). For her forthcoming doctoral thesis she is studying the Soviet ideological utopia through photographic representations of cosmic space.

Dario Llinares is at the University of Leeds, in the final year of completing his PhD thesis entitled '*Idealized*' *Masculinity and the Cultural Mythology of the Astronaut*. His thesis conceptualizes the way the media has constructed the astronaut as a mythic exemplar of masculinity transcending social-cultural shifts from modernity to post-modernity. The interdisciplinary nature of his work is reflected in the wide range of subjects on which he has lectured at both the University of Leeds and Leeds Metropolitan University. These include courses based on gender, 'race', globalization, media, politics and film. He is currently working on a new paper that theorizes the relationship between heteromasculinity and the aesthetics of queer in contemporary cinema.

Martin Parker is Professor of Organization and Culture at the University of Leicester School of Management. His recent publications include *Against Management* (Polity, 2002), *For Business Ethics* (Routledge, 2005) and *The Dictionary of Utopias and Alternative Organization* (Zed, 2007).

Daniel Sage is a Research Associate at the Department of Civil and Building Engineering at Loughborough University. In 2007 he completed his PhD ('Cosmic Subjects: An Imaginative Geography of the American Space Programme') at the Institute of Geography and Earth Sciences at Aberystwyth University. Drawing upon various performative ontologies, this diverse project examined the socio-technical dis/organization of spatial registers both within and around NASA. He has published on geopolitics, frontier geographies and NASA's art programme. His present research work is a socio-technical study of the spatialization of project management within the construction industry. d.j.sage@lboro.ac.uk

Stevphen Shukaitis is a lecturer in Ethics, Aesthetics, and Imagination at the University of Essex and a member of the Autonomedia Editorial Collective. He is co-editor (with Erika Biddle and David Graeber) of *Constituent Imagination: Militant Investigations // Collective Theorization* (AK Press, 2007). For more on his writing and activities, see http://stevphen.mahost.org.

Warren Smith was employed for nine years as a lecturer in Organizational Studies at the School of Management, University of Leicester, after a PhD at the University of Keele. Since 2006 he has worked as an Associate for the School and also the Open University. He is interested in questions of engagement, accountability and authenticity, and has written on conspiracies, violence and science fiction, amongst other things.

Amanda Taylor is a Master's student in English Composition and Literature at California State University, San Bernardino. Her research interests focus on posthuman subjectivity, the cultural studies of science, intersections between Romanticism and science-fiction, and the materiality of language. The working title of her thesis is 'Welcome to the World of Tomorrow Today: Matt Groening's *Futurama* as Posthuman Mediator.' Her thesis will explore relationships between humans and machines and the impact of those relationships on (post)human subjectivity.

Brian Woods is currently an Honorary Fellow at the Department of Sociology, Anthropology, and Applied Social Sciences at the University of Glasgow. He graduated from the University of Edinburgh in 1999 with a PhD on which the empirical part of this current work is based. His research interests in the sociology of science and technology are varied and, along with the Space Shuttle, he has published on a range of diverse topics including wheelchair history, the social impact of geo-demographics, and the sociology of food allergy and food intolerance. brian.woods@lawcol.co.uk

Acknowledgement

Thanks to Kelvin Jenkins for the original design for the cover.

Index